KU-261-170

FROM THE HEART

Voices of the American Indian

Edited and with Narrative by

LEE MILLER

PIMLICO

To the memory of
Grandma Maggie Axe Wachacha,
Most Beloved Woman.
My most beloved friend.

PIMLICO
An imprint of Random House
20 Vauxhall Bridge Road,
London SW1V 2SA

Random House Australia (Pty) Limited
20 Alfred Street, Milsons Point, Sydney
New South Wales 2061, Australia

Random House New Zealand Limited
18 Poland Road, Glenfield, Auckland 10, New Zealand

Random House South Africa (Pty) Limited
Box 2263, Rosebank 2121, South Africa

Random House UK Ltd Reg. No. 954009

First published by Knopf, Inc. 1995
Pimlico edition 1997

3 5 7 9 10 8 6 4

© Pathways Productions, Inc. 1995

The right of Lee Miller to be identified as the author
of this work has been asserted by her in accordance with
the Copyright, Designs and Patents Act, 1988

This book is sold subject to the condition that it shall not, by way
of trade or otherwise, be lent, resold, hired out, or otherwise circulated
without the publisher's prior consent in any form of binding or cover
other than that in which it is published and without a similar condition
including this condition being imposed on the subsequent purchaser

Papers used by Random House UK Limited are natural,
recyclable products made from wood grown in sustainable forests.
The manufacturing processes conform to the environmental
regulations of the country of origin

Printed and bound in Great Britain
by Mackays of Chatham PLC

ISBN 0-7126-7357-1

Contents

Acknowledgments

There are many people I wish to thank, not only in the making of *From the Heart*, but for their help all along the way. First, a very special thanks to Jack Leustig, senior producer and director of the *500 Nations* television series, for making this book possible, and whose drive and vision turned a dream into reality; and in addition, to Kevin Costner, Jim Wilson, and Tig Productions, whose support allowed traditional Indian voices to be heard. To the Hodenosaunee Grand Council and my friends at Onondaga and Akwesasne, thanks from the bottom of my heart for showing me what it means to be traditional and helping me to be who I am. More than anyone I know, you embody the spirit of this book, and you helped me to see that the past is still alive and the teachings never go away. Thanks to Grandma Lucinda for giving me a place that will always be home, and to my brother Enoch Crow, Jr., for giving me some of the best advice I ever had. I also want to thank Dr. John Hébert and Barbara Loste at the Library of Congress for bringing every opportunity my way; and Dave Kelly and the research librarians on staff for their enthusiastic assistance. A special thanks to my friend Diana Chung in Washington, who made my stay there possible; to Derek Milne at UCLA; to Brigid Brink at the University of Oklahoma Press for her generosity to our series; and to Gloria Dellow, without whom few projects I have ever undertaken would be complete. And finally, to my Mom and Dad—for everything.

Introduction

My friends, I have been asked to show you my heart. I am glad to have a chance to do so. I want the white people to understand my people. Some of you think an Indian is like a wild animal. This is a great mistake. I will tell you all about our people, and then you can judge whether an Indian is a man or not. . . . I will tell you in my way how the Indian sees things . . . it does not require many words to speak the truth. What I have to say will come from my heart, and I will speak with a straight tongue.
—*Inmutooyahlatlat (Chief Joseph), Nez Percé*

When Joseph spoke these words in a Washington, D.C., interview more than a century ago, most Americans were not ready to listen. For four hundred years, the world had failed to understand Indian people, and the watchword of the day was change—change for Indian people, not understanding of them.

And so the United States government furthered what the Europeans had initiated, and Indian nations were herded onto military reservations and kept under close supervision. As part of an aggressive campaign to assimilate them into American society, government boarding schools were established whose stated purpose was the obliteration of Indian languages and the total eradication of cultures. Indian parents experienced the agonizing pain of having their children forcibly wrenched from them and sent to these schools to become "civilized." Acculturation was unleashed as a weapon of war.

The tragedy was that many victims of the boarding school experience came away with a distorted perception of themselves. For years they had been told that to be Indian was bad, and the good Indians were those who were able to throw the past away and become Americans. Successful "civilized" Indians were held up as role models and placed in positions of authority by the federal government in matters relating to Indian affairs.

But these same children whisked away to boarding schools came from nations who continued to regard themselves as the sovereign entities that they were. Seeing no reason to adhere to customs and mores that were in many cases the antithesis of their own, Indian nations felt no compunction to accept as role models those whom white people chose for them. In the end, what Americans achieved was little more than an artificial "Indian," a fabricated image painstakingly nurtured through a policy of cultural genocide.

As part of the acculturation policy, Indian people were denied heroes from their past. White people had an abundance of them—a whole pantheon, in fact. They had fictitious ones and real ones, those who fought for independence, and those who forged new trails west. They even had men who became heroes for no other reason than that they killed Indians.

Today, the exploits of these white heroes are taught in elementary schools. Indian children, who are forced to attend these schools, are told that George Washington is a hero—he beat the British in the revolutionary war; he was the first American president, the father of the country. But white children never learn what Indian children know—that George Washington killed Indians; that he betrayed Indian national governments by illegally conscripting them to fight in colonial wars; or that his grandfather gunned down Indian leaders under a white flag of truce.

In American schools, Indian children are taught that Abraham Lincoln emancipated slaves. But white children are never told that this emancipation only pertained to black slaves. Indian slavery existed in California until long after the Civil War, at a time when that state's legislators were arguing so vehemently against African slavery.

Ulysses S. Grant was responsible for the death of Apaches; Andrew Jackson killed Creek, Seminole, and Cherokee; Thomas Jefferson sanctioned the massacre of Shawnee and Kickapoo in the Ohio Valley—this from a man who himself claimed to be a descendant of Pocahontas. These are America's heroes; they are not ours.

After the United States celebrated the conclusion of its last "Indian War"; after it had taken Indian children away to erase their cultures; after it had obliterated all means for economic independence; after it had destroyed Indian governments and replaced them with a leadership based on its own model; after the languages were fast disappearing; after alcoholism had replaced hope and despair replaced living; then in the middle of this century could it dare at last to suggest that Indian people had heroes.

But once again the false Indian image America had forged dictated that the heroes they selected were not the valiant freedom fighters who gave their lives to preserve their nations and cultures intact but those individuals who were willing to become assimilated. Yet there were still Indian people who measured a man's worth differently; they kept their heroes.

If Indian people did not fit the image America created for them then, who were they? The answer is that they were (and are) more than five hundred sovereign and distinct nations, each with its own unique history, traditions, language, and laws. They were (and continue to be) a people who lived with a belief in God, possessed a moral sense of right and wrong, and acted according to honored teachings tested by time. Above all, they were a people who had a right to come to their destiny in their own way.

But didn't Americans, at least, recognize this? Didn't they pride themselves for their self-reliance and courage, even as they shouted liberty toward Europe? Where did this pioneer spirit come from? Perhaps it originated from the land . . . or maybe, just maybe, it resulted from observing the independence enjoyed by Indian nations. It may have developed as the colonials were confronted by people who lived in freedom and democracy long before these notions were considered in Europe. Or perhaps it was the fiery Indian resistance that challenged their advance every step of the way that made Americans desire to be as strong. Without question, Indian nations tempered the American mold—and after allowing themselves to be shaped by this experience and forging still another image of a noble savage, they later returned with a fury and attempted to reshape the Indian.

The speeches in this book are not the words of stereotypical alcoholics, welfare recipients, or people without hope. They are the voices of leaders, freedom fighters, and champions. They are our heroes. This is our image of who we were. This is who we are.

The intent of this book is to destroy the flawed image of the Indian created so long ago. We are neither unintelligent nor lazy nor helpless nor without feeling. We no longer have to measure our worth according to Western standards of success. We have a right to our sovereignty. We can create our own destiny. The old, false image of ourselves has power only if we choose to accept it. The time has come to invalidate this image and render it unrecognizable, both to ourselves and to the world. We have the means to reforge our identity. And to do this, we look to the wisdom of the past.

So let us reexamine Indian history for a moment. After Cristóbal Colón sailed into the Caribbean in 1492, a part of the world forever changed. Like it or not, nations on the North American continent would be introduced to Spaniards, English, Dutch, French, Swedes, Russians, and settlers from many other nations who persuaded themselves that they had found a free new world.

But in a larger sense, there was a very important aspect of this world that never changed, and ultimately represents the most significant part. It is the one thing that no one could take away, though everyone tried. It remained hidden, because it was manifested on the inside, from the heart, and was made up of the teachings and beliefs that rendered the nations alive and gave meaning and order to their world. It was the belief in the efficacy of the teachings that generated strength . . . and heroes.

If there is one thing that genocide does, it creates heroes. That isn't to say that Indian people wouldn't have had their champions anyway, for all the nations prided themselves on wisdom, oratory, strength, and exemplary action. But there is something about genocide, perhaps, that brings out these qualities more clearly than any other way.

When freedom was taken away, there were those who dared to demand it back. When the cultures were destroyed, there were those who kept the traditions alive for future generations to enjoy; when the whole world said no, others defiantly said yes, for they answered to a higher authority . . . and when their lives were threatened, they confronted death boldly. How do you defeat a man who is not afraid to die? who has weighed his life and determined that it is more valuable given to his people as a sacrifice than all the comforts of living? Such heroes made the people strong, and made them survivors.

Against this backdrop, then, Indian history is far from defeatist. Instead, it is a story of triumph, of courage in the face of adversity, of victory in the midst of defeat. Those whom we honor as heroic martyrs lend us strength and in the process teach us something of what we are worth. Christians call this redemption: bringing the good out of a bad situation. Indian people call it life.

This book, like the *500 Nations* television series, is written in honor of these heroes and their descendants who continue to carry on the traditions. Boarding schools took away a very important sense of history and wonder. If these speeches can repair decades of destructive deculturation in some small way, then this compilation will have achieved its goal. It is hoped, as a consequence, a rethinking of American and European attitudes toward other cultures will result.

Finally, the ideas expressed in these speeches are presented to our children so that they will judge them with admiration and honor, realizing that the value of their culture is greater because of the sacrifices made for it. May it give them something to believe in, and may it help them know that the same unfaltering strength exists inside each one of them, without compromise and without fear.

From the Heart

. . . the tongues of dying men
Enforce attention like deep harmony:
Where words are scarce, they are seldom spent in vain,
For they breathe truth that breathe their words in pain.
                              —*Richard II,* ACT II, SC. I

Why, fellow-citizens, if, from Philip of Pokanoket down to Black Kettle on the far plains and prairies, the Indian had not resisted us inch by inch for every acre of land that we stole from him, I should be ashamed of the soil that fed him and the sun that looked down upon him. What is to give our children courage? . . . The Indian who taught us what this American continent can make of manhood has written that record in a resistance that neither the omnipotence of civilization nor the overwhelming numbers of forty millions of people could ever reduce into yielding to us tamely. I thank him. I am only proud of my country as a continent, because the race that preceded us was no race to yield up tamely their rights. . . .

The civilized man approaches his victim, demoralizes him with his vices and then crushes him under his feet. And if we were to measure the justice or the merit of civilization by the fringe which comes in contact with barbarism, as we advance we should have to cover our faces . . . for it is a record of infamy . . . and the only and the brightest spot in that section of our history is that the Englishman, with all his art, with all his wonderful superiority, with all the omnipotence of his warlike machinery, with his overwhelming numbers, has never yet met the Indian and frightened him anywhere. . . .

From Massachusetts Bay back to . . . [the Plains] every few miles is written down in imperishable record as a spot where . . . [Indian nations] made a stand for justice and their own rights . . . the future will recognize it as a glorious record of a race that never melted out and never died away, but stood up manfully, man by man, foot by foot, and fought it out for the land God gave him, against the world, which seemed to be poured out over him. I love the Indian because there is something in the soil and climate that made him that is fated in the thousand years that are coming to mold us, and I hope we shall always produce heroes as persistent as Philip and Moketavata. . . . [To] the . . . reproach that the press of America [hurls] at the Indian, "You defend yourselves savagely!" the haughty chief replied, "Sir, if you knew how sweet freedom was, you would defend it even with axes!" That is what the Indian says to us. . . . If you knew how sacred justice was and how sweet liberty, you would recognize that I was right. . . .

—Wendell Phillips, *United States*

The Caribbean

How much damage, how many calamities, disruptions, and devastations of kingdoms have there been? How many souls have perished in the Indies over the years, and how unjustly? How many unforgivable sins have been committed?
— *Fray Bartolomé de Las Casas*, Spain

In 1492 Genoan seaman Cristóbal Colón sailed between the islands studding the tropical waters of the Caribbean and claimed the land for Spain. Although Colón was wrong in believing that he had entered the Asian kingdom of Cathay, he was correct in assuming that the peoples who thronged to greet him belonged to civilizations as profoundly ancient as any in Europe.

Colón was hailed enthusiastically as Taíno leaders welcomed him as a valuable ally and trading partner. He dined onshore as a dignitary, was received into Taíno homes, and was plied generously with food and gifts. Yet the first encounter was marred by appalling cultural misunderstanding: during much of the time, Colón believed he was being revered as a God (as indeed his reception might have led him to think), while the Taíno proceeded under the blithe assumption that the Spaniards would act according to the rules of any foreign nation and trading partner. The Taíno's generosity would prove their downfall.

Incredibly, Colón mistook his hosts' civility for submission and returned to Spain with grandiose tales of a tropical paradise, of gold, and of docile island natives who existed in the world solely to serve Spain. To his queen he wrote, "They are fit to be ordered about and made to work, to sow and do aught else that may be needed, and you may build towns and teach them . . . to adopt our customs."

And in that one phrase—"teach them to adopt our customs"— began the most egregious error, the most profound example of moral amnesia, that the world would ever know. The notion that Europe possessed a superiority to all other cultures was the one thing that the disparate powers who came to this continent would hold in common. And once they had deemed non-European cultures immoral and wrong, they firmly believed in a God-given mandate to eradicate them from the face of the earth.

In 1493 Colón returned to the Caribbean for the second time and founded the Spanish colony of Isabela on the island of Hispaniola. Spain had gained a foothold, and the grip was deadly. Almost immediately, gold was discovered in the Vega Real, a region along the central cordillera of Hispaniola. Mines were opened, and indigenous peoples were enslaved to work them. Plantation estates were carved out of the ever shrinking lands of the indigenous chiefdoms of Magua, Xaragua, Maguana, Higuey, and Ciguayo, and, under the system of *repartimiento*, Spaniards were granted the legal right to dispose of the Taíno as labor. And so age-old villages, governments, alliances, leagues, and polities were obliterated, and local leaders were forced to turn over both tribute and subjects to Spain.

Witness to the agony and human destruction that followed was the Dominican friar Bartolomé de Las Casas. By 1515 abuses had grown so blatant that Las Casas returned to Spain, where he was granted an audience at the court of King Ferdinand. As a result of this mission, he was awarded the title of "Protector of the Indians" and, although few reforms actually were implemented, his pen unrelentingly spewed forth the bitterness of the Taíno's destruction.

In 1542 Las Casas gained the long-sought-after reforms called the New Laws, which recognized the rights of Indian people—but by then there were few Taíno left. Subjugation, massacres, rebellions, famine, and plague had waged an unrelenting assault: by the turn of the century there reportedly were none left alive and, although that was not entirely true, the islands that once thronged with people lay barren.

As Las Casas caustically noted, "from 1494 ... to 1508, over three million people had perished from war, slavery and the mines. Who in future generations will believe this?" Who, indeed?

. . . neither better people nor land can there be . . . the houses and villages are so pretty. . . . They love their neighbors as themselves, and they have the sweetest speech in the world; and [they are] gentle and are always laughing. . . . And the memory that they have! They want to see everything and ask what it is and what it is for!   —Cristóbal Colón, *Genoa*

Now I have ordered [my men] to build a tower and a fort . . . not that I believe it to be necessary . . . for it is obvious that with these men that I bring, I could subdue all of this island . . . since [the people] are naked and without arms. . . . But it is right that this tower be made . . . so that with love and fear they will obey. . . .   —Cristóbal Colón, *Genoa*

And this may be also a generall rule, that the Spaniards to what ever part of the Indies they did come . . . ceased not to exercise their abominable slaughters, tyrannies, and execrable oppressions upon the poor people, and being delighted with new kindes of torments, daily encreased their cruelty and rage.   —Fray Bartolomé de Las Casas, *Spain*

First Fight   (1494)

Gold is discovered in the Vega Real district of Hispaniola, and a chain of Spanish forts are flung up in haste to protect the mines. Rumors of Indian unrest spur Colón to send a force of four hundred troops across the Vega with orders to terrorize the Taíno into submission. Along the Río del Oro, five Taíno men are accused of stealing the clothing of Spaniards whose burdens they are forced to carry. When their village leader refuses to indict them, he, his brother, and his nephew are seized. They are taken prisoner to Colón and sentenced to be decapitated. Later he relents and frees them unharmed, but the Taíno near the fort of Santo Tomás do not know this. They menacingly surround five soldiers, hoping to secure the release of their leader. A mounted Spaniard viciously drives them back. The first Taíno blood is shed; for them, it will be a war without end.

> The worst and gravest crime was to capture a King living peacefully in his own domain, and to chain him was an ugly and atrocious crime . . . [Colón] should have taken pains to bring love and peace and to avoid scandalous incidents. . . . Instead, he inspired fear and displayed power, declared war and violated a jurisdiction that was not his but the Indians'; and it seems to me this is not using the door but a window to enter a house, as if the land were not inhabited by men but by beasts.　　　—Fray Bartolomé de Las Casas, *Spain*

Caonabo　(1495)

In the Vega Real, Taíno rise in resistance. The Spaniards vow that for every European killed, one hundred Taíno will die. The ruler Caonabo in the kingdom of Maguana is declared the most powerful threat to Spanish security; it is no coincidence that his land contains the richest deposits of gold. Alonso de Hojeda works his way through the mountainous passes of Maguana. He is greeted by Caonabo and treated very cordially. The Spaniard presents a gift in the name of Colón—polished silver manacles, which are placed on Caonabo's wrists like shining bracelets. Hojeda proposes to visit the seaside and, like it or not, Caonabo will go. On the coast, he is packed aboard a Spanish vessel to be taken on a diplomatic mission to Spain. His wife, Anacaona, wonders why he is bound in chains.

News arrives from the open sea. Water has entered the compartment where Caonabo is secured. He is reported drowned within the hold, lost at sea. Spain is rid of its most worthy opponent.

War in the Vega   (1495–1497)

In the Vega Real, war continues. Fourteen powerful Taíno leaders form an alliance to drive the Spaniards from their lands. It is reported that more than one hundred thousand Taíno have gathered in resistance. But Spanish muskets, cavalry, and attack dogs scatter the field, and plague, famine, and demoralization follow. Many take to the hills, only to be hunted down and enslaved.

. . . [The Taíno] began to think what way they might take to expell the Spaniards out of their Countrey. But good God! what sort of Armes had they? such as were available to offend or defend as bulrushes might be. Which when the Spaniards saw, they came with their Horsemen well armed with Sword and Launce, making most cruel havocks and slaughters among them. Overrunning Cities and Villages, where they spared no sex nor age; neither would their cruelty pity Women and childe, whose bellies they would rip up, taking out the infant to hew it in pieces. They would often lay wagers who should with most dexterity either cleave or cut a man in the middle, or who could at one blow soonest cut off his head. The children they would take by the feet and dash their innocent heads against the rocks, and when they were fallen into the water, with a strange and cruel derision they would call upon them to swim.

—Fray Bartolomé de Las Casas, *Spain*

Once the Indians were in the woods, the next step was to form squadrons to pursue them, and whenever the Spaniards found them, they pitilessly slaughtered everyone like sheep in a corral. It was a general rule among Spaniards to be cruel; not just cruel, but extraordinarily cruel so that harsh and bitter treatment would prevent Indians from daring to think of themselves as human beings or having a minute to think at all.   —Fray Bartolomé de Las Casas, *Spain*

Repartimiento   (1500)

The island of Hispaniola fills with Spaniards; their towns dot the countryside. Estates are carved out of Indian lands, and the Taíno population is dispensed as property to labor upon them. The system, called *repartimiento,* is the official handiwork of Comendador Francisco de Bobadilla, although Colón himself first enslaved the Taíno. The early Spanish landholders on the island are mostly convicts—charged with homicide and other heinous crimes too awful to mention, and have chosen a life in Hispaniola over punishment at home. On the island, they live like lords, forcing the Taíno into fiendish servitude.

Thus [the Spaniards] grew more conceited every day. . . . They no longer felt like walking any distance. Having neither mules nor horses, they rode the backs of Indians . . . they also had Indians carry large leaves to shade them from the sun and others to fan them with goose wings. I saw many an escort follow them loaded like a donkey with mining equipment and food, many of them with scars on their shoulders like working animals. . . . To console them for their services, they beat and insulted the Indians, hardly calling them anything but "dog." Would to God they treated them as such, because they would not have killed a dog in a million years, while they thought nothing of knifing Indians by tens and twenties and of cutting slices off them to test the sharpness of their blades.   —Fray Bartolomé de Las Casas, *Spain*

Taíno Boys and a Parrot

Two Taíno boys, as yet unhardened by the tyranny under which they live, walk alone along a footpath. Perched on their shoulders are pet *guuacamay*, parrots whose brilliant feathers are much prized by the Taíno. Coming toward them along the same footpath are two Spaniards. But why are they grinning? The boys hesitate uncertainly, they freeze. Their feet die beneath them—they are like lead. Fear bursts trembling upon them as the Spaniards reach toward the shimmering parrots. The boys feel the agitation of the birds, the nervous shifting of their feet. There is a terrible squawking and fluttering of wings. The boys cry out and the Spaniards laugh. With a great blow of their gleaming swords, the boys' heads roll to the ground.

And who, down to the lowest idiot, will not think blind and downright malicious those who dared spread this belief and defame so many people, saying Indians need tutors because they are incapable of organization, when, in reality, they have kings and governors, villages, houses and property rights, and communicate with one another on all levels of human, political, economical and social relations, living in peace and harmony? . . . They should have loved and praised the Indians, and even learned from them, instead of belittling them by publicizing them as beastly; instead of stealing, afflicting, oppressing and annihilating them, making as much of them as they would a heap of dung on a public square.

—Fray Bartolomé de Las Casas, Spain

Gold and Cuba   (1511)

In Cuba, the Taíno hide their gold. Those who know the Spaniards all too well come forward to submit to the king of Castile. They return home, confident in their security, and sleep soundly for the first time in many nights. In the darkness, Diego Velásquez, under orders from Colón's brother, mobilizes troops. Quietly, they enter a sleeping village and, one by one, the houses are set on fire. The screams of the dying fill the night air. Men, women, and little children escape from the flames, only to be captured as slaves and branded with hot irons. Others are tortured to disclose where the gold is. The same is repeated across the island. Eight hundred thousand Taíno are killed in the carnage. Later, visitors to Cuba note the workers' bodies, scarred and burned.

In the gold mines, work is brutal. With little more than pick-axes, the Taíno are forced to burrow into the bowels of the earth. When water fills the caverns, they must scoop it out by hand. Husbands are separated from wives and families for eight months out of the year. They are ill fed, and thousands die of starvation. The women, too, are overworked in the fields, raising the food that feeds the Spaniards. Infant mortality climbs—seven thousand Taíno babies die in Cuba in a three-month period. Taíno who escape are hunted down by special police and whipped until left for dead. On the sacred Day of the Body of Christ in Hispaniola, the king's accountant throws a lavish banquet, and the saltcellars are filled with grains of gold.

It is not possible to recount the hundredth part of what I have seen with my own eyes. A man had need to have a body of iron to undergo the labor they endure in getting gold out of the mines. They must delve and search a hundred times over in the inner parts of the mountains till they dig them down from top to bottom; they must work the very rocks hollow.
    —Fray Bartolomé de Las Casas, *Spain*

You know that the Christians are coming here; and you know how they treated the chiefs and people of Haiti. They come to do the same here. Do you know perhaps why they do it? . . . They do it . . . because they have a god whom they greatly adore and love. To make us adore him they strive to conquer us and take our lives. . . . Behold [this gold,] here is the God of the Christians. They seek him everywhere, in the rocks and under the ground. . . . If we preserve this gold, they will finally have to kill us, in order to take it from us. Let us throw it into this river.   —Hatuey, *Taíno*

. . . they were so relentlessly persecuted and pursued with their wives and children up into the hills—so tired, hungry, and harassed . . . [and] there went with them disease, death, and misery. . . . Just as if they had been killed in the wars . . . they died of hunger and sickness that surrounded them, and the fatigue and oppression that followed. . . . [After] 1496 . . . no more than a third remained of the multitudes that had been on the island.

—Fray Bartolomé de Las Casas, *Spain*

Wherefore many went to the woods and there hung themselves, after having killed their children, saying it was far better to die than to live so miserably. . . . Some threw themselves from high cliffs down precipices; others jumped into the sea . . . and others starved themselves to death.

—Girolamo Benzoni, *Italy*

Anacaona   (1503)

The widow Anacaona rules the province of Xaragua, inherited at the death of her brother Beheccio. Xaragua remains only nominally under Spanish control; Anacaona continues to resist demands for labor, though she pays food tribute to Spain. On a Sunday afternoon, she graciously accompanies Nicolás de Ovando, the new governor of Hispaniola, into her statehouse. Inside, eighty regional leaders are gathered for talks.

But Ovando has other plans. The leaders are bound with ropes and a firebrand is lowered against the thatched roof. The flames jut skyward, melting the grass, turning the writhing bodies within to charred ash.

Outside, mounted soldiers charge through Xaragua, lancing civilians. The few who survive are condemned to slavery. Anacaona is spared because of her royal station, only to be hung.

... [Ovando] decided to perform what Spaniards always perform on arrival in the Indies, that is to say, when they come to a heavily settled area, being so outnumbered that they make sure all hearts tremble at the mere mention of the name Christians; therefore they terrorize the natives by performing a large-scale and cruel massacre ... great were the ravages and cruelties done to men, old people and innocent children, and great was the number of people killed.

—Fray Bartolomé de Las Casas, *Spain*

The Bahaman Lucayos   (1509–1513)

The Caribbean is fast becoming depopulated. Enterprising Spaniards search farther afield for slaves to work the mines and plantations. In the Bahamas the harvest of the Lucayos begins. Villages are raided at night; the holds of ships are crammed full of thousands of prisoners. In Hispaniola the Spaniards draw lots. The Lucayos, those who have not poisoned themselves, are distributed among them. A Lucayan man lashes together yauruma wood and builds a small raft. He places his family on board and fills gourds of water for the trip. They steal away from Hispaniola and float toward the Bahamas, and freedom.

But fifty leagues away from the Hispaniola shore, a Bahaman ship bears down upon them. It is full of Lucayan slaves. Desperately, the small raft tries to dodge the oncoming vessel; but it is seen. The flight is over. Torn from the raft, they are returned to the corral where other Lucayan slaves are held awaiting distribution.

. . . they used to stuff shipholds with hundreds of Indians of both sexes and all ages, pack them like sardines and close all the hatchways to prevent escape, thus shutting off air and light. And, since ships carried food and water only for the Spanish crew, the Indians died and were thrown into the sea, and the floating corpses were so numerous that a ship could find its course by them alone, without need of a compass, charts, or the art of navigations. . . . no ship ever raided the Lucayos that did not . . . have to throw overboard one-third or one-fourth of its human cargo. . . .

—Fray Bartolomé de Las Casas, *Spain*

The Lucayos are reported extinct. In vain, a ship combs the Bahamas Islands in search of survivors. After three years, it returns with only eleven persons. Among them is an old man.

I stood there staring at them, especially at the old man, who was tall and venerable and had a long face, dignified and authoritative . . . and thinking how many like him there were all over these islands, and how in so short a time and almost under my eyes they had been destroyed without offending us in the least, nothing was left for us to do but lift our eyes to Heaven and tremble at divine judgment.

—Fray Bartolomé de Las Casas, *Spain*

Enrique's Resistance   (1519–1533)

From out of the carnage of the massacre of Xaragua stands a little boy named Enrique. His father, Magicorex, ruler of the lands of Bahoruco, lies dead and smoldering beneath the state-house ruins.

When Enrique reaches manhood, he assumes leadership of his people, but they are not free. Their lives belong to a planter named Valenzuela, who treats the Taíno with contempt: they are animals, they have no feelings. When he rapes Enrique's wife, it is the final insult in a long list of abuses. Enrique leads his people into the wilds of the Bahoruco mountains. His action brings a flash of hope to many, and hundreds of Taíno escape to join him. With military genius, Enrique defends the mountain passes; army after army of Spaniards are repelled. His followers adore him; he gives them a moment of freedom, a moment to live as Taíno. Fourteen years later, an embarrassed Spain sues for peace. Enrique is victorious.

In a more just world Enrique would have been the master. . . . Valenzuela viewed Enriquillo as a slave and valued him less than manure in the street.

—Fray Bartolomé de Las Casas, *Spain*

The Spanish came to call him the rebel Enrique, and those who followed him were termed rebels and insurgents, although in truth they were not rebelling, but only fleeing from

Sixteenth-century engraving of a Taíno from the island of Hispaniola.
Although the engraving is based on eyewitness descriptions, the
European engraver never saw any Taíno in person.

their cruel enemies, who were misusing and destroying them, just as a cow or an ox tries to escape from the slaughterhouse.
—Fray Bartolomé de Las Casas, *Spain*

. . . the Indian kings and chiefs never did recognize the superiority of the Castilian King. From the day of discovery to the present, they have been tyrannized . . . killed in cruel wars and oppressed into a most inhuman servitude. . . . Nor was there ever any justice here . . . and where there is no justice, the oppressed are entitled to right their own wrongs.
—Fray Bartolomé de Las Casas, *Spain*

You have come a powerful man to these lands unknown to you, and you have inspired great fear wherever you have gone. I want to tell you that we believe in the life hereafter. Departing souls go in two directions: one is bad, full of darkness, where those who do evil to men go; the other is good and happy, and peace-loving people go there. Therefore, if you feel you must die and believe that every man answers for his deeds after death, you will not harm those who do not harm you. . . .
—(Name not given), *Taíno*

[The Spaniards] . . . are violent and perfidious men, and [only] seek to shed the blood of innocent people: [and because of this], I will neither enter into relations with you, nor form any alliance with so false a people.
—Mayobanex, *Ciguayo*

I know the Spanish very well, because they killed my father and . . . grandfather and all the people of the kingdom of Xaragua, and reduced the population of the entire island of

Española. . . . I have fled to my own land, where . . . neither [I] nor any of my followers are harming anyone, but are simply defending ourselves against those who came to capture and kill us. I need not talk to another Spaniard.

—Enrique, *Taíno*

Mexico

I am intoxicated, I weep, I grieve,
I think, I speak,
within myself I discover this:
indeed, I shall never die,
indeed, I shall never disappear.
There where there is no death, there where death is overcome,
let me go there,
Indeed I shall never disappear.
                    —Nezahualcoyotl, Texcoco Nahuatl

By 1499 Spain had extended her enterprise as far west as Cubagua Island off the Venezuelan coast, where the discovery of pearl fisheries electrified the nation. By the early decades of the sixteenth century, the Spanish had reconnoitered Panama and Honduras and were growing relatively familiar with Central America. As caravels crisscrossed the Caribbean, it was inevitable that they would encounter peoples from the Mexican mainland. The first mention of the Maya was made during the fourth and final voyage of Cristóbal Colón in 1502, when a canopied Mayan vessel intercepted his ship. Luckily for the Maya, Colón's star had set at court; but the reprieve would not last long.

In 1517 a Spanish slave expedition under Francisco Hernández de Córdoba probed the Yucatán. In return for this sinister version of Spanish greeting, the Maya extended a welcome of their own, and Indian armies beat back Córdoba all the way along the coast until he was driven into the sea. However, in this brief encounter, the Spaniards managed to raid a Mayan temple and carry away coffers of gold. In Cuba, the vision of wealth and the unlimited possibility of slaves dizzied even sober minds and prompted the immediate outfitting of an expedition to the Yucatán.

This party, led by Juan de Grijalva, had no sooner put onto the Mexican shore when it unexpectedly encountered a Taíno woman from Jamaica. It is tempting to think that the poor reception accorded the Spaniards in the Mayan country might have owed more to prior knowledge of their practices than anything else. In any case, Grijalva was shown more gold and then wisely told that it lay farther to the west, in the country of the Aztec.

Grijalva raced back to Cuba with a full report. The samples of gold brought back by the expedition inflamed the wildest passions. The Spanish king immediately was petitioned for right of conquest, and royal authorization was granted to Hernándo Cortés. In 1519 Cortés landed on the Mayan coast at Cozumel with an army of six hundred men, sixteen cavalry, and cannon. After a brief and none-too-pleasant encounter, he sailed north out of the Mayan country, toward the land of the Aztec gold.

In the sixteenth century, the sweeping Valley of Mexico was the seat of the powerful Aztec Empire. Formed nearly a century earlier by the Triple Alliance of the Mexica, Texcoco, and Tlacopán, the Aztec domain quickly extended across much of central Mexico. Many nations welcomed allegiance to the powerful Aztec, but others were forced into it by bloody conquest. Feelings ran high among the Aztecs' enemies, chafing under heavy tributes, at the same time that the Spanish unwittingly were putting in an appearance along the shore. As it happened, Cortés made landfall in the coastal nation of Tlaxcala, said to be the most formidable opponent of the Aztec, and one of the regions farthest from its control.

Aztec prophecies foretold the empire's destiny. Belief in a cyclical revolution of time portended the day when the conquerors inevitably would become the conquered and the mighty Toltec predecessors in the Valley of Mexico would return to reclaim their kingdom. This was to occur in the year One Reed—the year in which kings would fall. Cortés landed in Mexico on April 22, 1519: in the calendrical year One Reed.

Beyond the massive military of the Aztec Empire was a world filled with beauty. Watered causeways led into the capital city of Tenochtítlan, whose graceful temples rose in architectural grandeur. Gardens resplendent with flowers, aviaries aflutter with the plumage of royal birds, and open markets filled with exotic perfumes, teaks, fruits, and vegetables graced the city. There were universities and military schools, musicians and artists, shopkeepers and gem cutters. Poets and philosophers sang the praises of their world. Truly, this was México.

> *Extended lies the city, lies México,*
> *spreading circles of emerald light,*
> *radiating splendor like a quetzal plume . . .*
> *O author of life, your house is here! . . .*
> *Your song is heard on earth; it spreads among the people.*
> *Behold México . . .*
>
> —Aztec poem

The Arrival   (1519)

On the shore, emissaries sent by Moctezuma watch the Spaniards closely. Important among them is a scribe, charged with the faithful execution of everything he sees and hears. The emissaries hail Cortés and are taken aboard the vessel. They taste the white stuff they say looks like tortillas, though it is leavened. They drink the red wine, which makes the world reel. They talk of Moctezuma and offer the presents he has sent. It is the first act of diplomacy between the two nations. Cortés initiates the second. To demonstrate Spanish might, a match is lowered against the wick of a cannon. Fire leaps from the muzzle, the deck pitches to the thunder, a tree struck on shore splinters into a thousand fragments. Cortés eagerly anticipates their reaction. Are the emissaries struck dumb with fear? Are they immobilized? No—anxiously, they prod the scribe to record; there the poor man sits, furiously drawing.

Cholula   (1519)

Cortés, his army swelled by allies from Tlaxcala, begins the inland march toward the Aztec capital. He repeatedly has ignored all of Moctezuma's entreaties to advance no farther. At Cholula, the first town in Moctezuma's great alliance, the soldiers eagerly grasp at the rich presents of gold and feathers brought from the capital as a peace offering, but sneer at the oft-repeated message not to enter Tenochtítlan.

The Cholulans are instructed to offer resistance. Soldiers are sent from the Aztec capital. Cortés suspects an ambush and fires into the crowded plaza, striking civilians. The streets are awash with gore; flies buzz around corpses. When Cortés withdraws, six thousand Cholulan citizens lie dead in the streets.

24

They gave the Spaniards banners of gold, banners of quetzal feathers, and gold necklaces. And when they had given them these gifts they broke into smiles, they were overjoyed, filled with bliss. They were like monkeys, running their fingers over the gold and holding it high, sitting delightedly before it, as if it renewed them and brightened their hearts.

Truly this is what they lust after and thirst for. For this they puff up their bodies in vanity; they are famished for gold, like hungry pigs they desire it.

And they eagerly tore down the gold banners, they wave them about, admire them on every side. They are like fools babbling in tongues; every utterance is in a savage language.
—Aztec chronicler

Then there arose from the Spaniards a cry summoning all the noblemen, lords, war leaders, warriors, and common folk; and when they had crowded into the temple courtyard, then the Spaniards and their allies blocked the entrances and every exit. There followed a butchery of stabbing, beating, killing of the unsuspecting Cholulans armed with no bows and arrows, protected by no shields . . . with no warning, they were treacherously, deceitfully slain.   —Aztec chronicler

Moctezuma (1519)

Inside the palace, Moctezuma is informed of the Cholulan massacre. Cortés has not been stopped—the army marches on. In near-panic, Moctezuma orders maguey plants set into the ground to conceal the thoroughfare into the city and sends Cortés an emissary who poses as the Aztec leader. But Cortés only laughs, and demands to be taken to the real Moctezuma. Disdainfully, the maguey plants are kicked aside. The army marches on.

Terror grips Tenochtítlan. Moctezuma is paralyzed with fear, a pitiable figure. Palsied into inaction, he can do little but hold his head and give vent to grief. Inside the houses, the people live dying, weighed down by the oppressive knowledge that the world as they know it has come to an end. And then, as they wait, the army appears on the horizon.

[The city] rose in tumult, alarmed as if by an earthquake, as if there were a constant reeling of the face of the earth.

—Aztec chronicler

Shocked, terrified, Moctezuma himself wept in the distress he felt for his city. Everyone was in terror; everyone was astounded, afflicted. Many huddled in groups, wept in foreboding for their own fates and those of their friends. Others, dejected, hung their heads. Some groups exchanged tearful greetings; others tried mutual encouragement. Fathers would run their hands over their small boys' hair and, smoothing it, say, "Woe, my beloved sons! How can what we fear be happening in your time?" Mothers, too: "My beloved sons, how can you live through what is in store for you?"

—Aztec chronicler

The iron of their lances . . . glistened from afar; the shimmer of their swords was as of a sinuous water course. Their iron breast and back pieces, their helmets clanked. Some came completely encased in iron—as if turned to iron. . . . And ahead of them . . . ran their dogs, panting, with foam continually dripping from their muzzles.   —Aztec chronicler

We were astounded. . . . the majestic towers and houses, all of massive stone and rising out of the waters, were like enchanted castles we had read of in books. Indeed, some of our men even asked if what we saw was not a dream.

—Bernal Díaz, *Spanish Army*

[Your Highness,] . . . there is so much to describe that I do not know how to begin even to recount some part of it . . . [Moctezuma has] all the things to be found under the heavens . . . fashioned in gold and silver and jewels and feathers . . . no smith in the world could have done better, and in jewels so fine that it is impossible to imagine with what instruments they were cut. . . . There are in the city many large and beautiful houses [with] large . . . rooms and . . . very pleasant gardens of flowers both on the upper and lower floors. . . . Along one of the causeways to this great city run two aqueducts . . . [and] good fresh water . . . flows into the heart of the city and from this they all drink.

—Hernándo Cortés, *Spain*

What now, my warriors? We have come to the end. We have taken our medicine. Is there anywhere a mountain we can run away to and climb? —Moctezuma, *Aztec*

Do the former rulers know what is happening in their absence? O that any of them might see, might wonder at what has befallen me—at what I am seeing now that they have gone. For I cannot be dreaming. —Moctezuma, *Aztec*

Moctezuma, the ninth Aztec emperor in a line of succession
dating back to the poet-ruler Nezahualcoyotl, was the last to
begin his reign before the Spanish conquest.

Moctezuma's own property was then brought out . . . precious things like necklaces with pendants, arm bands tufted with quetzal feathers, golden arm bands, bracelets, golden anklets with shells, rulers' turquoise diadems, turquoise nose rods; no end of treasure. They took all, seized everything for themselves . . . as if it were theirs.   —Aztec chronicler

Massacre and Death of Moctezuma   (1520)

The Spanish occupy Tenochtítlan. Inside the palace, the army breaks through a sealed doorway, bursting into a room filled with golden treasure. The sight turns them mad with greed, and they determine to have Tenochtítlan for their own. Moctezuma is seized and held prisoner inside the Imperial Palace. Cortés assumes his tribute over neighboring states, glutting himself with Aztec wealth.

In April, at the height of the Aztecs' most sacred religious celebration, the Spaniards attack. Aztecs fall dead and dying in all directions. Humiliated and dejected, the once-powerful Moctezuma is dragged before his people in chains and, from the summit of the Imperial Palace, is ordered to command his army not to resist.

But the Aztec know that Moctezuma no longer belongs to himself. They elect his brother Cuitlahuac leader. Days later, Moctezuma is found dead. The Spaniards claim that the Aztec have killed him, but his loyal subjects disagree. Moctezuma was strangled inside his own palace.

. . . they charged the crowd with their iron lances and hacked us with their iron swords. They slashed the backs of some. . . . They hacked at the shoulders of others, splitting their bodies open. . . . The blood of the young warriors ran like water; it

gathered in pools. . . . And the Spaniards began to hunt them out of the administrative buildings, dragging out and killing anyone they could find . . . even starting to take those buildings to pieces as they searched. —Aztec chronicler

La Noche Triste (1520)

The Aztec under Cuitlahuac mount a spirited resistance. The Spaniards are pinned inside the Imperial Palace, where they are besieged for many weeks. Two months after the massacre, desperate for food and water, they attempt to steal away in the middle of a rainy night; but their lust for gold is too great and the loot weighs them down. As they escape across the aqueducts leading out of the city, they sink beneath the water like falling stones. Two-thirds of the Spanish army never live to reach the outskirts of the city. The Spaniards forever after recall the event as "The Sad Night." But the Aztec can only wonder.

That night, at midnight, the enemy came out, crowded together, the Spaniards in the lead, the Tlaxcallans following. . . . Screened by a fine drizzle, a fine sprinkle of rain, they were able undetected to cross the canals . . . just as they were crossing, a woman drawing water saw them. "Mexicans! Come, all of you. . . . They are already leaving! They are already secretly getting out!" Then a watcher at the top of the temple . . . also shouted, and his cries pervaded the entire city. —Aztec chronicler

The canal was filled, crammed with them. Those who came along behind walked over . . . on corpses. . . . It was as if a mountain of men had been laid down; they had pressed against one another, smothered one another. . . .

—Aztec chronicler

The Final Fall (1521)

The Aztec who think the Spanish have gone for good do not know Spain. Cortés waits with diabolical patience as the army spends a year rebuilding, regaining strength. New alliances are made with neighboring city-states as other allies of Moctezuma back away, demoralized.

. . . at about the time that the Spaniards had fled from Mexico . . . there came a great sickness, a pestilence, the smallpox. It . . . spread over the people with great destruction of men. It caused great misery. . . . The brave Mexican warriors were indeed weakened by it. It was after all this had happened that the Spaniards came back.

—Aztec chronicler

Less than a year later, the army returns. But by now, the Aztec are crippled from European illnesses that have ravaged the capital. Cuitlahuac is dead of smallpox; Cuauhtémoc is successor. For seventy-five days, Tenochtítlan withstands the siege. As they advance, the Spaniards raze the city, tearing down the beautiful architecture, and filling in the canals. The glory and triumph of the Aztec wither under the trampling feet of the invaders. Inside the royal aviaries, hot orange fire spurts, deliberately set. The innocent birds fly frantically against the cages as the smell of fire fills the air. The Aztec are much like these birds, trapped within the confines of their besieged city. In the streets of Tenochtítlan, hundreds of thousands of gaunt and starving Aztec citizens die. They have astounded the Spaniards by their undaunted resistance, but finally Cuauhtémoc is forced to surrender. Later, he is executed.

Ah, captain, I have done everything within my power to defend my kingdom and deliver it from your hands. But as fortune has not favored me, take my life; it will be most fitting; and in so doing you will bring an end to the Mexican kingdom, for already you have ruined and destroyed my city and my people. —Cuauhtémoc, *Aztec*

Fighting continued, both sides took captives, on both sides there were deaths . . . great became the suffering of the common folk. There was hunger. Many died of famine. . . . The people ate anything—lizards, barn swallows, corn leaves, saltgrass. . . . Never had such suffering been seen. . . . The enemy pressed about us like a wall . . . they herded us. . . . The brave warriors were still hopelessly resisting.
—Aztec chronicler

Great was the stench of the dead. . . . Your grandfathers died, and with them died the son of the king and his brothers and kinsmen. So it was that we became orphans, O my sons! So we became when we were young. All of us were thus. We were born to die! —Aztec chronicler

Finally the battle just quietly ended. Silence reigned. Nothing happened. The enemy left. All was quiet, and nothing more took place. Night fell, and the next day nothing happened, either. No one spoke aloud; the people were crushed. . . . So ended the war.   —Aztec chronicler

Proudly stands the city of México—
Tenochtítlan,
here no one fears to die in war . . .
Keep this in mind, O princes . . .
Who could attack Tenochtítlan?
Who could shake the foundations of heaven?

—Aztec poem

The North Atlantic

*Learn now, my brother, once for all, because I must open to thee
my heart: there is no Indian who does not consider himself infinitely more happy and more powerful than the French.*
— (*Name not given*), Micmac

In 1534 Jacques Cartier sailed between the high, rolling cliffs of
the Gaspé and claimed the land of the Micmac for France. The
Micmac, who had every right to be incredulous, monitored
the progress of his ships along the coast. Failing to subscribe to the
popular European theory that natives either ran in dread or fell
prostrate in veneration, the Micmac chose their own response.
Cartier and his companions "sawe two companies of boates of
wilde men going from one land to the other: their boates were in
number about fourtie or fiftie. One part of the which . . . went on
shore making a great noise, beckening unto us that wee should
come on land, shewing us certaine skinnes upon pieces of wood
. . . wee would not goe to them . . . they seeing us flee, prepared to
follow us . . . making many signes of joy and mirth, as it were de-
siring our friendship. . . ."

Cartier was not the first European to coast Micmac waters.
John Cabot in 1497, Giovanni da Verrazano in 1524, and Estéban
Gómez in 1525, among others, had preceded him. And for years,
Basque and Breton fishermen had probed the region for cod and

brought home tales of a fabled golden city called Norumbega. European interest was fueled, and when the Englishman Bartholomew Gosnold entered the Gulf of Maine for the first time in 1602, he was stunned to find Micmac traders navigating the coast in their own Basque shallops.

Following Cartier came the establishment of the first permanent French colony on the North American continent. In 1608 Samuel de Champlain built Quebec City along the banks of the Saint Lawrence River in the country of the Huron, where the French soon indulged in the dishonorable pursuit of obliterating indigenous religions. Jesuit priests poured into New France. And although there were many converts, there were many others who resisted.

Other than scattered coastal enclaves and hardy black-robed Jesuits, so intent on their mission that they seemed impervious to the cold, few braved the frigid climate. For a long time, much of the interior remained free of extensive European settlement. But although the cold dissuaded permanent occupation, Europeans coveted an item that abounded there, which they went to great lengths to obtain: fur. And for this, the Indian nations were indispensable.

The early decades of European-Indian interaction were ones of accommodation—largely of French entrepreneurs to the regional Indian polities who set the standards for an evolving fur trade. The Montagnais, in the cold Laurentides north of the Saint Lawrence, had long traded hides and moose meat for Huron corn, as did Micmac along the frigid North Atlantic coast. Spring was the time of coming together when Indian families, which had dispersed into the hinterland for the winter hunt, reunited to feast, trade, and hold their national ceremonies. When the Micmac, Huron, Montagnais, Algonquin, and other northern nations discovered the French interest in furs, they easily incorporated the Europeans into their centuries-old system of exchange. French *coureurs de bois,* who had learned enough of

Indian cultures to fit no longer into their own, became middlemen and somewhat of a New World curiosity. And even when trading posts cheated Indian businessmen by falsifying measurements, the latter quickly demonstrated that the Europeans had more than met their match, by wetting hides and forcing the scales to reflect the same.

The British were not far behind the French in developing the fur trade and soon vied with them by erecting permanent posts, such as those at Hudson Bay and York Factory, where they saved time and money by encouraging Indian traders to bring their wares to them. Gradually, the fur trade, which had begun so much in Indian favor, shifted. The old relationship between Indian hunter and animals changed as musk-bearing mammals were slaughtered at an impressive rate. Village cohesion felt the strain as younger men pursued the economic opportunities of the trading post rather than the traditional round of the village. Tribal authority was undermined as European economics established new rules of conduct and offered substantial incentives for individuals to operate outside of prescribed cultural patterns. Finally, regional stability was disrupted as tribes who formerly traded together to promote peace found themselves in competition over scarce resources—and enemy nations became armed with deadly European weapons. Although the nations ultimately survived, this period in their history is remembered as one of turmoil that was not without cost.

By the mid-eighteenth century, France and England were engaged in a bitter struggle over the hegemony of the region. The series of conflicts that culminated in the French and Indian War led to the fall of New France in 1760. Although the northern limits of the Montagnais and Nascapi country still remained, at best, sparsely inhabited, the southern reaches along the coasts of Nova Scotia, New Brunswick, and Maine had taken on a complex frontier aspect. Frenchmen, Englishmen, trappers, settlers, and priests freely intermingled with Indian leaders, businessmen, and individuals on a personal basis. Negotiating boundaries and cultural distance became increasingly difficult, yet Indian nations maintained their integrity and clearly demonstrated that no European power held sway over them when it came to the subject of sovereignty.

I am only a poor little animal that goes cringing upon the earth; you Frenchmen are the giants of the world, who make all else tremble. . . . You say that the French have come to live at Quebec to defend us, and that you will come into our country to protect us. . . .

You tell us to guard what we do, you grip our arms and we shudder; then you grip at the heart, and all our body trembles.
                                                                    —Capitanal, *Montagnais*

Cartier (1534)

The Frenchmen aboard Cartier's ship wonder about the inhabitants of New France. Europeans once thought that the people of America were monsters, with eyes in the center of their foreheads like the great Cyclops. All that is past; now they know better. The men on the ship also wonder what the Indian people will think of them and whether their reaction will be one of hostility or fear. In all likelihood they believe, as many European explorers have, that the native inhabitants will be awed. After all, when they come at the ships, touching and making exclamations of joy, are they not revering them?

[The] . . . event created such a stir that the noted men were called to discuss the matter and to see what must be done about it, and on their getting together it was decided that there shall be some good spiritual men selected and sent on along the coast to watch the strange people's movements. . . . Whether they were creatures with the speech or not, none knew because no one had heard them talk. However, it was determined to have them watched and this watching to continue until his true description and habits had been learned. . . . Just at this time an exciting news was brought from the extreme north to the effect that the white man's big canoe had come again, and had landed its people who are still remaining on the land on the north shore of the "Maquozz-bem-to-cook, Lake River," and have planted some heavy blocks of wood in the form of a cross. These people are white and the lower part of the faces of the elder ones are covered with hair, and the hair is in different colors, and the eyes are not alike, some have dark while others have light colored eyes. . . . They have shown nothing only friendship. . . . When this news spread, the people took it so quietly and talked about it in such a way, there was no excitement, but everybody took it as though it were an old affair, yet it had such effect upon them, that it was evident that the general desire was, that the habits of the strange people must be well learned, and all agree to wait and see what kind of a treatment they will extend to the red people.

—Joseph Nicolar, *Penobscot*

Hochelaga (1535)

Taignoagny and Domagaia stand again upon their native soil. After spending a year in France, where they have been taken by Jacques Cartier to learn the language, they have returned. But in Europe, they have learned more than a few French words. They have learned of French numbers, of power, of glory—and they have learned that they do not want the French to take a foothold on their land. In France they have learned one more thing: they have learned not to trust.

Hoping that Cartier will soon leave their country, they are stricken to realize that his plan is to push up the mighty Saint Lawrence toward Hochelaga, a fortified town situated on an island within the river. Vigorous attempts to prevent him from going fail; Cartier will see Hochelaga.

The town sits quietly along the river, ringed by heavy palisades. Cornfields fall away on all sides, giving way to oak and flaming maple that push up the slopes of a mountain so beautiful that Cartier calls it Mount Royal. Inside Hochelaga, people touch him in greeting, and Cartier imagines that he is being revered as a God. Boldly, he enters their longhouses, noting the furnishings and tubs bursting with corn; the crowd presses close behind him. As he prepares to leave, women block his path and offer dishes of food, but he has no taste for it. Unwittingly, he insults their hospitality, for to feed is to honor a guest. Impressed, Cartier remembers Hochelaga well.

Years later when the French return, the town has vanished without a trace. They shrug, and on the site of Hochelaga, build Montreal.

Sickness   (1535)

After his uninvited visit to Hochelaga, Cartier returns to the village of Stadacona. Although the leader Donnacona offers every hospitality, Cartier insists on building a fort for security. As the winter snows begin to deepen, a strange sickness grips his men. Symptoms are severe, and an alarming number die. To mask their weakened condition, Cartier implores his dying men to bang on the insides of the ship as though making repairs. The Stadaconans also appear ill, but they recover. Though his men die fast, Cartier cannot bring himself to save them by asking help of a people he considers inferior. Fear, mistrust, and prejudice are costly.

... then did their legges swell, their sinnowes shrinke as blacke as any cole ... their mouth became stincking, their gummes so rotten, that all the flesh did fall off, even to the rootes of the teeth which did also almost fall out. ... That day Philip Rougemont, borne in Amboise, died, being 22 yeeres olde ... our Captaine caused him to be ripped (open)

to see if, by any meanes possible we might know what it was
. . . he was found to have his heart white, but rotten, and
more than a quart of red water about it . . . his lungs blacke
and mortified, his blood was altogither shrunke about the
heart. . . . In such sort did the sicknesse continue and en-
crease, that there were not above three sound men in the
ships. —Jacques Cartier, *France*

Out of desperation, Cartier belatedly turns to Domagaia for
help. The Stadaconans instruct him to drink a tea made of bark.
Cartier is so distressed that he orders an entire tree felled. Within
days, his men are cured of the scurvy that has sickened them, and
the French are forced to admit that in the eyes of the Stadaconans,
they are children.

After this medicine was found . . . there was such strife about
it, who should be first to take of it, that they were ready to kill
one another, so that a tree as big as any Oake in France was
spoiled and lopped bare . . . and it wrought so well, that if all
the phisicians of Mountpelier and Lovaine had bene there
with all the drugs of Alexandria, they would not have done so
much in one yere, as that tree did in six dayes. . . .
—Jacques Cartier, *France*

The earth is our mother. She nourishes us; that which we put
into the ground she returns to us, and healing plants she gives
us likewise. If we are wounded, we go to our mother and seek
to lay the wounded part against her, to be healed. Animals
too, do thus, they lay their wounds to the earth.
—Bedagi (Big Thunder), *Penobscot*

I am greatly astonished that the French have so little clever-
ness . . . in the effort to persuade us to convert our poles, our
barks, and our wigwams into those houses of stone and of
wood which are [as] tall and lofty, according to their account,
as these trees. Very well! But why now . . . do men of five to
six feet in height need houses which are sixty to eighty? For,
in fact, as thou knowest very well thyself . . . do we not find in
our own all the conveniences and the advantages that you
have with yours, such as reposing, drinking, sleeping, eating,
and amusing ourselves with our friends when we wish?

—(Name not given), *Micmac*

The Capture of Donnacona   (1536)

The mistrust which Taignoagny and Domagaia place in Cartier is
well founded. They remain determinedly aloof when the French
prepare to leave in the spring and warn Donnacona not to enter
the fort. But Donnacona cannot believe that the French will harm
an ambassador and a leader. Sensing their distrust, Cartier pub-
licly declares that no one will be carried into France as before—
and Taignoagny smiles with relief.

Cartier is lying. In truth, he plans to seize the leading men of
Stadacona and take them prisoner to France to confirm to the king
what he has seen, and to induce Donnacona to repeat the statement that rubies and gold abound in the country of Saguenay.
Donnacona, Taignoagny, Domagaia, and eight others are captured.

About two of the clocke in the afternoone they came, & being
come neere our ships, our Captaine went to salute Donnacona, who also shewed him a mery countenance, albeit very
fearefully his eyes were still bent toward the wood. . . .
Taignoagny . . . had bid Donnacona hee should not come

aboord our ships. . . . Presently . . . [Donnacona] entred into
the Fort with the Captaine, but . . . Taignoagny came to make
him come out again. Our Captaine seeing that there was no
other remedy, began to call unto them to take them.

—Jacques Cartier, *France*

The Stadaconans scream and cry at the side of the ship, pleading Donnacona's release. Twenty-four chains of wampum are
flung at Cartier's feet for ransom. He heeds them not. He has
promised a safe return the following year; and Donnacona is carried helplessly away. Four years pass. Cartier returns; but the
ship's hold is empty. Donnacona, Taignoagny, Domagaia, and the
others have died, prisoners in a foreign land. Only one little girl,
ten years old, is still alive. She is never returned from France.
Along the Saint Lawrence, Donnacona's wife holds in her lap the
empty frying pan her husband has given her—his present from the
French as they bore him away.

. . . the people of [Stadacona] came to our shipps . . . [and
when they] inquired of the Captaine where Donnacona and
the rest were, the Captaine answered . . . [t]hat Donnacona
was dead in France, and that his body rested in the earth, and
that the rest stayed there as great Lords, and were maried,
and would not returne backe into their Countrey. . . .

—Jacques Cartier, *France*

Thou reproachest us, very inappropriately, that our country is
a little hell in contrast with France, which thou comparest to
a terrestrial paradise. . . . Thou sayest of us also that we are
the most miserable and most unhappy of all men, living without religion, without manners, without honour, without social order, and, in a word, without any rules, like the beasts in

our woods and our forests. . . . Well, my brother, if thou dost not yet know the real feelings which our Indians have towards thy country and towards all thy nation, it is proper that I inform thee at once.

I beg thee now to believe that, all miserable as we seem in thine eyes, we consider ourselves nevertheless much happier than thou in this, that we are very content with the little that we have; and believe also once for all, I pray, that thou deceivest thyself greatly if thou thinkest to persuade us that thy country is better than ours. For if France, as thou sayest, is a little terrestrial paradise, art thou sensible to leave it? . . . Besides, since we are wholly convinced of the contrary, we scarcely take the trouble to go to France . . . we find all our riches and all our conveniences among ourselves, without trouble and without exposing our lives to the dangers. . . .

Now tell me this one little thing, if thou hast any sense: which of these two is the wisest and happiest—he who labours without ceasing and only obtains, and that with great trouble, enough to live on, or he who rests in comfort and finds all that he needs in the pleasure of hunting and fishing?

—(Name not given), *Micmac*

Fur Trade (1606)

Monsieur de Poutrincourt searches the Bay of Chouakoet for lands to settle. The Kennebec leader Olmechin knows all about French trade goods, and what they can buy in regional prestige.

Monsieur de Poutrincourt imagines that he will trade a little— distribute a few knives, scarves, and glass beads as he has done all along the coast. In amazement, he stares out at the sea covered with boats, filled with Kennebec men seeking trade. Six hundred additional canoes are promised to arrive the following day. Monsieur de Poutrincourt skirts the bay, ignoring the throngs on shore entreating him to land. He does not stop. They follow along the coast, outrunning the ship. At last, Monsieur de Poutrincourt drops anchor.

There follows a headlong dash to the water's edge. A man rips open his foot on a sharp rock. He falls. They cradle his head in their lap and refuse the entreaties of the French surgeon. At last, the doctor prevails and administers the wound by wrapping the foot in a binding cloth. The trade continues. Two hours later, the patient returns—limping, but otherwise well. He wears the binding cloth round his head.

The beaver does everything perfectly well, it makes kettles, hatchets, swords, knives, bread; and, in short, it makes everything.　　　　　　　—(Name not given), *Montagnais*

Baptizing the Micmac　　(1610)

Monsieur de Poutrincourt returns to the Micmac country after a European sojourn, to revive the abandoned French settlement at Port Royal. His first act—after planting corn, of course—is the "salvation of souls." Twenty-one Micmac are baptized from the household of the leader Membertou. They are given the names of great and worthy people of Europe. Membertou becomes King Henry; Actaudinech is Pope Paul. Membertou's wife is Queen Marie. And Mombertocoichis, alias Judas, walks along the beach with Lewes Lord Dauphin, Membertou's oldest son.

Kennebec Singing　　(1611)

The frost has turned the maple leaves a flaming red, and the evenings fall black and chill. Two camps pause for the night among the trees, separated only by the cold water of the Kennebec River. They are unsure of each other. Along one bank, huddled next to a fire for warmth, are French soldiers accompanied by the Jesuit priest Father Biard. The outline of their cannon is illuminated by the dancing flames.

Across the river, clear of the cannon's mouth, is a party of Kennebec. As the night wears on, the stillness is broken by the sound of their singing.

In the French camp, Father Biard's blood chills; he is convinced the songs are for the Devil. He quickly commands the uncouth soldiers beside him to sing the Ave Maria. Across the water, the Kennebec abruptly fall silent. When the French soldiers exhaust their repertoire of sacred hymns, they, too, lapse into silence. The Kennebec singing resumes. The priest becomes frantic. The soldiers loudly break into an imitation of the Kennebec songs and dance in disrespectful mime of the silhouetted figures along the bank. Again, the Kennebec stop to watch and listen. When the French grow tired, the Kennebec begin again, and in this way, songs and discordant sounds fill the air on both sides of the river throughout the cold night. Biard remarks that it is comical—two choirs coming together through song. One can only wonder what the Kennebec think.

Jesuits (1611)

When the Jesuits first arrive in New France, they are more a curiosity than an intrusion. They desire neither land nor furs, and ask only to live in an Indian household that they might study the language. Their verbal stumbling is a source of amusement; their quiet manners make them liked.

But there is one thing that makes these learned men poorly educated. They have not learned that God has made all religions, and they come here to tell people who already believe in a Creator that such a One exists. Although the people have faith in an afterlife, and practice a religion that enables them to live well with one another and the world, they are told that they are wrong, and must follow a new way. The missionaries cannot see that they are dividing communities and undermining faith, destroying civilizations that the Creator made in the Beginning, when He taught them how to pray.

Who do you think Pigarouich is? He is a big tree strongly rooted in the earth; do you think to hack it down all at once? Strike, strike heavy blows of the axe, and continue a long time, and at last you will overthrow it. It wants to fall, but it cannot, . . . its bad habits hold it down, in spite of itself. Do not lose courage; you will succeed in the end.

—Pigarouich, *Algonquin*

. . . I understand that your town is shaken by the words of the black robes, that several have already received Baptism, that a larger number desire it, and that you yourselves lend ear to these words which charm at the first impression. But without doubt you ignore, my brothers, where these promises of eternal life end. I have been among the French at Quebec and at Three Rivers; they taught me the foundation of their doctrine. But the more thoroughly I examined their mysteries, the less clearly I saw the light. They are tales invented to inspire us with true beliefs of an imaginary fire and, under the false hope of a good which never will come to us, engage us in inevitable unhappiness.

—Agouachimagan, *Algonquin*

A Century of Conflict (1650–1750)

European presence on the North Atlantic coast increases instability in the interior. Conflict is more frequent, the fallout more deadly.

English settlements pushing up from the south and French pressure bearing down from the north create a volatile environment. Although both England and France will expend much energy blaming the other for enjoining Indian nations to hostility, Indian leaders uphold their own sovereignty and side with the party least likely to threaten their interests.

Although several missionaries have come among us, sent by the French friars to break the peace between the English and us, yet their words have made no impression upon us. We are as firm as the mountains, and will so continue as long as the sun and moon endures.   —Bomazeen, *Kennebec*

The place where you are, where you make your dwellings, where you are building a fort, where you now want to enthrone yourself, this land of which you presently wish to make yourself absolute master, this land belongs to me, I have come from it as certainly as the grass, it is the very place of my birth and of my home, it is my land, me the Indian, yes I swear it, it is god who has given it to me to be my country forever . . . show me where I the Indian will lodge? you chase me from you; where do you want me to take refuge? you have taken possession of almost all this land in all its extent, there remains to me no more than Kchibouktouk. You envy me even this morsel. . . . Your residence at Port Royal does not make me greatly angry because you see that I have left you there tranquilly for a long time, but now you force me to speak out on account of the great theft you do to me.

—Micmac delegation

Penobscot Pirates   (1724)

The Penobscot carefully watch as English fishermen put ashore for wood and water. One by one, they steal their vessels. The English have brought war to their land; now, the Penobscot will fight back on the sea.

Fifty Penobscot pirate ships bear down upon eight English vessels along Fox Island. The English surrender. Their fleet increased, the Penobscot capture fourteen more, bringing their total to twenty-two vessels and fifty small boats. The British call them "powerful and desperate," and declare that they terrify all the shipping along the coast. Great sea battles are carried out, but attempts to take British forts fail. Two Penobscot shallops filled with combustibles are sent rollicking toward Saint George's garrison, but they are discovered and extinguished moments before impact. Still, the pirates keep navigation disrupted during the summer of 1724.

We were driven from our corn last year by the people about Kennebeck, and many of us died. We had no powder and shot to kill venison and fowl with, to prevent it. If you English were our friends as you pretend you are, you would not suffer us to starve as we did.

—Madokawando, *Penobscot*

You know your people do my Indians great deal wrong. They abuse them very much—yes they murder them; then they walk right off—nobody touches them. This makes my heart burn. . . . Some time ago a very bad man about Boston, shot an Indian dead. Your people said surely he should die, but it was not so. In the great prison house he eats and lives to this day. Certainly he never dies for killing [an] Indian.

—John Neptune, *Penobscot*

Rasle's War (1724)

Eleven hundred English soldiers and Indian allies surround the unfortunate Kennebec border town of Nanrantsouak, situated midway between British and French lines. For thirty years, the Kennebec have sustained French Jesuit Father Rasle at their town. When the English are unable to win Kennebec friendship, they blame Rasle for preaching hatred against the Protestants.

The dense underbrush conceals the soldiers' approach. Suddenly, musketshot explodes into the Kennebec cabins, riddling them with two thousand rounds. The Kennebec men, numbering only fifty, desperately hold off the army, while their women and children flee across the river. Father Rasle, his hands raised in supplication, is gunned down in front of a wooden cross in the center of the village. The odor of burning corn suffocates Nanrantsouak. It was to be the Kennebec food for the coming winter. But now there are fewer mouths to feed. Down the streets of Boston, the soldiers parade twenty-six Kennebec scalps. Fourteen are those of children.

[The raid was] the greatest slaughter we have made upon them for many years, or indeed ever on the Eastern Tribes.
—John Wentworth,
New Hampshire lieutenant governor

The *Indians* were under amazing Terror; yet in their surprise some of them snatch'd up their Guns and fired: but their hands shook and they did no Execution. They immediately betook themselves to flight, and in running fell on the very muzzles of our Guns that lay in Ambush. Our Men pursued them so warmly, that several were slain on the spot; more got into their Canoos, & others ran into the River; which was so rapid and the falls in some places so great, that many of them

were drowned. . . . The number of the dead which we sculpt, were twenty six. . . . The number in all that were kill'd and drown'd were supposed to be eighty, but some say more. . . .
—Samuel Penhallow, *New Hampshire Royal Council*

We hear on all sides that this Governor and the Bostonians say that the Abenakis are bad people. 'Tis in vain that we are taxed with having a bad heart. It is you, brother, that always attack us; your mouth is of sugar but your heart of gall. In truth, the moment you begin we are on our guard. . . . We have not yet sold the lands we inhabit, we wish to keep the possession of them. Our elders have been willing to tolerate you, brothers Englishmen, on the seaboard as far as Sawak-wato, as that has been so decided, we wish it to be so. But we will not cede one single inch of the lands we inhabit beyond what has been decided formerly by our fathers . . . we expressly forbid you to kill a single beaver, or to take a single stick of timber on the lands we inhabit. If you want timber we'll sell you some, but you shall not take it without our permission. . . .

Who hath authorized you to have those lands surveyed? . . . On condition that you will not encroach on those lands we will be at peace. . . . I repeat to you . . . that it depends on yourselves to be at peace with the Abenakis. Our [French] Father who is here present has nothing to do with what we say to you; we speak to you of our own accord . . . [he is] only as a witness of our words. We acknowledge no other boundaries of yours than your settlements whereon you have built, and we will not, under any pretext whatsoever, [let] . . . you pass beyond them. The lands we possess have been given us by the Master of Life. We acknowledge to hold only from him. We are entirely free.
—Atiwaneto, *Cowasuck*

I Panaouamskeyen, do inform ye . . . of what has passed between me and the English in negotiating the peace that I have just concluded with them. . . . My reason for informing you, myself, is the diversity and contrariety of the interpretations I receive of the English writing in which the articles of peace are drawn. . . . These writings appear to contain things that are not, so that the Englishman himself disavows them in my presence, when he reads and interprets them to me himself.

First, that I did not commence the negotiation for a peace, but he, it was, who first spoke to me on the subject, and I did not give him any answer until he addressed me a third time. . . . I did not give him for answer—I am come to ask your pardon; nor, I come to acknowledge you as my conqueror; nor, I come to make my submission to you; nor, I come to receive your commands. . . . Thereupon, he said to me—Let us observe the treaties concluded by our Fathers, and renew the ancient friendship which existed between us. I made him no answer thereunto. Much less, I repeat, did I become his subject, or give him my land, or acknowledge his King as my King. . . . He again said to me—But do you not recognize the King of England as King over all his states? To which I answered—Yes, I recognize him King of all his lands; but I rejoined, do not hence infer that I acknowledge thy King as my King, and King of my lands. Here lies my distinction—my Indian distinction. . . .

What I tell you now is the truth. If, then, any one should produce any writing that makes me speak otherwise, pay no attention to it, for I know not what I am made to say in another language, but I know well what I say in my own. . . .

—Panaouamskeyen, *Penobscot*

Last of the Beothuk (1819)

They call themselves the Beothuk. To the Basques, they are the Red Indians of Newfoundland, because their skin is dyed red with ochre. Because of them, the name "redskin" will be applied to all the nations of the continent, but the Beothuk will be remembered for little more. The Europeans will see to that. Fishermen along the coast of Newfoundland shoot them for sport, and trappers joke that they would rather kill a Beothuk than a deer. Governor Charles Hamilton offers 100 pounds to anyone who brings a Beothuk alive to Nova Scotia to be "civilized."

It is March, and a hard snow covers the ground along Red Indian Lake. An armed party wends along the shore. At their approach, the Beothuk flee in all directions across the frozen lake and into the pinewoods. Demasdoweet, a woman with a small child, runs slower than the others. They grab her. In vain, her husband Nonosbawsut tries to save her. With each effort, he is stabbed and repeatedly shot.

Nonosbawsut's blood congeals on the frozen lake as he lies dead upon the ice. The man who murders him cries, "It is only an Indian, and I wish I had shot a hundred instead of one." Demasdoweet is taken prisoner; her child dies along Red Indian Lake. There are now only twenty-seven Beothuk left alive.

Mary March, renamed for the month in which they captured her, is taken to Nova Scotia and clothed in all the best shops. Luck now seems to be with her, for in a rush of humanity, the governor ordains that she will be returned to her people. But Mary March dies aboard the vessel that carries her home. Now she lies inside a pine box, along the empty shore of Red Indian Lake.

The rude fishermen, hunters and trappers of those days were a rough lawless order of men, little disposed to try conciliation or kindness on a tribe of savages whose presence in the country was felt to be an annoyance. That they treated the poor Beothucks with brutal cruelty admits of no doubt. In fact, for two hundred years they seem to have regarded the red men as vermin to be hunted down and destroyed.

—Rev. Moses Harvey, *Canada*

New England

The times are Exceedingly Alter'd, Yea the times have turn'd everything upside down, or rather we have Chang'd the good Times, Chiefly by the help of the White People, for in Times past, our Fore-Fathers lived in Peace, Love, and great harmony, and had everything in Great plenty. . . . But alas, it is not so now, all our Fishing, Hunting and Fowling is entirely gone.
—(*Name not given*), Mohegan

In 1609 Henry Hudson, of the Dutch East India Company, entered New York harbor and coasted inland, up the river that now bears his name. Luckily for him, and rather unluckily for the Indian nations along the river, Hudson arrived in the fall, and Mahican and Catskill farmers pressed him with fat orange pumpkins, grapes, and other produce of a bountiful harvest. Although he had not found China as hoped, Hudson was so gratified with his reception, and especially with the beaver and otter pelts received, that the voyage was considered a tremendous success.

To the north was a much different situation. In 1620 the Pilgrims landed at Plimouth Rock, amid a countryside strangely desolate. Throughout the cold winter, they encountered no living people, but found evidence of many Indian graves. Thomas Morton described the shocking mortality that swept New England: "the hand of God fell heavily upon [the natives], with such a mortall stroake, that they died [in] heaps. . . . And the bones and skulls upon the severall places of their habitations made such a spectacle . . . it seemed to mee a new-found Golgotha."

The following spring, a Pemaquid leader from the coast of Maine hailed the tiny Plimouth settlement, startling them greatly by speaking English. His name was Samoset. He had learned their language from ships' captains trading along the coast. The Pilgrims' astonishment only increased the following day when Samoset returned with yet another man who spoke fluent English. He was introduced as Tisquantum, a Patuxet, upon whose lands Plimouth was built.

Tisquantum related the grim story of his capture by English captain Thomas Hunt. In the service of Captain John Smith, Hunt had come along the New England coast in 1614. Among the Nauset and Patuxet, he made a business filling the hold of his ship not only with fish, as per his instructions, but with Indian people for the slave market. Among them was Tisquantum. Hunt unloaded his human cargo in Málaga, Spain, where Tisquantum made his escape, spent two years in London, and finally shipped passage back to his homeland. He arrived at Patuxet only to find his village deserted.

Soon after Tisquantum's capture, an appalling epidemic contracted from the Europeans had struck the coast with deadly fury. The Patuxet nation was annihilated. They were not alone. The contagion sped through New England, obliterating entire nations. The Massachusett and Pocumtuck suffered devastating losses totaling 90 percent of their populations.

Upon learning of the awful fate of the rightful owners of the lands they occupied, the Pilgrims were exuberant. Governor William Bradford declared that "there is neither man, woman, nor child remaining, as indeed we have found none; so there is none to hinder our possession, or to lay claim unto it."

As the months unfolded, Massasoit, of the neighboring Pokanoket nation of Wampanoag, established formal diplomatic relations with Bradford. Both sides pledged mutual support and protection. As proof of their sincerity, Tisquantum was sent to instruct the Pilgrims how to cultivate the land, a politically advantageous position he gladly seized. At the end of the year, the Pilgrims celebrated their first Thanksgiving, but for the Pokanoket, the only thing unique about it was that it was celebrated with Pilgrims.

The Pilgrims did not long bask in their hegemony over New England. In 1626 the Dutchman Peter Minuit negotiated for the sale of Manhattan Island. Although two nations shared the territory—the Canarsee in the south and the Reckgawawanc in the north—Minuit obliged the Canarsee to sell the entire island, an act later challenged vigorously by both the Reckgawawanc and the Staten Island Canarsee.

On Manhattan Island, the Dutch West India Company built Fort Amsterdam, from which New Netherland carried on a thriving trade with nearby Algonquian nations. North in the Hudson River valley, a second post was opened at Fort Orange that catered to the Mahican and Mohawk. During the tenure of New Netherland governor Willem Kieft, Indian-Dutch relations deteriorated rapidly. Kieft proved manipulative and abusive in his interaction with the nations. Their resistance led to the implementation of extermination policies, which were set into motion against several groups, including the Raritan and Wecquaesgeek.

Below Fort Orange, Dutch settlements sprang up in the Catskill Mountains engendering almost immediate conflict with the Esopus nation. This resulted in yet another planned extermination, this time of the Esopus, by Kieft's successor, Governor Peter Stuyvesant. Many Esopus were captured and sold into slavery at Curaçao in the West Indies, although some were returned following a feeble peace. It was a horror-filled period for the Esopus and Catskill nations and for the Dutch settlers alike—although the latter's abuses had caused the problem—and fearful stories abounded for years to come of the dark and foreboding Catskill hollows, of headless horsemen, and of dead and dying Esopus.

Closer to the Pilgrims at Plimouth, other English colonies took hold—at Massachusetts Bay, Rhode Island, and Connecticut.

When New Sweden lay claim to the lands about Delaware River and Bay, the European iron grip on the coast was complete. And north of them all loomed France, the most formidable power in the scramble for control of the lucrative fur trade.

By the time of Massasoit's death in 1660, the peace diligently preserved for forty years with the Plimouth colony was not without cost. New England Indian nations precariously held their lands, which threatened at any moment to be engulfed by expanding settlement. Untold abuses were suffered at the hands of the colonials, for which Indian people had no redress. If only Massasoit had not so honorably upheld his end of the bargain and instead had demanded retribution for the first offense! Expecting mercy from the very people who had come to their shore seeking refuge, they received none, and many Indian people found themselves servants or slaves to English masters.

The Europeans arrived on the continent bearing the prejudices of their culture, and rather than adapt to their hosts' manner of living, they cleared lands and erected enclosures, and then insisted that Indian nations do the same. When Indian leaders doggedly refused, cattle and hogs overran their fields, and Indian people became repeat offenders in colonial courts for various crimes in connection with defending their lands. How and when the English conceived that the Pokanoket and others were under their jurisdiction is unclear, but Puritan leaders demanded that Indian nations observe their laws, and punishment fell heavily upon any Indian person found in violation.

When King Philip succeeded his father, Massasoit, he strenuously resisted encroachment on the sovereignty of his people. Relations deteriorated rapidly and in 1675 the bitter confrontation known as King Philip's War broke out, which ultimately involved most of the Indian nations of New England.

At the end of the war, many of the smaller nations allied to Philip were destroyed or scattered. On the one hand, King Philip's War dramatically demonstrated that the ability of Indian leaders to dictate to Europeans—a position they had enjoyed in 1620—

was lost. On the other hand, the conflict merely hardened the position of Indian nations and Europeans alike. And when Grey Lock's War broke out in 1723, neither the English, nor the colonials, nor the French looking on, could fail to recognize the determination of Indian nations to maintain their sovereignty, with or without European sanction.

Hackensack Incident   (1643)

A Dutchman lies dead on the ground near the trading house outside the village of Ackingh-sack. The death is senseless and might have been prevented had the Dutch at Heer Vander Horst's colony not been so inclined to cheat their Indian customers. But profit at the trading house is everything. So when a Hackensack trader arrives with an armful of beaver to truck, they offer him brandy, against the expressed wish of the Hackensack leadership.

Into the brandy, the Dutch pour a half measure of water. The Hackensack trader replies that he can scoop water out of the river himself for free, and refuses to buy it. Turning around, he finds that the beaver-skin coat he has laid on a chair is missing; so are his goods. The Dutch soldiers inside the post do not help. Instead, they join in the abuse. The man departs with the rum bottle and returns with his weapons.

A Dutchman lies dead on the ground near the trading house outside the village of Ackingh-sack, and an observant planter named DeVries blames the soldiers inside.

We wonder how the sachem at the fort dares to exact such things from us. He must be a very shabby fellow; he has come to live in our land when we have not invited him, and now comes to deprive us of our corn for nothing.

—Tappan delegation

Are you our friends? You are only corn-thieves.

—Montauk delegation

Why do you sell brandy to our young men? They are not used to it—it makes them crazy. Even your own people, who are accustomed to strong liquors, sometimes become drunk, and fight with knives. Sell no more strong drink to the Indians, if you would avoid mischief.   —Hackensack delegation

Kieft's Massacre   (1643)

Nearly one hundred Wecquaesgeek and Tappan, fleeing from a party of Mahican, seek the protection of Fort Amsterdam. They cannot know that Willem Kieft, director-general of the fort, has argued for their extermination because they refuse to pay Dutch tribute. Nor can they know that the Mahican who have come from Fort Orange demanding similar payment have, in all probability, been sent by Kieft himself. Some of the refugees camp at the Hackensack town along the Oysterbank near the fort, while others cross the river to the Montauk village of Rockaway.

After the evening meal, when a cold darkness has settled, the planter Willem DeVries is invited by Kieft to view the scene unfolding outside the fort. Below, soldiers gather, and in the middle of the night DeVries's blood chills as the sound of shrieking fills the air.

When it was day, the soldiers returned to the fort, having massacred or murdered eighty Indians, and considering they had done a deed of Roman valour, in murdering so many in their sleep; where infants were torn from their mother's breasts, and hacked to pieces in the presence of the parents, and the pieces thrown into the fire and in the water, and other sucklings were bound to small boards, and then cut, stuck, and pierced, and miserably massacred in a manner to move a heart of stone. Some were thrown into the river, and when the fathers and mothers endeavoured to save them, the soldiers would not let them come on land, but made both parents and children drown. . . . Many fled from this scene, and concealed themselves in the neighbouring sedge, and when it was morning, came out to beg a piece of bread, and to be permitted to warm themselves; but they were murdered in cold blood and tossed into the water. Some came by our lands in the country with their hands, some with their legs cut off, and some holding their entrails in their arms. . . . After this exploit, the soldiers were rewarded for their services, and Director Kieft thanked them by taking them by the hand and congratulating them.   —Willem DeVries, *Netherlands*

Eighty severed heads are displayed inside the fort while the Dutch engage in celebration. Cornelius Van Tienhoven's mother joyfully kicks a ball about the street . . . but it is not a ball. It is a human head.

Our chief has sent us to know why you have killed his people, who have never laid a straw in your way, nor done you aught but good?   —Montauk delegation

When you first came to our coasts, you sometimes had no food; we gave you our beans and corn, and relieved you with our oysters and fish; and now, for recompense, you murder our people.   —(Name not given), *Montauk*

When the [English] arrived [on the coast], they looked about everywhere for good spots of land, and when they found one, they immediately and without ceremony possessed themselves of it; we were astonished, but still we let them go on, not thinking it worth while to contend for a little land. But when at last they came to our favourite spots . . . then bloody wars ensued: we would have been contented that the white people and we should have lived quietly beside each other; but these white men encroached so fast upon us, that we saw at once we should lose all, if we did not resist them. . . . We were enraged when we saw the white people put our friends and relatives, whom they had taken prisoners, on board of their ships and carry them off to sea, whether to drown or sell them as slaves . . . we knew not, but certain it is that none of them have ever returned or even been heard of.   —(Name not given), *Lenape*

Peach War   (1655)

Hendrick Van Dyck—formerly Ensign Hendrick Van Dyck—surveys his orchard with eyes of fury. In the glory of his career, he participated in a military expedition into Connecticut that resulted in the slaughter of seven hundred unsuspecting Wecquaesgeek men, women, and children. Van Dyck is despicable. But what is that he sees in his orchard? Marauding Indians, come to steal, come to plunder his possessions. Small minds imagine small deeds. He runs for his rifle, aims, and fires. A lone figure drops to the ground in the orchard. It is a woman, and in her hand she holds a peach.

Sixty-four canoes filled with Esopus, Tappan, Hackensack, and their allies land at dawn along the sandy shore of New Amsterdam. Inside their homes, the Dutch are awakened from sleep by a steady movement from house to house. Doors are opened, rooms searched, but nothing is taken. No one is harmed. They are looking for someone. In the evening they find him. He is Hendrick Van Dyck, and now an arrow protrudes from his chest, though he does not die. Justice served, the men return to the shore. But as they reach the canoes, Cornelius Van Tienhoven, burgher corps and former ensign under Kieft, arrives along the sandy spit at the head of a drunken mob. Shots fire into the Indian canoes, and the Peach War has begun.

For his involvement in the affair, Van Tienhoven is charged with drunkenness, debauchery, and the instigation of an Indian war. With "clouded brains, filled with liquor" he has escalated the suffering Van Dyck began. When ordered "to render his accounts" in November 1656, Van Tienhoven stages his own death and disappears forever.

Once a preacher came and began to explain to us that there was a God. We answered—"Dost thou think us so ignorant as not to know that? Go back to the place from whence thou camest." Then again another preacher came and began to teach us, and to say—"You must not steal, nor lie, nor get drunk, etc."—We answered—"Thou fool, dost thou think that we don't know that? Learn first thyself, and then teach the people to whom thou belongest, to leave off these things. For who steals, or lies, or is more drunken than thine own people?"   —Tschoop, *Mahican*

Grave-Robbing the Massachusett   (1620)

The Pilgrims have established their fledgling colony at Plimouth and now begin to look at the countryside about them. Wandering in the woods one day around Namskekit searching for stores of Indian corn, they stumble upon a Massachusett burial site. Within it lies the fresh grave of a woman, the mother of Chick-ataubut, a Massachusett leader. Greed overcomes them. They open the grave. Inside, draped over the body, are two bearskins carefully stitched together. The Pilgrims help themselves to the covering.

The Massachusett nation is enraged, but none feels the pain as greatly as Chickataubut. When the English next come ashore, his men fall upon them. After a stiff fight, the Massachusett retreat, leaving the Pilgrims to reflect upon Indian barbarity.

We brought sundry of the prettiest things away with us, and covered the corpse up again . . . there was a variety of opinions amongst us about the embalmed person.
> —"Mourt's Relation," *Plimouth colony*

. . . much troubled, and trembling at that doleful sight, a spirit cried aloud, "Behold! My son, whom I have cherished . . . canst thou forget to take revenge [on] those wild people that hath my [grave] defaced in a despiteful manner; disdaining our ancient antiquities, and honorable customs? See now the Sachem's grave lies like unto the common people . . . defaced. Thy mother doth complain, implores thy aid against this thievish people [the English] now come hither; if this be suffered, I shall not rest in quiet. . . ."
> —Chickataubut (House-on-Fire), *Massachusett*

Massasoit Questions King James   (1621)

At their first meeting with the Pilgrims at the Pokanoket capital of Montaup, Massasoit has many questions. The Pilgrims are strange people, with even stranger customs. Mostly, he wants to know about the English king James. He grieves to hear that the queen is dead, leaving the monarch a widower. But when he learns that he has not remarried, Massasoit starts in surprise and wonders what is wrong with the king. A Wampanoag leader would not long remain alone.

First of the Mohegans   (1634)

Events are tumultuous in New England—no less so within Indian nations than without. The Pequot leader Sassacus is engaged in a bitter power struggle with one of the twenty-six war captains of his nation. At stake is who will control the grand sachemship. The English welcome the conflict and maintain friendly relations with the opponents of Sassacus, who call themselves Mohegan. In fact, they encourage the dissension. The war captain breaks away from the nation and leads his people north along the Pequot River. Here they will build themselves into a mighty people, and their name will be made famous. Their leader, Uncas, becomes the First of the Mohegans.

Pequot Massacre   (1637)

The Pequot are formidable. From the Montauk nation on Long Island, famous for wampum manufacturing, they receive an ample supply of shell beads in tribute. They are wealthy. In addition, their country includes the Connecticut Valley, one of the richest fur-producing areas in New England. The strategic valley is coveted by both the English and Dutch, and both wish that the Pequot were at least more tractable, if not out of the way altogether.

Uncas, ever the antagonist of Sassacus, shrewdly hints that the Pequot are fomenting a strike against English settlements creeping into the valley. The death of two traders—one at the hands of the Western Niantic, the other by the Narragansett—are wrongly blamed on the Pequot. At last, both wampum and the coveted Connecticut Valley seem more attainable than ever. Instead of attacking Sassacus's indomitable fort, the English, bolstered by Uncas's Mohegans, embark upon an even less noble strategy: they obliterate the Pequot village of Mystic, where, instead of engaging worthy Pequot fighters, they oppose women and children.

The attack commences at dawn. The first fire that rips through the Mystic palisades hits Pequot citizens fast asleep. Scaling the fort, the soldiers rush through the town, shooting and stabbing even women and children found cowering beneath their beds for protection. A flaming brand is lowered against the woven mat covering of a Pequot house. Captain John Underhill orders the troops to surround the burning town. As the Pequot escape the flames, they are gunned down without mercy.

By some estimates, as many as seven hundred innocent Pequot lose their lives at the Mystic massacre. Two hundred survivors surrender to the Narragansett but are seized by the English, and the women and children are sold into slavery in the West Indies. Twenty-eight adult men who subsequently surrender are executed, their bodies thrown into the sea.

These Indians had not done one single wrong act to the whites, but were as innocent of any crime as any beings in the world. . . .

In 1647, the Pilgrims speak of large and respectable tribes. But let us trace them for a few moments. How have they been destroyed, is it by fair means? No. How then? By hypocritical proceedings, by being duped and flattered; flattered by informing the Indians that their God was a going to speak to them, and then place them before the cannon's mouth in a line, and then putting the match to it and kill thousands of them. We might suppose that meek Christians had better gods and weapons than cannon. . . . But let us again review their weapons to civilize the nations of this soil. What were they: rum and powder, and ball, together with all the diseases, such as the small pox, and every other disease imaginable; and in this way sweep off thousands and tens of thousands.   —William Apess, *Pequot*

Poisoning of Wamsutta   (1662)

Massasoit is dead. His son Wamsutta, also called Alexander, has taken his place. He is not like his father; he is less yielding to English demands. Rumors circulate in Boston that he is planning war.

Armed guards surround Wamsutta's camp. He is ordered to Plimouth for a meeting with the governor, where he will be made to answer to these charges. A guard lowers a pistol against his chest; they will take him by force. Wamsutta wrests away from the escorts' hold. He can walk alone.

The meeting in Plimouth is cut short not long after it is begun. The company of Pokanoket wend their way home. Wamsutta is deathly ill, and cannot travel without assistance. His wife, Weetamoo, is with him. Before they have gone halfway to Montaup, Wamsutta is dead. The English claim he has contracted a fever. But the Pokanoket know differently. They say that Wamsutta was poisoned.

[My] brother . . . came miserably to die, by being forced to Court and poisoned. . . . If 20 of our honest Indians testify that an Englishman has done us wrong, it is as nothing, and if but one of our worst Indians testifies against any Indian or [myself] when it pleases the English, that is sufficient.

—King Philip, *Wampanoag*

. . . the pilgrims landed at Plymouth, and without asking liberty from any one, they possessed themselves of a portion of the country, and built themselves houses, and then made a treaty, and commanded them to accede to it. This, if now done, would be called an insult, and every white man would be called to go out and act the part of a patriot, to defend their country's rights; and if every intruder were butchered, it would be sung upon every hill-top in the Union, that victory and patriotism was the order of the day. And yet the Indians . . . without the shedding of blood, or imprisoning any one, bore it. And yet for their kindness and resignation towards the whites, they were called savages, and made by God on purpose for them to destroy.   —William Apess, *Pequot*

. . . the people were to blame, for they might have read [the Bible] for themselves; and they doubtless would have found that we were not made to be vessels of wrath, as they say we were. And had the whites found it out, perhaps they would not have rejoiced at a poor Indian's death; or when they were swept off, would not have called it the Lord killing the Indians to make room for them upon their lands. . . . But it is certain the Pilgrims knew better than to break the commands of their Lord and master; they knew that it was written, "thou shalt not kill."   —William Apess, *Pequot*

We have been the first in doing good to the English, and the English the first in doing wrong. When the English first came . . . [my] father was as a great man, and the English as a little child. He constrained other Indians from wronging the English, and gave them corn and showed them how to plant . . . and [we] have let them have a hundred times more land, than now . . . [I] have for my own people.

—King Philip, *Wampanoag*

King Philip's War (1675)

Metacomet, known as King Philip, succeeds his brother Wamsutta. The Pokanoket suffer uncounted abuses from their English neighbors: settlers encroach on their lands; they cannot practice their customs without insult; their guns are taken and broken; their livestock stolen and killed. With hunting lands shriveling up, many Pokanoket are forced into domestic servitude at the homes of English planters, where they work alongside Indian slaves.

A Christian Massachusett Indian named John Sassamon warns the English of a plot afoot against them. The Pokanoket brand him a traitor. In the winter, Sassamon's body is found floating beneath the ice of Assawomset Pond. As a result, three of Philip's men are charged by Plimouth with murder and executed. Philip reacts with vehemence; his nation alone has legal right to try the accused. Pokanoket sovereignty is breached.

His complaints unheeded, and feeling that the English are bent upon his people's destruction, Philip is left with little choice but to defend the integrity of his nation. War begins. Pokanoket victories are swift. The towns of Swansey, Taunton, Middleborough, and Dartmouth fall in quick succession. An eyewitness writes that Indian people congregate at the outskirts of the settlements "like the lightning on the edge of the clouds." By the following summer, fifty-two of New England's ninety villages will feel the Wampanoag strength.

Indian nations flock to the side of Philip. Weetamoo, Alexander's widow and leader of the Pocasset, brings three hundred

King Philip gave his life in the struggle to keep his nation free
from the descendants of the Pilgrims, whom his father, Massasoit,
had greeted in 1621.

men to the field in support. Other bands of Wampanoag follow suit, along with the Nipmuc, Pocumtuck, and Sokoki. The war spreads to Maine when English soldiers toss a Saco chief's baby into the water to see "if young Indians could swim naturally like animals of the brute creation." The baby drowns, and the war advances up the coast and into the interior to nations who have their own grievances against the English. Only the powerful Narragansett have yet to commit.

Brothers,—You see this vast country before us, which the [Creator] gave to our fathers and us; you see the buffalo and deer that now are our support.—Brothers, you see these little ones, our wives and children, who are looking to us for food and raiment; and you now see the foe before you, that they have grown insolent and bold; that all our ancient customs are disregarded; that treaties made by our fathers and us are broken, and all of us insulted; our council fires disregarded, and all the ancient customs of our fathers; our brothers murdered before our eyes, and their spirits cry to us for revenge. Brothers, these people from the unknown world will cut down our groves, spoil our hunting and planting grounds, and drive us and our children from the graves of our fathers, and our council fires, and enslave our women and children.

—King Philip, *Wampanoag*

I understand the captain is come to kill me and the rest of the Indians here. Tell him we know it, but fear him not, neither will we shun him; but let him begin when he dare, he will not take us unawares. —Peksuot, *Wampanoag*

Know by this paper, that the Indians that thou hast provoked
to wrath and anger will war this twenty-one years if you will.
There are many Indians yet. We come three hundred at this
time. You must consider the Indians lose nothing but their
life. You must lose your fair houses and cattle.

—James the Printer, *Nipmuc*

Great Swamp Massacre   (1675)

Unconfirmed reports reach Boston that the neutral Narragansett
are harboring Wampanoag refugees. Some say that Philip himself
is among them. An army of fifteen hundred assembles, headed by
Benjamin Church, and made up of soldiers from Massachusetts
Bay, Plimouth, and Connecticut.

On December 19, a light snow falls. The Narragansett town on
the edge of the Great Swamp is braced for the impending storm. A
thick palisade surrounds the settlement, and tubs of corn are
stacked around the inside of the houses for protection. The village
consists of five hundred dwellings; many of the residents are
women and children.

The soldiers scale the breastworks and enter the village under
heavy fire. Hand-to-hand combat ensues for three hours. The soldiers slash and hack their way through the town; the butchered
and mangled fall like snow upon the ground. In confusion, some
Narragansett turn and rush into the flames of their burning homes.
A lucky few escape across the ice and disappear into the swamp.
The Narragansett proclaim the death toll at one thousand.

Brothers, we must be one as the English are, or we shall soon
all be destroyed. You know our fathers had plenty of deer and
skins, and our plains were full of deer and of turkeys. . . . But,
brothers, since these English have seized upon our country,
they cut down the grass with scythes, and the trees with axes.

Their cows and horses eat up the grass, and their hogs spoil our beds of clams; and finally we shall starve to death! Therefore, stand not in your own light, I beseech you, but resolve with us to act like men.   —Miantunnomoh, *Narragansett*

If your love be such, and it bring forth such fruits, how cometh it to pass, that when we come to Patuxet, you stand upon your guard, with the mouth of your pieces presented towards us?   —Caunbitant, *Narragansett*

The Capture of Canonchet   (1676)

At the time of the Great Swamp Massacre, Canonchet is the head sachem of the Narragansett. After the bloody slaughter, he plunges angrily into the war. Narragansett victories are swift. Along the Pawtucket River, Captain Michael Peirse makes a last stand, and all the soldiers in his party are killed.

The next day, four companies of Connecticut soldiers march against Canonchet. With them are Mohegan, Pequot, and Niantic fighters. Canonchet is ill-prepared. His people have dispersed to replant corn that the English have destroyed. Only seven men are at his side. Canonchet sees the army. Like a deer pursued by hunters, he flees. His breathing comes sharply, painfully; they are gaining. Across the cold, slippery river he runs. One foot slides on on a rock; his gun falls into the water. The chase is over; his life is gone. They say he might be spared if he surrenders his nation. Canonchet regards his captors with disdain . . . and chooses death.

The body is drawn and quartered. In Hartford, Connecticut, spectators gawk at the head of a great man, sent as a trophy to the Governing Council. It is Canonchet, leader of the Narragansett, ally of King Philip.

I like it well; I shall die before my heart is soft, or have said any thing unworthy of myself.

—Canonchet, *Narragansett*

The Reverend John Eliot   (1646)

The missionary John Eliot has mastered the Massachusett tongue. On October 28, for the first time, he preaches in that language to an assembled crowd at the town of Nonantum. The questions posed to him are thoughtful. How does he know Jesus? Why does the second commandment say that the child must suffer for the sin of its parents? Tremendously encouraged by the congregation's interest, the Reverend Eliot holds a second meeting two weeks later. After delivering a moving sermon, he again asks if there are questions. One man stands up. Why is the sea water salty, and river water fresh?

Praying Towns

The Christian Massachusett make their first settlement at Natick. Eliot believes that to know God, they must reform their lives. They must live apart from their heathen relatives, where Christian example will be the most effective. The settlement at Natick is only the first of a great number of such "praying towns" established across New England. Many incur the wrath of those who adhere to the religion and customs of their ancestors. The Mohegan leader Uncas goes so far as to lodge a protest at the court at Hartford against the laying out of another praying town, declaring that all the chiefs in the country are against it.

Despite the best designs of the church, the advent of King Philip's War sees the desertion of large numbers of Christian Indians. Those remaining neutral find themselves bitterly hated and feared. Some lose their lives at the hands of their white Christian brothers.

Fifteen praying Massachusett from Marlborough are dragged through the streets of Boston, tied together by the neck like galley slaves. Slowly, they shuffle toward the gallows, where they are to be hung for complicity with Philip. The Boston Court of Assistants intervenes and declares that the majority are not guilty. A crazed mob attempts to lynch them anyway.

As public sentiment mounts, five hundred Christian Indians are compounded on a military reservation on Deer Island in Boston Harbor. There they wait out the war, suffering through the bitter winter of 1676 without adequate food, shelter . . . or justice.

Indian Slaves   (1676)

The fiery victories which mark the beginning of the war are fast dying away. Philip suffers a series of staggering defeats. Indian men, women, and children captured by the British are sent as slaves to the Caribbean, Spain, Portugal, the Southern colonies, and the Azores. Along the Taunton River on July 30, Church's Rangers kill Philip's uncle and capture his sister.

The Pokanoket are now on the run, but they have their families, wives, and children with them, slowing them down. Church's Rangers have no one. On August 1, the Rangers burst upon Philip's camp. He escapes, but 130 Pokanoket are captured. Among them are his wife, Wootonekanuske, and his little boy. In Plimouth, the clergy decide their fate: they will be sold into slavery in Bermuda. All that is dear to Philip is gone.

My heart breaks, now I am ready to die.

—King Philip, *Wampanoag*

... they took a part of my tribe, and sold them to the Spaniards in Bermuda, and many others; and then on the Sabbath day, these people would gather themselves together. . . . And there is no manner of doubt but that all my countrymen would have been enslaved if they had tamely submitted . . . [They] even put an end to their own wives and children, and that was all that prevented them from being slaves; yes, *all*. It was not the good will of those holy pilgrims that prevented, no. But I would speak, and I could wish it might be like the voice of thunder, that it might be heard afar off, even to the ends of the earth. He that will advocate slavery, is worse than a beast. . . . And he that will not set his face against its corrupt principles, is a coward, and not worthy of being numbered among men. . . .   —William Apess, *Pequot*

How they could go to work to enslave a free people, and call it religion, is beyond the power of my imagination, and outstrips the revelation of God's word.

—William Apess, *Pequot*

Death of King Philip   (1676)

Philip sleeps. It is only a fitful slumber—he has been hunted from place to place like an animal, and now he returns to his father's capital at Montaup. He has decided where he will make his last stand, and where he will die.

On the dawn of August 12, Philip stumbles into a carefully laid ambush at the edge of his camp and is shot and killed. The English do not allow him to be buried. The body is drawn and quartered.

A lonely wind swirls around Montaup. The army is gone. Little remains of what has transpired on this spot; but suspended from the branches of four trees pieces of a body swing slowly in the breeze. In Plimouth, Philip's severed head is hoisted upon a gibbet, where it remains for twenty years, exposed to public scorn.

It is said that in the Christian's guide, that God is merciful, and they that are his followers are like him. How much mercy do you think has been shown towards Indians, their wives and their children? Not much, we think. No. . . . Have you any regard for your wives and children, for those delicate sons and daughters? Would you like to see them slain and laid in heaps, and their bodies devoured by the vultures and wild beasts of prey? and their bones bleaching in the sun and air, till they moulder away, or were covered by the falling leaves of the forest, and not resist? No. Your hearts would break with grief, and with all the religion and knowledge you have, it would not impede your force to take vengeance upon your foe, that had so cruelly conducted thus. . . . Can, or do you think we have no feeling?   —William Apess, *Pequot*

. . . during the bloody contest, the pious fathers wrestled hard and long with their God, in prayer, that he would prosper their arms, and deliver their enemies into their hands. . . . Nor could they, the Pilgrims, cease crying to the Lord against [King] Philip, until they had prayed the bullet through his heart. . . . If this is the way they pray, that is bullets through people's hearts, I hope they will not pray for me; I should rather be excused.   —William Apess, *Pequot*

The Northeast

The Iroquois laugh when you talk to them of obedience to kings;
for they cannot reconcile the idea of submission with the dignity
of man. Each individual is a sovereign in his own mind; and as
he conceives he derives his freedom from the [Creator] alone, he
cannot be induced to acknowledge any other power.
—John Long, England

In 1664 England assumed control of Dutch holdings in North America, and the territory formerly designated New Netherland became part of New York. For the Indian nations in the region, relations hardly changed. The English already had incurred the enmity of the Wappinger bands around the Hudson River for assisting the Dutch in a bloody war against them in 1644. Along the Connecticut River, on a wintry night under a full moon, seven hundred Wecquaesgeek were indiscriminately slaughtered by an English and Dutch force; afterward, the soldiers bivouacked on the crimson snow.

On Long Island, reservations were created as early as 1666. The Shinnecock, Unquachog, and Montauk grabbed hold of them, knowing that at least some small part of their holdings were guaranteed safe from settlement. Many other nations around lower New York wisely moved west into Pennsylvania, beyond the frontier line. Later, as that state became settled, an "everlasting peace" was concluded with William Penn, that the Quakers—in the early days at least—honored.

To the north, south of Lake Ontario, lay the country of the Hodenosaunee. Theirs was a powerful confederacy of five nations based on the principles of unity and peace, not war. It was not always the case. In the years before the formation of the league, warfare tore the nations apart, as bitter conflict swept the region. Then, around A.D. 900, a peacemaker arrived from the Huron village of Kahanahyenh. Through his guidance, the Confederacy was born.

Immortalized, for better *and* worse, by Henry Wadsworth Longfellow, Hiawatha was a very real and heroic figure. An Onondaga leader who defended the ideals of peace at the risk of his own life, he assisted the Peacemaker in establishing the Great Law, a system of organizing principles for the Hodenosaunee Confederacy that continues to this day. To Europeans, the Hodenosaunee stood as a formidable barrier, a moral censure that demanded attention. The Americans who forged an identity on this land cultivated a healthy respect for the Hodenosaunee, and in the process learned much about themselves.

In 1671, Thomas Batts and Robert Fallam effected the first trans-Allegheny crossing, paving the way for expanding European settlement west to the mountains. Although the nations there lived well in advance of the frontier line, and very few had been in direct contact with Europeans, the region quickly destabilized. European presence along the coast jabbed into the side of Indian society like a sharp thorn. European trading patterns upset age-old mechanisms of promoting international peace through exchange, while former methods of resolving disputes were thrown into disarray by the introduction of powerful new weapons. As diplomacy broke down, the result often was raging warfare in the interior, where European footsteps had never even trod. When the frontier did push west to the Appalachians and Europeans surveyed the chaos around them for the first time, they failed to grasp that it was of their own making. Instead, the "myth of the savage" was born.

To Indian nations, the series of European conflicts that culminated in the French and Indian War were little more than a continuation of the frontier turbulence that had been raging in their lands for a century. And although historians typically portray Indian nations as caught in a power struggle between England, France, and Spain, it is hardly likely that Indian leaders viewed the situation similarly. For them, the issue was their own sovereignty—political, cultural, and territorial. Each nation responded according to what it perceived as its best interest.

Peace was concluded between the French and English in 1763, but for the Indian nations, the issues remained unresolved. Instead, they were manifested in the attempts made during this period to regain their independence, struggles that unfortunately have become known only under English names such as Pontiac's "Rebellion," Tecumseh's *War* of 1812, and Black Hawk's *War*. Such designations deny their true importance. These conflicts, as well as the prophetic movements that arose among the Hodenosaunee, Lenape, Shawnee, Potawatomi, and Winnebago in the Northeast, were acclaimed by Indian nations as heroic efforts to maintain that level of cultural and political sovereignty which guarantees the continuity of a people.

The Doeg Incident and the Destruction of the Susquehannock (1675)

The Maryland colony fears the Susquehannock nation that rides on her northern border. The latter's dealings with first the Swedes, then the Dutch threaten Maryland's expansionist plans and disrupt the fur trade. In desperation, Maryland "invites" the Susquehannock to move within her borders, where the situation can be brought under control.

Later that year, a wealthy planter along the Potomac River cheats Doeg nation traders out of money. Several Doeg are killed, and the retaliatory death of the planter's herdsman prompts the Virginia militia into action. Under pretext of a parley, the militia guns down ten Doeg negotiators in an attack upon their village. Fourteen resident Susquehannock are shot and killed.

A new Virginia militia is raised to make "full inquiry" into the matter. Abetted by Maryland troops, the total force equals one thousand. Heading the militia is Colonel John Washington, whose grandson will be the first president of a new United States. The colonel's Mount Vernon plantation, lying across the river from the Indian settlement, is carved out of Doeg lands. Washington blames the Susquehannock for recent depredations. It is an argument that is always used to lay claim to Indian lands.

From their fort opposite Mount Vernon, five Susquehannock leaders hurry forward under a white flag, carrying with them a peace medal issued by Lord Calvert. The militia encircling their town outnumbers them ten to one. The leaders are accused of murdering a plantation overseer, an act that they stridently deny. Colonel Washington remarks: "Should we keep them any longer? Let us knock them on the head." One by one, they are executed. Following the promised "full inquiry," the militia fires upon the Susquehannock town in a siege that lasts six weeks. Later, Washington is tried for murder, but never convicted.

I will justifie that the Conquest of the Susquehannocks was noe just conquest nor managed like a just conquest, for noe cause of warr was given by them and they then were betrayed out of their lives. . . . Oh, it is much to be feared that the Cry of soe much innocent blood will at some time or other bring downe God's wrath upon the Children yet unborn in Maryland though I heartily wish it otherwise.

—William Penn, *Pennsylvania governor*

My brother, it seems your friends have not done you justice in your education; they have not well instructed you in the rules of common civility. You see that we, who understand and practice those rules, believe all your stories: why do you refuse to believe ours?

—(Name not given), *Susquehannock*

Our forefathers were under a strong persuasion (as we are) that those who act well in this life will be rewarded in the next according to the degrees of their virtues; and, on the other hand, that those who behave wickedly here will undergo such punishments hereafter as were proportionate to the crimes they were guilty of. This has been constantly and invariably received and acknowledged for a truth through every successive generation of our ancestors. It could not, then, have taken its rise from fable; for human fiction, however artfully and plausibly contrived, can never gain credit long among people where free inquiry is allowed, which was never denied by our ancestors. Now we desire to propose some questions. . . . Does he think that we who are zealous imitators in good works, and influenced by the same motives as we are, earnestly endeavoring with the greatest circumspection to tread the path of integrity, are in a state of damnation? . . . Let us suppose that some heinous crimes were committed by some of our ancestors, like to that we are told of another race of people. In such a case God would certainly punish the criminal, but would never involve us that are innocent in the guilt. Those who think otherwise must make the Almighty a very whimsical, evil-natured being. . . . In a word, we find the Christians much more depraved in their morals than we are; and we judge from their doctrine by the badness of their lives.

—(Name not given), *Susquehannock*

Whose Land Is This? (1684)

There seems to be some misunderstanding among the French as to who really owns the Hodenosaunee territory. The French think it is they who control the Great Lakes, although the Hodenosaunee are making it abundantly clear that they are mistaken. When Seneca along the western frontier impede French travel to interior posts, their animosity affords the English great pleasure. Later, when the Hodenosaunee make overtures of peace, the French attempt to awe them into submission. An army is marched into the capital at Onondaga to attend the treaty conference. A bout of sickness prevents many of the fifteen hundred soldiers and their Indian allies from leaving Quebec; nevertheless, a sizable force is mustered. The Onondaga are unimpressed.

You must have believed, when you left Quebec, that the sun had burnt up all the forests, which render our country inaccessible to the French, or that the lakes had so far overflown the banks, that they had surrounded our castles, and that it was impossible for us to get out of them. Yes, surely, you must have dreamed so, and the curiosity of seeing so great a wonder has brought you so far. *Now* you are undeceived. I, and the warriors here present, are come to assure you, that the Senecas, Cayugas, Onondagas, Oneidas and Mohawks are yet alive. . . . I do not sleep. I have my eyes open. The sun, which enlightens me, discovers to me a great captain at the head of a company of soldiers, who speaks as if he were dreaming. He says, that he only came to the lake . . . [to make peace] with the Onondagas. But *Garangula* says, that he sees the contrary; that it was to knock them on the head, if sickness had not weakened the arms of the French . . . We carried the English into our lakes, to trade there with the [Odawa] and [Miami], as the Adirondacks brought the French to our [lands] to carry on a trade, which the English say is theirs.

We are born free. . . . We may go where we please, and carry with us whom we please, and buy and sell what we please. . . . Take care for the future that so great a number of soldiers as appear there, do not choke the tree of peace planted in so small a fort. It will be a great loss, if, after it had so easily taken root, you should stop its growth, and prevent its covering your country and ours with its branches. —Garangula, *Onondaga*

Walking Purchase (1737)

The Lenape glance at the treaty held out by John Penn for their inspection and are told that it is a deed to their lands. It was signed in 1686 by none other than William Penn and Lenape leaders Mayhkeerickkishsho, Taughhoughsey, and Sayhoppy. Their signatures are on the document; the Lenape cannot know it is a forgery. The deed, they are told, cedes away all the lands between the Delaware River and Neshaminy Creek that "a man can walk in a day and a half." John Penn smiles. The deed has never been walked.

The Lenape are distraught, but even more so when they discover that Pennsylvania has selected the three swiftest athletes in the colony to be employed for the walk. In the days preceding the event, teams of workers clear underbrush from the path, and the athletes are trained over the terrain.

On the day of the walk, crowds line the route offering refreshments and cheering the walkers on. When the race begins, the Lenape repeatedly call upon them to walk and not run. Of the three athletes, two die from their exertions. Only one lives to the end, covering sixty-five miles in a day and a half. The Lenape are forced into exile onto Hodenosaunee refugee lands.

And indeed, the unfairness practiced in the walk, both in regard to the way where, and the manner how it was performed . . . were the common subjects of conversation in our neighborhood, for some considerable time after it was done.
—Thomas Furniss, *American colonist*

. . . this very ground that is under me was my land and inheritance, and is taken from me by fraud. . . . When I have sold lands fairly, I look upon them to be really sold. A bargain is a bargain. Tho' I have sometimes had nothing for the lands I have sold but broken pipes or such triffles, yet when I have sold them . . . I look upon the bargain to be good. Yet I think that I should not be ill used on this account by those very people who have had such an advantage in their purchases, nor be called a fool for it. Indians are not such fools. . . .
—Teedyuscung, *Lenape*

Nanticoke Exodus   (1744)

After the Walking Purchase removes the Lenape from central Pennsylvania, allied nations find themselves alone and unprotected. On the eastern shore of Delaware and Maryland, the Nanticoke nation has lost one of their strongest allies at a time when English encroachment and injuries increase. They soon discover that a firm position against the English will earn nothing but extermination. Threatened by the Maryland government, the Nanticoke accept a Hodenosaunee offer to relocate to a refugee area in Wyoming Valley (Pennsylvania). Part of the nation immediately removes, but others are detained by Maryland and not allowed to leave. In the end, a number of Nanticoke remain in their homeland, unwilling to relinquish it, no matter the cost.

Our kindness to you ought to be received more thankfully as We have it in Our Power to take all Your Lands from you, and use you as your ill Designs against Us have deserved, whereas you cannot make any War upon Us, but what must end in your own Destruction. —Maryland Assembly

. . . they were known to go from [the] Wyoming [refugee center] . . . to fetch the bones of their dead from the Eastern shore of Maryland. . . . I well remember having seen them between the years 1750 and 1760, loaded with such bones, which, being fresh, caused a disagreeable stench, as they passed through the town of Bethlehem.
—Rev. John Heckewelder, *Moravian*

We now speak in behalf of our Couzins the Nantycokes. You know that on some differences between the People of Maryland & them we sent for them & placed them at the Mouth of Juniata, where they now live; they came to Us while on our Journey & told us that there were three Settlements of their Tribe Left behind in Maryland who wanted to come away, but the Marylanders kept them in fence & would not let them; we desire, therefore (being urg'd thereto by our Couzins the Nantycokes), that you write to the Govr. of Maryland & use your utmost Interest that the fence in which they are confin'd may be taken away . . . that they may be allowed to come & settle where the other Nantycokes are & Live with them amongst us. We have further to tell you that the People of Maryland do not treat the Indians as you & others do, for they make Slaves of them & sell their Children for Money & this makes us more importunate with you to get the rest of our Couzins from among them. . . .

—Canassatego,
Onondaga, with the Nanticoke delegation

About seven Years ago [1754] we went down to Maryland, with a Belt of Wampum, to fetch our Flesh and Blood, which we shewed to some Englishmen there, who told us they did not understand Belts, but if we had brought any order in writing from the Governor of Pennsylvania, they would let our Flesh and Blood then come away with us; but as this was not done, they would not let them come. . . .

—Tokahaio, *Cayuga,* with the Nanticoke delegation

French and Indian War (1754–1760)

The French and Indian War begins as a power struggle between France and England for control of the North American continent, but ultimately involves Indian nations all the way from Maine to Georgia. Violence and warfare have become endemic to the frontier, and the French and Indian War is nothing new. For Indian nations, the issue is sovereignty—and the right to life, liberty, and the pursuit of happiness within their national boundaries. The Europeans think the nations are taking sides with them; but that is so much egocentrism. The nations know why they are at war. To them, this is not a European conflict, but a threat to their own survival and for this, and this alone, they willingly give their lives. At the Battle of Lake George in 1755, the Mohawk leader Hendrick realizes that his men are outnumbered by the French, and that they will probably die. During the fighting, Hendrick is killed.

If they are to fight, they are too few. If they are to be killed, they are too many.   —Thoyanoguen (Hendrick), *Mohawk*

Defeat of Jumonville   (1754)

The young lieutenant colonel George Washington marches into the Allegheny wilderness toward the first campaign of his career. He is to drive French commander Joseph Coulon de Villiers, sieur de Jumonville, back across the British line, an act which will trigger the French and Indian War. He gratefully welcomes the support of Tanacharison's Indian forces and, in a pelting rain, they proceed to Jumonville's encampment.

In horror, Tanacharison watches as the inexperienced Washington bursts into the French clearing, his troops fully exposed. Jumonville suffers a stunning defeat, but it is owing to the Indian forces concealed in the woods. Afterward, Tanacharison vents his disgust at the European method of fighting and teaches Washington a lesson that will serve well in the Revolutionary War.

The Colonel is a good-natured man, but has no experience . . . he by no means takes advice from . . . [us]; he . . . made no fortifications at all but that little thing upon the meadow, where he thought the French would come up to him in open field . . . the French acted as cowards and the English as fools. . . .   —Tanacharison (Half-King), *Oneida*

. . . we told them . . . that we looked upon this War as a War between the English and French only, and did not intend to engage on either side; for that the French and English made War and Peace at Pleasure, but when the Indians once engaged in Wars they knew not when it would end. We also told the French that they knew, and all the World knew, the Countries on which we were Settled, and particularly the Lakes were ours, and therefore if they would fight . . . the English, they ought to fight on the Salt Water. . . .

—Canassatego, *Onondaga*

. . . it is you who are the disturbers in this land, by coming and building your towns; and taking it away unknown to us, and by force. We kindled a fire, a long time ago, at a place called Montreal, where we desired you to stay, and not to come and intrude upon our land.

—Tanacharison (Half-King), *Oneida*

. . . [The Grand Council] heard the white People had begun to settle on their side of the Blue Mountains. . . . As our Boundaries are so well known, and so visibly distinguish'd by a range of high Mountains, we could not suppose this could be done by mistake . . . we, therefore, thought it was become necessary to proceed & to make our Complaints, to hear what the Governments had to say on an Affair whereby we are likely to be very much hurt.   —Ogaushtosh, *Seneca*

[The English] have called us down to this Council Fire, which was kindled for Council Affairs, to renew Treaties of Friendship. . . . But here we must hear a Dispute about Land, and our Time is taken up, but they don't come to the Chief Point. The English first began to do Mischief; we told them so; They only thanked us for our Openness and Advice, and said they would take Care for the future, but healed no wounds. . . . I fear they only speak from their Mouth, and not from their Heart. —Tokahaio, *Cayuga*

When you mentioned the affair of the Land Yesterday, you went back to old Times, and told us, you had been in possession of the Province of Maryland above One hundred Years; but what is one hundred years in comparison to the length of Time since our Claim began? Since we came out of this Ground? For we must tell you, that long before One hundred years Our ancestors came out of this very Ground, and their Children have remained here ever since. You came out of the Ground in a Country that lyes beyond the Seas, there you may have a just Claim, but here you must allow Us to be your elder Brethren, and the Lands to belong to us long before you knew anything of them.

—Canassatego, *Onondaga*

We thought the Boundaries had been settled between Us and the White People. . . . We have several times desired the Governor of Pennsylvania to remove his People from our lands, and We understand he has done his utmost Endeavours for that purpose except using Force, which We do not desire he should. . . .

What we are now going to say is a Matter of great Moment, which We desire you to remember as long as the Sun and Moon lasts. We are willing to sell You this large Tract of Land for your People to live upon, but We desire this may be considered as Part of our Agreement that when We are all dead and gone your Grandchildren may not say to our Grandchildren that your Forefathers sold the Land to our Forefathers, and therefore be gone off them. . . . Your Grandchildren . . .

will say We were Fools for selling so much Land for so small a matter, and curse Us; therefore let it be a Part of the present Agreement that We shall treat one another as Brethren to the latest Generation, even after We shall not have left a Foot of Land. . . .

We desire You would content yourself with what We shall now grant you. We will never part with the land at Shamokin and Wyomink; our Bones are scattered there, and . . . We reserve it to settle such of our Nations upon as shall come to us from the Ohio. . . . Abundance of Indians are moving up and down, and We shall invite all such to come and live here, that so We may strengthen ourselves.

—Thoyanoguen (Hendrick), *Mohawk*

Aftermath of the French and Indian War (1763)

The French and Indian War officially ends in 1760. With French defeat, British settlers pour across the Alleghenies, onto lands only sparsely settled by the French. In the Lenape nation, a prophet named Neolin warns against further assault on their lands and culture. Pushed west from the coast to the mountains and now beyond them, the Lenape have little to hope from the renewed advance of settlement. Neolin calls for a return to traditions and the renunciation of European culture. Among the Odawa in the Great Lakes, Pontiac heeds the warning.

The nations of the Great Lakes and the Ohio Valley quickly unite under Pontiac for the common cause of driving the settlers back across the Alleghenies. In May 1763 Pontiac's allies seize the British fort at Sandusky. British holdings fall like dominoes. By the end of the month, Pontiac holds nine of eleven forts; only Detroit and Fort Pitt remain.

PONTIAC.

Pontiac, Odawa leader of an Indian confederacy. His efforts to
drive the English from their lands resulted in the Proclamation
Line of 1763, making the Ohio River the boundary of
white settlement.

I stand in the path you travel in, till tomorrow morning.
—Pontiac, *Odawa*

It is important for us, my brothers, that we exterminate from our land this nation which only seeks to kill us. . . . When I go to the English chief to tell him that some of our comrades are dead, instead of weeping for the dead . . . he makes fun of me and of you. When I ask him for something for our sick, he refuses, and tells me that he has no need of us. You can well see by that he seeks our ruin. . . . There is no more time to lose, and when the English shall be defeated, we shall see what to do, and we shall cut off the passage so that they cannot come back to our country. —Pontiac, *Odawa*

I have warriors, provisions, and ammunition, to defend [Fort Pitt] three years against all the Indians in the woods; and we shall never abandon it as long as a white man lives in America. I despise the Ottawas, and am very much surprised at our brothers the Delawares, for proposing to us to leave this place and go home. This is our home. You have attacked us without reason or provocation; you have murdered and plundered our warriors and traders. . . . Therefore, now, Brothers, I will advise you to go home to your towns, and take care of your wives and children. Moreover, I tell you that if any of you appear again about this fort, I will throw bombshells, which will burst and blow you to atoms, and fire cannon among you, loaded with a whole bag full of bullets.
—Captain Simeon Ecuyer, *British Army*

[symbol]

I wish there was not an Indian Settlement within a thousand miles of our Country, for they are only fit to live with the Inhabitants of the woods: (i.e., wild beasts), being more allied to the Brute than the human Creation.

—Colonel Henry Bouquet, *British Army*

[symbol]

Why do you complain that our young men have fired at your soldiers, and killed your cattle and your horses? You yourselves are the cause of this. You marched your armies into our country, and built forts here, though we told you, again and again, that we wished you to remove. My Brothers, this land is ours, and not yours.

—Shingas and Turtle's Heart, *Lenape*

[symbol]

Englishman! Although you have conquered the French you have not yet conquered us! We are not your slaves. These lakes and these woods and mountains were left to us by our ancestors. They are our inheritance and we will part with them to none. Your nation supposes that we, like the white people, cannot live without bread and pork and beef! But you ought to know that He—the Great Spirit and Master of Life—has provided food for us in these broad lakes and upon these mountains.   —Mihnehwehna, *Ojibway*

[symbol]

I do not see any good that it would do me to put a bullet through your body—I could not make any use of you when dead; but I could of a rabbit or turkey. As to myself, I think it more wise to *avoid* than to put myself in the way of harm; I am under apprehension that you might hit me. That being the case, I think it advisable to keep my distance. If you want to try your pistols, take some object—a tree, or anything about my size; and if you hit that, send me word, and I shall acknowledge, that had I been there you might have hit me.

—Kahkewaquonaby, *Ojibway*

Germ Warfare   (1763)

Pontiac's allies are sick. Smallpox rages among the Odawa, Mingo, Lenape, and Shawnee. By spring, the great alliance falters, and Pontiac's Rebellion grinds to an end. The British can congratulate themselves, for they will go down in infamy as the first "civilized" nation to use germ warfare.

Could it not be contrived to send the Small Pox among those disaffected tribes of Indians? We must on this occasion use every stratagem in our power to reduce them.

—Sir Jeffrey Amherst, *Commander of British forces*

I will try to inoculate the [Indians] with some blankets that may fall in their hands, and take care not to get the disease myself. As it is a pity to expose good men against them, I wish we could make use of the Spanish method, to hunt them with English dogs, supported by rangers and some light horse, who would, I think, effectually extirpate or remove that vermin.

—Colonel Henry Bouquet, *British Army*

You will do well to try to inoculate the Indians by means of blankets, as well as to try every other method that can serve to extirpate this execrable race. I should be very glad your

scheme for hunting them down by dogs could take effect, but England is at too great a distance to think of that at present.
—Sir Jeffrey Amherst, *Commander of British forces*

When I view my situation, I consider myself as an object of compassion. . . . When I look upward, I see the sky serene and happy; and when I look on the earth, I see all my children wandering in the utmost misery and distress.
—Mashipinashiwish, *Ojibway*

The Ottawas were greatly reduced in numbers on account of the small-pox. . . . This small-pox was sold to them shut up in a tin box, with the strict injunction not to open their box on their way homeward, but only when they should reach their country; and that this box contained something that would do them great good, and their people! . . . Accordingly, after they reached home they opened the box; but behold there was another tin box inside, smaller . . . and when they opened the last one they found nothing but mouldy particles in this last little box! . . . But alas, alas! pretty soon burst out a terrible sickness among them. . . . Lodge after lodge was totally vacated—nothing but the dead bodies lying here and there in their lodges—entire families being swept off with the ravages of this terrible disease. The whole coast of Arbor Croche, or Waw-gaw-naw-ke-zee, where their principal village was situated, . . . is said to have been a continuous village some fifteen or sixteen miles long . . . was entirely depopulated and laid waste . . . this wholesale murder of the Ottawas by this terrible disease sent by the British people, was actuated through hatred, and expressly to kill off the Ottawas and Chippewas. . . .   —Andrew Blackbird, *Odawa*

Paxton Boys   (1763)

As the war progresses, feelings run high against Indian people, even in places far removed from the frontier. Near Lancaster, Pennsylvania, twenty remaining Susquehannock live peacefully on the lands of their forefathers. They are much liked by their neighbors, and earn a living selling handmade brooms, baskets, and wooden bowls.

On a wintry day, riders thunder toward the Susquehannock settlement. Nearly everyone is away in Lancaster, trucking their wares. Only six people are left behind, including four women, an old man named Shehaes, and a little boy, Christy. Christy is a playmate of the Quaker children in town; he makes them bows and arrows. The riders are an armed vigilante mob known as the Paxton Boys. In a blast of gunfire, they tear through the Susquehannock settlement. No one is spared. Old Shehaes, asleep in his bed, is butchered with an axe and scalped.

The Paxton Boys ride into Lancaster with bloody axes hanging from their saddles. Two little Quaker boys recognize Christy's gun. Kindly neighbors rush the fourteen surviving Susquehannock to the town jail for their own protection. On December 27, the Paxton Boys—now fifty-seven strong—ride into Lancaster, and bash open the jail door. The Paxton Boys do not regard themselves as animals. Far from it—they are Presbyterians and, two days after Christmas, have come to carry out the Scriptures' instructions to Joshua—to rid the world of heathens.

Those cruel men . . . by violence broke open the [jail] door, and entered with the utmost fury. . . . When the poor wretches saw they had no protection . . . nor could possibly escape . . . they divided into their little families, the children clinging to the parents. . . . Men, women, and little children were every one inhumanly murdered!—in cold blood! . . . The bodies of the murdered were then brought out and exposed in the street, till a hole could be made in the earth, to receive and cover them. But the wickedness cannot be covered, the guilt will lie on the whole land. . . . The blood of the innocent will cry to heaven for vengeance.

—John Penn, *Pennsylvania governor*

Near the back door of the prison lay an old Indian and his [wife], particularly well known and esteemed by the people of the town . . . His name was Will Soc. Around him . . . lay two children, about the age of three years, whose heads were split with the tomahawk and their scalps taken off. Toward the middle of the jail-yard, along the west side of the wall, lay a stout Indian . . . shot in his breast. His legs were chopped with the tomahawk, his hands cut off, and finally a rifle-ball discharged in his mouth, so that his head was blown to atoms, and the brains were splashed against and yet hanging to the wall for three or four feet around. . . . In this manner lay the whole of them—men, women, and children—spread about the prison-yard, shot, scalped, hacked, and cut to pieces.

—William Henry, *American colonist*

These poor people have been always our friends. Their fathers received ours with kindness and hospitality. . . . Behold the return we have made them! . . . Unhappy people! To have lived in such times and by such neighbors!

—Benjamin Franklin, *American colonist*

Many of our old People are dead, so that we are now left as it were Orphans in a destitute Condition, which inclines us to leave our old Habitations. When we are gone, ill-minded People may tell you Stories to our Prejudice; but we assure

You that Distance will not alter our Affections for You. Therefore give no Ear to such Stories, as we on our Part will not think you can lose your Regard for Us, tho' there are some who would persuade Us that we are now not so much regarded by you as we have been.

—Cataradirha, *Susquehannock*

Logan Massacre (1774)

The frontier is bloody with violence. Vigilante mobs roam the countryside. The Cayuga leader Logan has sworn off bloodshed. He participated in neither the French and Indian War nor Pontiac's alliance. Now, as hostilities continue to defile the peace, Logan removes his people out of harm's way to a secluded spot along Yellow Creek.

Screams shatter the silence. Logan, away hunting, cannot hear them. He cannot hear a tomahawk slice through the belly of his pregnant sister, or the groans of his family as they die slowly along Yellow Creek. Logan, away hunting, is alone.

In the spring of 1774, a robbery and murder occurred in some of the white settlements on the Ohio, which were charged to the Indians, though perhaps not justly, for it is well known that a large number of civilized adventurers were traversing the frontiers at this time, who sometimes disguised themselves as Indians, and who thought little more of killing one of that people than of shooting a buffalo.

—Benjamin Thatcher, *United States*

I appeal to any white man to say, if ever he entered Logan's cabin hungry, and he gave him not meat; if ever he came cold and naked, and he clothed him not. During the course of the last long and bloody war, Logan remained idle in his cabin, an advocate for peace. Such was my love for the whites, that my countrymen pointed as they passed, and said, "Logan is the friend of white men." I had even thought to have lived with you but for the injuries of one man. Colonel Cresap, the last spring, in cold blood and unprovoked, murdered all the relations of Logan, not even sparing my women and children. There runs not a drop of my blood in the veins of any living creature. This called on me for revenge. I have sought it: I have killed many: I have fully glutted my vengeance. For my country, I rejoice at the beams of peace. But do not harbor a thought that mine is the joy of fear. Logan never felt fear. He will not turn on his heel to save his life. Who is there to mourn for Logan?—Not one.   —Tahgahjute (Logan), *Cayuga*

Revolutionary War (1775–1783)

When the Revolutionary War erupts between American colonists and the British, the Hodenosaunee willingly lend advice to the fledgling colonials. A representative form of government, based upon union, has kept the Hodenosaunee powerful and free for centuries. To the colonials, they urge the same.

We heartily recommend Union and a good agreement between you. . . . Our wise forefathers established Union and Amity between the Five Nations. This has made us formidable. . . . We are a powerful Confederacy; and by your observing the same methods, our wise forefathers have taken, you will acquire such strength and power.

—Canassatego, *Onondaga*

Soon after the Revolution begins, both British and Americans strive to enjoin Indian nations to fight on their side. The Hodeno-saunee are unwilling to offer anything more than advice. They, along with the Lenape, Shawnee, and Wyandot, are determined to remain neutral. The battle is not theirs to fight; Indian represen-tatives issue strict injunctions that their national borders are not to be crossed during the war.

Efforts are stepped up to break the neutrality. While Hodeno-saunee delegates lodge in Independence Hall to acknowledge the new colonial government and renew the pledge of peace, the Con-tinental Congress is forging plans to involve them in the war. The British do the same.

Individual members of the Hodenosaunee ultimately join the British while others abet the Americans—yet the neutrality of the Grand Council is never rescinded. The situation amounts to noth-ing less than civil war among the Hodenosaunee, and both Amer-icans and British are too occupied drawing rebel Hodenosaunee away from their national government to care.

At first I looked upon it as a family quarrel, in which I was not interested!—However, at length it appeared to me, that the father was in the right; and his children deserved to be pun-ished a little!—That this much be the case, I concluded from the many cruel acts his offspring had committed from time to time, on his Indian Children; in encroaching on their lands, stealing their property, shooting at, and murdering without cause, men, women, and children!—Yes! even murdering those, who at all times had been friendly to them. . . .

—Pachgantschihilas, *Lenape*

You have told us we had nothing to do with the war between you and the British. But the war has come to our doors. . . . If we sit still on our lands, and take no means of redress, the

British, following the customs of you white people, will hold them by conquest; and you, if you conquer Canada, will hold them on the same principles, as conquered from the British.
— Sagoyewatha (Red Jacket), *Seneca*

The resolutions of the Six Nations are not to be broken or altered. . . . This then is the determination of the Six Nations, not to take any part, but as it is a family affair, to sit still and see you fight it out.   — Little Abraham, *Mohawk*

I am appointed by the Six Nations to take care of this country, that is of the nations on the other side of the [Allegheny River], and I desire you will not think of an expedition against Detroit for, I repeat, we will not suffer an army to pass through our country.   — Guyashuta, *Seneca*

Some time ago you put a war-hatchet into my hands, saying "take this weapon and try it on the heads of my enemies, the [Americans], and let me know afterwards if it was sharp and good." . . . At the time you gave me this weapon, I had neither cause nor wish to go to war against a foe who had done me no injury. . . . You may perhaps think me a fool, for risking my life at your bidding—and that in a cause in which I have no prospect of gaining any thing. For it is your cause, and not mine—you have raised a quarrel among yourselves—and you ought to fight it out. . . . Many lives have already been lost on *your account*—The tribes have suffered, and been weakened. . . .

You say you love your children, the Indians.—This you have often told them; and indeed it is your interest to say so to them, that you may have them at your service. . . .

Pay attention to what I am going to say. While you, Father,

are setting me on your enemy, much in the same manner as a hunter sets his dog on the game; [and] while I am in the act of rushing on that enemy of yours, with the bloody destructive weapon you gave me, I may, perchance, happen to look back to the place from whence you started me, and what shall I see? Perhaps, I may see my father shaking hands with the [Americans] . . . I may *then* see him laugh at my folly for having obeyed his orders; and yet I am now risking my life at his command! . . . The warrior is poor, and his cabin is always empty; but your house, Father, is always full.

—Hopocan (Tobacco Pipe), *Lenape*

Sullivan Campaign (1779)

As punishment for Hodenosaunee rebels aiding the British, George Washington determines to crush the Confederacy and render it useless. In 1779 the Sullivan campaign is inaugurated. Five thousand American troops under General John Sullivan sweep through the Hodenosaunee country. Insatiably they advance across the land, destroying and burning everything that lives. In the end, only two Seneca towns—of the scores that once existed—remain unscathed, and thousands from all the nations are left homeless to face one of the most bitter winters in memory.

Sullivan's campaign will forever blight the record of George Washington. After the battle of Newtown, Sullivan's rangers mutilate the Seneca and Lenape dead, and bootlegs are made from their skin. At the end of the war, Washington rewards the same soldiers who have desolated the Hodenosaunee countryside with estates carved from their lands. Some of these lands are taken not from the neutral or pro-British Hodenosaunee, but from members of the very nations who have aided the Americans.

Caroline Parker, Seneca. Hodenosaunee women were
active in the government of their confederacy, and they equally
bore the brunt of George Washington's 1779 Sullivan
campaign aimed at civilians.

The expedition you are appointed to command is to be directed against the hostile tribes of the Six Nations of Indians. . . . The immediate objects are the total destruction and devastation of their settlements, and the capture of as many prisoners of every age and sex as possible . . . parties should be detached to lay waste all the settlements around . . . that the country may not be merely overrun, but destroyed . . . we may then listen to propositions for peace, and endeavour to draw further advantages from their fears.

—George Washington, *instructions to Sullivan*

A part of our corn they burnt, and threw the remainder into the river. They burnt our houses, killed what few cattle and horses they could find, destroyed our fruit trees, and left nothing but the bare soil and timber. . . . Accordingly we all returned; but what were our feelings when we found that there was not a mouthful of any kind of sustenance left, not even enough to keep a child one day from perishing with hunger. —Dickewamis (Mary Jemison), *Seneca*

Father: The voice of the Seneca nation speaks to you. . . . When your army entered the country of the Six Nations, we called you the Town Destroyer; and to this day, when that name is heard, our women look behind them and turn pale, and our children cling to the necks of their mothers. . . .

When our chiefs returned from the treaty at Fort Stanwix, and laid before our council what had been done there, our nation was surprised to hear how great a country you had compelled them to give up to you, without your paying to us any thing for it. Every one said that your hearts were yet swelled with resentment against us. . . . We asked each other, "What have we done to deserve such severe chastisement?" . . . You then told us that we were in your hand, and that by closing it you could crush us to nothing, and you demanded from us a great country, as the price of that peace which you had offered us; as if our want of strength had destroyed our rights.

... a man of the name of Phelps has come among us, and claimed our whole country northward of the line of Pennsylvania ... that it did not belong to us, for the great king had ceded the whole of it, when you made peace with him. ... He demanded it; he insisted on his demand, and declared that he would have it *all*. It was impossible for us to grant him this, and we immediately refused it. ... He then threatened us with immediate war, if we did not comply. Upon this threat, our chiefs held a council, and they agreed that no event of war could be worse than to be driven, with our wives and children, from the only country which we had any right to, and, therefore, weak as our nation was, they determined to take the chance of war, rather than submit to such unjust demands, which seemed to have no bounds. ...

Before you determine on a measure so unjust, look up to God, who has made *us* as well as *you*. We hope He will not permit you to destroy the whole of our nation. ... The land we live on, our fathers received from God, and they transmitted it to us, for our children, and we cannot part with it.   —Cornplanter, *Seneca*

They must have a plenty of money, to spend it buying false rights to lands belonging to Indians.

—Sagoyewatha (Red Jacket), *Seneca*

The news that came last night by our men from Albany made this a sick day in Oneida. All our children's hearts are sick, and our eyes rain like the black clouds that roar on the tops of the trees of the wilderness ... in the white man's land Skenando's name has gone far, and will not die. He has spoken many words to make his children straight. Long has he said, drink no strong water, for it makes you mice for white men, who are cats. Many a meal have they eaten of you. Their mouth is a snake, and their way like the fox. Their lips are sweet, but their heart is wicked. Yet there are good whites and good Indians. I love all good men. . . . The great chief at the setting sun . . . says the whites have made us wicked like themselves, and that we have *sold* them our land. We have *not* sold it—*we have been cheated.* . . .

—John Skenando, *Oneida*

Formerly we enjoyed the privilege we expect is now called freedom and liberty; but since the acquaintance with our brother white people, that which we call freedom and liberty becomes an entire stranger to us; and in place of that comes in flattery and deceit, to deprive poor . . . people of their properties, and bring them to poverty and, at last, to become beggars and laughing stocks to the world.

—Ohnawiio, Oteatohatongwan, and
Teholagwanegen, *Mohawk*

At our meeting last fall, at Fort George, you . . . desired us to point out the land we claimed in this State. . . . You then brought in several objections against our claim, but we could not find either of them to be reasonable. . . . If we had ever sold any of our lands, either to the King of France or Britain or either of the United States, we should of course have signed our names to the agreements . . . but, [we did] so far from any thing of this kind, that we bid defiance to the world to produce any deed, or sale, or gift, or lease, of any of the lands in question, or any part of them . . . to either the King of

France or Britain, or to either of the United States, or to any individual. . . .

You produced us a copy of a deed from several Mohawks, for eight hundred thousand acres of land, which those Mohawks had as good a right to sell as they have to come and dispose of the city of New York . . . you, at the treaty of last fall, pointed those people out to us to be too just a people, you thought, to do a thing of the kind; but what makes them just in your eyes, we expect, is because they stole from us, and sold to you. This is what makes them a just people. . . .

Had we, several years ago, done as those have, whom you call a just people, that is, had we sold off all our lands, then underhandedly sold our brother's, then fled our country, took up arms, and come and killed men, women, and children indiscriminately; burnt houses, and committed every other act of devastation; and, in short, done every thing we could against our once nearest friends, then, according to what you say of those Mohawks, you would have esteemed us a just people, and therefore would not have disputed our claim. . . .

It seems that, before a nation can get justice of another, they must first go to war, and spill one another's blood; but, brothers, we do not like this mode of settling differences; we wish justice to be done without. . . .

—Ohnawiio, Oteatohatongwan, and
Teholagwanegen, *Mohawk*

That land of Ganono-o, or "Empire State" as you love to call it, was once laced by our trails from Albany to Buffalo—trails that we had trod for centuries—trails worn so deep by the feet of the Iroquois that they became your own roads of travel as your possessions gradually eat into those of my people. . . . The land of Ganono-o, the Empire State, then is our monument! We shall not long occupy much room in living; the

single tree of the thousands which sheltered our forefathers—one old elm under which the representatives of the
tribes were wont to meet—will cover us all; but we would
have our bodies twined in death among its roots, on the very
soil on whence it grew! Perhaps it will last no longer being
fertilized by their decay. . . .

Have we, the first holders of this prosperous region, no
longer a share in your history? Glad were your fathers to sit
upon the threshold of the Long House, rich did they then
hold themselves in getting the mere sweeping from its door.

Had our forefathers spurned you from it when the French
were thundering at the opposite end to get a passage through
and drive you into the sea? Whatever has been the fate of
other Indians, the Iroquois might still have been a nation;
and I, instead of pleading for the privilege of living within
your borders—I . . . might have had a country!

—Waowowanoonk (Peter Wilson), *Cayuga*

Missionaries and Handsome Lake   (1800)

Missionaries are on Hodenosaunee land. They are building
houses, teaching the people to plant, and instructing them how to
live. But the Hodenosaunee are a people who have always planted,
and they know quite well how to live. They have been doing both
since time began. However well-meaning, missionary attempts to
deprive them of their religion and culture only cause infinitely
more misery.

Postwar Hodenosaunee society experiences a difficult period of
reconstruction, as might be expected of any nation ravaged by war.
In the midst of the crisis, a Seneca prophet named Handsome
Lake guides the Hodenosaunee back to their traditions, ushering
in a period of returning prosperity.

With sweet voices and smiling faces, they offered to teach them the religion of the white people. Our brethren in the East listened to them. They turned from the religion of their fathers, and took up the religion of the white people. What good has it done? Are they more friendly one to another than we are? No, Brother! They are a divided people;—we are united. They quarrel about religion;—we live in love and friendship. . . . If you wish us well, keep away; do not disturb us. . . . We do not worship the [Creator] as the white people do, but we believe that the forms of worship are indifferent to the [Creator]. It is the homage of sincere hearts that pleases him, and we worship him in that manner. . . . You wish us to change our religion for yours. We like our religion, and do not want another.   —Sagoyewatha (Red Jacket), *Seneca*

Brother, listen to what we say. There was a time when our forefathers owned this great island. Their seats extended from the rising to the setting sun. The [Creator] had made it for the use of Indians. He had created the buffalo, the deer, and other animals for food. He made the bear and the beaver, and their skins served us for clothing. He had scattered them over the country, and taught us how to take them. He had caused the earth to produce corn for bread. All this he had done for his red children because he loved them. . . . But an evil day came upon us. Your forefathers crossed the great waters, and landed on this island. Their numbers were small. They found friends and not enemies. They told us they had fled from their own country for fear of wicked men, and come here to enjoy their religion. They asked for a small seat. We took pity on them, granted their request, and they sat down amongst us. We gave them corn and meat. They gave us poison in return. The white people had now found our country. Tidings were carried back, and more came amongst us. Yet we did not fear them. We took them to be friends.

They called us brothers. We believed them, and gave them a larger seat. At length their numbers had greatly increased. They wanted more land. They wanted our country.

Our eyes were opened, and our minds became uneasy. Wars took place. Indians were hired to fight against Indians, and many of our people were destroyed. They also brought strong liquors among us. It was strong and powerful, and has slain thousands.

Brother!—our seats were once large, and yours were very small. You have now become a great people, and we have scarcely a place left to spread our blankets. You have got our country, but are not satisfied. You want to force your religion upon us. . . . The [Creator] has made us all. But he has made a great difference between his white and red children. He has given us a different complexion and different customs. . . . Since he has made so great a difference between us in other things, why may we not conclude that he has given us a different religion according to our understanding? The [Creator] does right. He knows what is best for his children. We are satisfied. Brother!—We do not wish to destroy your religion, or take it from you. We only want to enjoy our own.
—Sagoyewatha (Red Jacket), *Seneca*

The South

*It was a strange and a hard matter; a thing which [the delega-
tion] had not explained to them . . . and could not explain to the
nation. It was with the utmost reluctance that they consented to
give the land away; it was like pulling out their hearts, and
throwing them away.*

—*Alexander Cornell*, Creek

In the South, a pattern of European occupation evolved similar
to that in the North, yet there were differences. In the latter,
colonization was prompted by the lure of finding the North-
west Passage and the subsequent development of the fur trade. In
the South, settlement was effected to check Spanish expansion
out of the Caribbean and, later, to promote a plantation-style
economy. By the mid-sixteenth century, Spain had traveled far
enough up the Atlantic coast to name the Chesapeake Bay "Madre
de Dios." The French had made similar headway along the South
Carolina and Florida shore, until driven off by the Spanish. The
English responded to these threats by establishing a colony in
North Carolina, and the race for dominance began. When the
scramble ended, Spain controlled Florida, England held the
southern coast from Maryland to Georgia, and France occupied
the Mississippi Delta region around New Orleans.

The Indian version of this same history has quite a different
ring. Spaniards, exploring north along the Atlantic coast, entered

the broad waters of the Chesapeake Bay. Before leaving, they seized a young boy who was, in all likelihood, from a ruling family of the Kiskiak nation near the bay. Twenty years later, he persuaded the Jesuits to begin a mission in his homeland. And so Don Luis (as he was baptized) secured a way home. Upon arriving he promptly escaped, leaving the good friars to their own devices along the Chesapeake Bay. Had they left him alone, all would have been right, but the missionaries were enraged at his perfidy and made repeated attempts to secure his return. The story ended tragically. Don Luis killed the friars in his own defense, and when Spaniards inevitably came to investigate the Jesuits' disappearance, the Kiskiak hopelessly donned the brown religious cassocks and strode along the beach, heads bowed, in the vain hope that the ship would leave. It did leave, but only after eight Kiskiak dangled lifelessly from her rigging.

Unaware of this tragedy, Sir Walter Raleigh's English expedition hastened to locate the Chesapeake Bay to wrest it from Spain, but missed the mark and planted the first English colony at Roanoke on the North Carolina coast. In 1584 and 1585, they were welcomed by the Secotan and treated to an abundance of crabs, shellfish, corn, and other produce, notwithstanding that pestilence spread wherever they traveled. Thomas Hariot, a chronicler with the expedition, noted that "within a few days after our departure . . . the people began to die very fast, and many in short space; in some townes about twentie, in some fourtie, in some sixtie, & in one six score . . . the like by report of the oldest men in the country never happened before, time out of minde."

In 1586, little more than a year after these good relations were established, the English could credit themselves with kidnapping and chaining the Chowanoc leader's son; holding his father hostage; and decapitating Pemisapan, the Secotan leader. Little wonder that when they came back the following year to colonize, they had no intention of returning to Roanoke Island, although their treacherous pilot deposited them there anyway. By 1590 the colony of 118 men, women, and children mysteriously had disappeared, forever destined to be remembered as the Lost Colony. No one bothered to ask the Secotan their whereabouts. It was easier to think that they had killed them (as indeed they had just cause), although a century later, the surveyor John Lawson believed he had located descendants of the colony living in the coastal Indian village of Hatteras.

By the early eighteenth century, the English were well established along the south Atlantic coast. Lord Calvert settled the colony of Maryland within the nation of the Piscataway and thereafter waged campaigns of extermination against Indian nations on the eastern shore. In Virginia, the formidable Powhatan engaged in three wars with the English at Jamestown and very nearly succeeded in driving them back into the bay, but in the end Jamestown emerged the winner. Pocahontas, favorite daughter of Powhatan leader Wahunsonacock, was kidnapped, married to an Englishman, and dead in the space of four years. Shortly thereafter, her father died, reportedly of a broken heart.

In Charleston, a thriving trade developed between the Siouan nations and the English. Unlike the northern fur trade, which concentrated primarily on pelts, the southern trade took on a more sinister aspect. Deer hides, Indian slaves, and rum formed its nucleus, and thousands of Indian people were acquired through barter and deliberately instigated wars. There was not a nation in the South that did not suffer from this brutal ravage of its people, the majority of whom were shipped to the West Indies to work the sugar plantations.

A notorious group of slave traders known as the Goose Creek Men emerged in South Carolina. Highly respected southern gentlemen and landed estate owners, they ran the politics of the South, served as officers in Indian wars, and at least one became a distinguished Indian agent. Many early proprietors of the colony hailed from plantations in Barbados. And so the system of Indian slave labor begun by the Spanish *repartimiento* continued through the colonial period and spread into the southern United States. When coastal Indian nations became decimated through disease and slavery, Africans were brought in to replace them. Had the Goose Creek Men been less successful and the economy forced to take on a different complexion, the history of the United States might have been quite different.

It was not only the British who engaged in the Indian slave trade. The French in Louisiana found it not only lucrative but a convenient way to dispose of "problematic" Indian nations who stood in the way of their commerce and expansion. Governors Bienville and Périer were the most notorious, and hapless individuals from the Chitimacha, Natchez, Yazoo, Koroa, Ofo, Tiou, and many other nations joined the countless thousands enslaved in the West Indies. For most, the life of misery would be short. Few survived beyond the first years.

As the fur trade diminished along the coast in the early 1700s, the British moved farther inland, contacting interior nations such as the Cherokee and Creek. This shift in interest left many of the remnant coastal nations out in the cold. Long ago having removed to the vicinity of trading posts called "factories," many had adopted European dress, depended on European firearms, lived in European-style houses, and spoke fluent English. When the factories suddenly closed, they were left stranded. Incoming Europeans, meeting Indians in remote valleys who spoke English and raised domesticated animals, were amazed, and wild stories of missing Welshmen, Lost Colonists, and other incredible tales were circulated freely. Later, these same Indian nations would be forced to "prove" their Indianness to a foreign government that had no right even to inquire.

By the time of the French and Indian War, southern Indian nations were plagued by the same turbulent disruptions faced by those in the North. The British steadily advanced west, while the French pushed north and east up the Mississippi River Valley and toward the Appalachians. Some nations, like the Creek, became wholly engulfed. Others, like the precariously situated Cherokee, were trapped between the two powers. Smaller nations were displaced entirely. In both the North and the South, larger countries such as the Cherokee, Creek, Chickasaw, Catawba, and Hodeno-saunee established refugee areas within their nations to accommodate those in need. Others sought asylum in remote back areas and swamps, where they maintained their independence until long after the colonial era. The entire length and breadth of the Appalachian frontier, from Maine to Georgia, was in turmoil and Indian nations all along it fought bravely to survive, and won.

In a situation so complex, it is not possible to dismiss all interaction as either good or bad. There were instances in which Indian nations manipulated European powers to their best advantage, and other times when Europeans got the better of them—abusing Indian leaders with threats, bribery, alcohol, and beatings. A local plantation family cheerfully called upon an Indian doctor to cure a sick family member at the same time that vigilante mobs roamed the frontier indiscriminately killing any Indian people they saw. Indian nations experienced civil wars and fought each other, as colonial powers did the same. But almost without exception, every Indian/white clash that was termed "an Indian depredation" invariably could be traced to an act of treachery on the part of a white settler against an Indian person, his stock, his goods, or his land. When Indian people retaliated, colonial officials could be sure that for every frontier settler killed, there previously had been an Indian person slain. To further upset the balance, early treaties stipulated that settlers found across Indian national boundary lines could be removed by the nations and their goods confiscated. Bloodshed inevitably resulted, and then (frontier justice!) Indian people were blamed.

Despite this complex interaction, whenever Indian testimony was taken, the frontier situation was summed up very clearly. Indian people were determined to maintain their nations, their cultures, and their lands, or die defending them.

Powhatan (1607)

Wahunsonacock considers what to do with the English settlement of Jamestown, which sits on his land. As leader of the powerful Powhatan Confederacy, he easily can destroy it. Yet this will come at cost of life, and loss of English goods that are useful tools in diplomacy with other nations. A decision is reached—the English shall be made tributary to the Powhatan and become the latest nation within the alliance. But Captain John Smith has no such inclination: "Powhatan, you must knowe as I have but one God, I honour but one king: and I live not here as your subject."

Instead, Smith arranges for Wahunsonacock to pledge allegiance to the King of England. The two are at diplomatic loggerheads.

... but a foul trouble there was to make him kneel to receive his crown, he neither knowing the majesty nor meaning of a crown, nor bending of the knee, endured so many persuasions, examples, and instructions, as tired them all; at last, by leaning hard on his shoulders, he a little stooped, and three having the crown in their hands put it on his head. . . .
—Captain John Smith, *Jamestown governor*

Yet, Captain *Smith* . . . some doubt I have of your comming hither, that makes me not so kindly seeke to relieve you as I would: for many do informe me, your comming is not for trade, but to invade my people and possesse my Country: who dare not come to bring you corne, seeing you [are] thus armed with your men. To cleere us of this feare, leave abord your weapons; for here they are needlesse, we being all friends and for ever *Powhatans.* —Wahunsonacock, *Powhatan*

Captaine *Smith*, I never used anie of [my] *Werowances* [leaders] so kindlie as your selfe; yet from you, I receave the least kindnesse of anie.   —Wahunsonacock, *Powhatan*

Count the stars in the sky, the leaves on the trees, and the sand upon the sea-shore—for such is the number of the people of England.   —Tomocomo, *Powhatan*

As the English increase, so does their contempt for the Powhatan. War erupts in 1610, and again in 1622 and 1644 after Wahunsonacock's death. Along the bank of the Potomac River, 250 Indian dignitaries lie dying. They have attended an English peace council, and have drunk a toast of poisoned wine. The English will win the war, but not with honor.

[The Powhatan are] . . . Soules drown'd in flesh and blood; Rooted in Evill, and oppos'd in Good; Errors of Nature, of inhumane Birth, The very dregs, garbage, and spawne of Earth; Who ne're (I think) were mention'd with those creatures Adam gave names to in their severall natures But such as comming of a later Brood, (Not sav'd in th'Arke) but since the generall Flood Sprung up like vermine of an earthly slime . . . Father'd by Sathan, and the sonnes of hell.

    —Christopher Brooke, *England*

I have seen two generations of my people die. Not a man of the two generations is alive now but myself. I know the difference between peace and war better than any men in my country. . . . Why will you take by force what you may have quietly by love? Why will you destroy us who supply you with food? What can you get by war? We can hide our provisions and run into the woods; then you will starve for wronging your friends. Why are you jealous of us? We are unarmed, and willing to give you what you ask, if you come in a friendly manner, and not with swords and guns, as if to make war upon an enemy. I am not so simple as not to know that it is much better to eat good meat, sleep comfortably, live quietly with my wives and children, laugh and be merry with the English, and trade for their copper and hatchets, than to run away from them, and to lie cold in the woods . . . and to be so hunted that I can neither eat nor sleep . . . so I must end my miserable life.   —Wahunsonacock, *Powhatan*

The Piscataway and Lord Calvert   (1634)

In 1632 King Charles I grants a charter of land called "Maryland" to Lord Baltimore, although the lands are not his to give. They belong to the Conoy, Choptank, Assateague, and other nations encompassed by the grant.

The day breaks warm and muggy along the Potomac River. Wannis, the Piscataway Emperor, stands along the shore waiting for the *Dove* to heave into sight. The night before, bonfires lit up the Potomac, spreading the news of Lord Calvert's approach. The Piscataway are secure in their strength—so much so that when the British pinnace pulls alongshore, Wannis engages in talks only indifferently. The question proposed by Lord Calvert demands a prompt answer. Shall the English colony stay or shall they go? Wannis offers only lukewarm response—if Lord Calvert has hoped for more, he will be disappointed.

Circumstances change. By the end of the century, English weapons of disease and encroachment are unleashed against the Piscataway. Both Maryland and Virginia plot their extermination. The Piscataway escape to an isolated island in the middle of the

Potomac River and once again are able to treat Maryland's demands with indifference. But indifference is not independence. Those Piscataway who do not escape to the Hodenosaunee refugee lands evade the colonists. They disappear deep within Zekiah swamp; they learn how to live free. The colonists cannot see that which is invisible; therefore the invisible must not exist. Within Zekiah swamp, the Piscataway reconstruct their lives.

I will not bid you [English] go, neither will I bid you stay, you must use your own discretion.   —Wannis, *Piscataway*

Let us have no Quarrels for killing Hogs. . . . Your hogs & Cattle injure Us You come too near Us to live & drive Us from place to place. We can fly no farther let us know where to live & how to be secured for the future from the Hogs & Cattle.
        —Mattagund, *delegation of Anacostank,*
        Zeag, and Patuxent nations

Wiccomiss Extermination   (1642–1669)

The eastern shore of Maryland, across the Chesapeake Bay, has become a spillway for settlers from the colony. Among the Indian nations displaced are the Wiccomiss. In 1642 they are declared enemies of the province and permission is granted to shoot any on sight.

Along a tidewater river, a Wiccomiss woman lies dead, murdered by an Englishman. Later, her kinsman Anatchcom is charged with slaying Captain John Odber in retaliation. Whether he is guilty or not does not matter; the extermination of the Wiccomiss begins in earnest. They are driven without mercy, hunted down in swamps and mires, and sold as slaves in Barbados. Jubilantly, the English report their total annihilation. On the same eastern shore, Virginia exterminates the Assateague and Pocomoke.

It is much more Prudence, and Charity, to Civilize, and make them Christians, than to kill, robbe, and hunt them from place to place as you would doe a wolfe.

—Father Andrew White, *England*

I am a Native of Patuxent. . . . I married a wife amongst the Wicomesses, where I have lived ever since, and they have sent me to tell you, that they are sorry . . . and hope you will not make the rash act of a few young men (which was done in heate) a quarrell to their Nation, who desire to live in peace and love with you. . . . It is the manner amongst us *Indians,* that if any such like accident happen, wee doe redeeme the life of a man that is so slaine, with a 100. armes length of *Roanoke* . . . and since that you are heere strangers, and come into our Countrey, you should rather conforme your selves to the Customes of our Countrey, [than] impose yours upon us. . . .   —(Name not given), *Patuxent,* with the Wiccomiss delegation

. . . [The Creator] was sorry he had made white men, because they drove the Indians from the . . . sea. I once owned all this land about here. . . . Here . . . is the very spot where my father lived. But white people gave him rum, and took it away, and I am not so well off as a Ratcoon. You white people make slaves of every thing, the wind, the water, the fire, and the earth. . . . [Yet] every thing makes slaves of you white people, and we Indians are free.   —Will Andrew, *Assateague*

To Divide and Conquer (1669)

Jean-Baptiste Le Moyne, sieur de Bienville and ruthless governor of Louisiana, impressively parades his batallion before the Choctaw and Chickasaw delegation, but few are moved. Bienville glares at the formidable assembly. Either nation alone is powerful enough, but acting in concert they represent an impenetrable barrier to French domination of the lower Mississippi. One delegate has the temerity to inquire if the French are more numerous in Europe than the few soldiers now before them: "If your countrymen are as thick, as you say, on their native soil as the leaves on the trees of our forests, why have they not sent more of their warriors here to avenge the death of those whom we have slain in battle? . . . And why is it that [their] places . . . are filled by so many little, weak, and bad looking men, and even boys?"

Bienville gives vent to passion and angrily declares that his forces have the strength to crush the entire Choctaw and Chickasaw nations. The delegates burst out laughing. "We would like to see that."

Europeans ultimately strain relations between the Choctaw and Chickasaw. When the French attack the neighboring Natchez, the Choctaw give asylum to the survivors and very clearly express their opinion of the French. Political intrigues later force the Choctaw to turn upon themselves in one of the bloodiest civil wars ever fought on American soil.

The Choctaws, whom I have set in motion against the Chickasaws, have destroyed entirely three villages of this ferocious nation, which disturbed our commerce on the river . . . it is a most important advantage which we have obtained, the more so, that it has not cost one drop of French blood, through the care I took of opposing those barbarians to one another.

—Sieur de Bienville, *Louisiana governor*

We neither respect you as a friend, nor fear you as an enemy.
We have extended the hand of friendship and safety to the
unfortunate Natchez, and . . . [will] protect them.

—Choctaw delegation

War among the Chitimacha   (1704)

The Chitimacha make a mistake. The French have stolen twenty
of their people for slaves, and the Chitimacha seek justice according to the laws of their nation. They have not yet learned that when
dealing with the French at New Orleans, it is better to suffer injustice than seek redress. When Governor Bienville learns that the
Chitimacha have killed four Frenchmen in retaliation, including a
missionary, he is moved to immediate action. The punishment is
extermination.

Do you not remember that, in 1704, the [Chitimacha] killed a
missionary and three other Frenchmen? . . . my wrath was
kindled, and I said to the neighboring Indian nations: "Bienville hates the [Chitimacha], and he who kills a [Chitimacha]
is Bienville's friend." When I passed this sentence upon
them, you know that their tribe was composed of three hundred families. A few months elapsed, and they were reduced
to eighty! They sued for peace at last, yielded to my demands,
and it was only then that the tomahawk, the arrow and the
rifle ceased to drink their blood.

—Sieur de Bienville, *Louisiana governor*

Thou knowest that a single man has killed . . . [a missionary], whose death has caused that of our best warriors: we have only old men, and women with their children remaining. . . . The sun was red before . . . the water troubled and stained with our blood; our women lamented without intermission the loss of their relations . . . at the least shriek of the birds of night all our warriors were on foot; they never slept without their arms; our huts were abandoned, and our fields lay fallow; we had all of us empty stomachs, and our faces looked long and meagre . . . the birds that perched near our habitations seemed, by their doleful notes, to sing us songs of death.

—Long Panther, *Chitimacha*

To Covet White Apple (1729)

Old Hair, the Natchez ruling Sun of the town of White Apple, stares across the table at the French commandant, Monsieur de Chopart. Despotic commander of Fort Rosalie, Chopart has been charged with abuse of power by his own officers.

The commandant of a fort built in the shadow of White Apple should have extended the most courteous regard toward the Natchez. Instead, Chopart holds them in contempt. Unceremoniously, Old Hair is ordered to vacate his capital so that investors can turn the site into a plantation. The Sun refuses with quiet dignity, and Chopart threatens to haul him to New Orleans in chains. In self-defense, the Natchez raze Fort Rosalie; French retribution knows no bounds. In the war that follows, nearly a thousand Natchez are deported as slaves to Santo Domingo. They are the lucky ones. In New Orleans, a crowd gathers for a night's entertainment. On top of a scaffold, a fire crackles, and an old Natchez woman is unchained and thrown on top of it like a rotten piece of wood.

Brother, such language was never before addressed to me; nor have your people ever before taken our property from us by force. What they wished of ours, we freely gave or they purchased. We prefer peace to war with your nation. What more can we do? In the center of the White Apple is our temple, in which the bones of our ancestors have reposed . . . and it is dear to our hearts.   —Old Hair, *Natchez*

Insolent barbarian! Call me not brother. Between thy race and mine are no kindred ties; nor do I parley with any of your race. Let it suffice you, that when I command, you must obey.
          —Monsieur de Chopart, *French commandant*

My white brother cannot be in earnest, but only desires to try the temper of the Indians. [Are you] ignorant of the fact that the Natchez built that village many thousand [years] ago, and have lived there ever since?   —Old Hair, *Natchez*

Extermination of the Chawasha   (1730)

An Indian scare grips the residents of New Orleans though, in truth, Indian nations have much more to fear from them. Louisiana governor Étienne Périer orders the extermination of the Chawasha nation as "a lesson" to those who try to oppose the French.

. . . the [Chawasha], a little tribe of only thirty warriors, dwelling a few miles above New Orleans, were even a subject of dread to the French. This induced me to have them destroyed by our negroes . . . setting an example before the

small tribes higher up the river. . . . If I had been so disposed
I could have destroyed all those nations, which are no service
to us.   —Étienne Périer, *Louisiana governor*

. . . in order to live in peace among ourselves, and to please
the supreme Spirit, we must indispensably observe the following points; we must never kill any one but in defence of
our own lives; we must never know any other woman besides
our own; we must never take any thing that belongs to another; we must never [lie] nor get drunk; we must not be
avaricious, but must give liberally, and with joy, part of what
we have to others who are in want, and generously share our
subsistence with those who are in need of it.
                                    —Guardian of the temple, *Natchez*

We have noticed for a long time that having the French as
neighbors has done us more harm than good. We old men see
it, but the young men do not. The supplies from Europe
please them, but of what use are they? . . . Before the French
came into our lands, we were men, we were happy with what
we had, we walked boldly upon all our paths, because then
we were our own masters. But today we tread gropingly, fearing thorns. We walk like the slaves which we will soon be,
since they already treat us as though we were. When they are
strong enough, they will no longer treat us with consideration. They will put us in chains. Has not their chief already
threatened ours with this affront? Is not death preferable to
slavery? . . . Since they are stronger in our region than any
place else, we shall be the first to wear their chains. When
they are powerful enough, they will do the same to all the
tribes.   —Natchez Council

Extermination of the Yazoo   (1731)

At the war's end, surviving Natchez flee as refugees to the Cherokee and Upper Creek. Many of their allies—the Yazoo, Koroa, and
Tiou—find themselves nearly exterminated. Within the Yazoo nation, a young man has lost his entire family and embarks upon a
journey across the country. In his travels west, he meets Indian
nations who live in dread of Europeans.

The cold was hardly gone, when I again embarked on the fine
river, and in my course I met with several nations, with whom
I generally staid but one night, till I arrived at the nation that
is but one day's journey from the great water on the west. This
nation live in the woods about the distance of a league from
the river, from their apprehension of bearded men, who come
upon their coasts in floating villages, and carry off their children to make slaves of them. These men were described to be
white, with long black beards that came down to their breast;
they were thick and short, had large heads, which were covered with cloth; they were always dressed, even in the greatest heats. . . . Those strangers came from the sun-setting, in
search of a yellow stinking wood, which dyes a fine yellow
color; but the people of this nation, that they might not be
tempted to visit them, had destroyed all those kind of trees.
Two other nations in their neighborhood, however, having no
other wood, could not destroy the trees, and were still visited
by the strangers. . . .   —Moncachtape, *Yazoo*

Catawba Joke   (1754)

The Catawba are continually reminded that the settlers invading
their country have no manners. In their nation, hungry travelers
are never turned away, but fed and well cared for. When the

settlers do not return such hospitality, the Catawba wonder at the insult. And while they take Catawba lands and drive away the game, the settlers never manage to learn the decorum of their Indian hosts. William Morrison testifies under oath that Catawba hunters have thrown a pail of water into his meal trough. When he prevents the action, he claims they push him away with their guns. Yet it is a Catawba man that is killed.

To the court, the Catawba reply that all they were intending to do was put a handful of the cornmeal into the water to make a mush drink as is their custom. Their testimony is demolished when three white settlers appear in defense of William Morrison. The Catawba are criminals indeed, for once they took bread and meat from them, and on another occasion attempted to abduct a child. It is unlikely that the settlers will ever adapt to the customs of the land or adopt the easygoing attitude of their hosts; but one thing is certain: they have provided the Catawba with unbounded food for thought.

As to our Liveing on those Lands we Expect to live on those Lands we now possess During our Time here for when the Great man above made us he also made this Island. He also made our forefathers and of this Colour and Hue. He also fixed our forefathers and us here and to Inherit this Land and Ever since we Lived after our manner and fashion.

—Arataswa (King Hagler), *Catawba*

... many times we are forced to go to Your houses when Hungry, and no sooner we do appear but your Dogs bark and as soon as You Discover Our Comeing You Imediately hide Your Bread Meal and Meat or any Other thing that is fit to Eat about your houses, and we being sensible that this is the Case, it is True we serch, and if we finde any Eatables in the house we Take some, and Especially from those who behave so Churlish and ungreatfull to us, as they are very well assured, of our great need. . . . If we ask a little Victuals you Refuse us & then we Owne we Take a Loaf of bread a little meal or meat to Eat, and then You Complain and say those are Transgressions, it is True there are many in those Settlements that are very kind and Curtious to us when or as often as we come they give us Bread and milk meat or Butter very freely . . . and if it should happen that they have nothing we goe away Contented with them, for we well know that if they had any thing ready we would have it freely and not Refused by them.

One of [our] Captains . . . Came to James Armstrong's house, the above Complaintant, who gave him a small Cake of Bread, and being very hungry he asked more for himself and his men, and being Told . . . that there was no more ready in the house One of the Indians Lifted up a bag that lay in the house Under which they Discovered Some Bread which they had Suspected was hid from them, and taking some of it the woman struck one of them Over the head. . . . You . . . accuse our People with attempting To take away a Child from one of Your People, but I hope you will not . . . Imagine it was done in Earnest, for I am Informed it was Only done by way of a joke by one of our wild Young men in Order to Surprize the People, that were the parents of the Child, to have a Laugh at the Joke.   —Arataswa (King Hagler), *Catawba*

The Appalachian Frontier   (1745–1783)

Everywhere, the story is the same. Settlers ignore Indian national boundaries and boldly settle on vital hunting grounds. When Indian nations seek redress, squatters resort to force of arms; and then Indian nations are blamed for depredations. As punishment for alleged frontier crimes, troops destroy the fertile Cherokee middle towns, whose fields are the nation's breadbasket.

We proceeded . . . to burn the Indian cabins. Some of the men seemed to enjoy this cruel work, laughing heartily at the curling flames, but to me it appeared a shocking sight. . . . But when we came . . . to cut down the fields of corn, I could scarcely refrain from tears. . . . I saw everywhere around, the footsteps of the little Indian children, where they had lately played under the shade of their rustling corn. When we are gone, thought I, they will return, and . . . with tearful eyes, will mark the ghastly ruin. . . . "Who did this?" they will ask their mothers, and the reply will be, "The white people did it,—the Christians did it!"

—Lieutenant Francis Marion, *British Army*

I tremble for my country when I reflect that God is just.
—Thomas Jefferson, *United States*

[The settlers] do not conceive that government has any right to forbid their taking possession of a vast tract of country . . . which serves only as a shelter to a few scattered tribes of Indians. Nor can they be easily brought to entertain any belief of the permanent obligation of treaties made with those people whom they consider, as but little removed from the brute creation.   —Lord Dunmore, *Virginia governor*

It is a little surprising that when we entered into treaties with . . . the whites, their whole cry is *more land!* Indeed . . . it seemed to be a matter of formality with them to demand what they knew we durst not refuse. . . . If . . . reconnoitering a country is sufficient reason to ground a claim to it, we shall insist upon transposing the demand, and your relinquishing your settlements. . . . Let us examine the facts of your present eruption into our country, and we shall discover your pretentions on that ground. What did you do? You marched into our territories . . . you killed a few scattered and defenseless individuals, spread fire and desolation wherever you pleased, and returned again to your own habitations. . . . Again, were we to inquire by what law or authority you set up a claim, I answer, *none!* Your laws extend not into our country, nor ever did. . . .

Indeed, much has been advanced on the want of what you term civilization among the Indians; and many proposals have been made to us to adopt your laws, your religion, your manners and your customs. But, we confess that we . . . should be better pleased with beholding the good effect of these doctrines in your own practices. . . . You say: Why do not the Indians till the ground and live as we do? May we not, with equal propriety, ask, Why the white people do not hunt and live as we do?

You profess to think . . . it is very criminal in our young men if they chance to kill a cow or a hog for their sustenance when they happen to be in your lands. We wish, however, to be at peace with you, and to do as we would be done by. We do not quarrel with you for killing an occasional buffalo, bear or deer . . . but you go much farther; your people hunt to gain a livelihood by it; they kill all our game. . . . The great God of Nature has placed us in different situations . . . he has not created us to be your slaves. *We are a separate people!* He has given each their lands . . . he has stocked yours with cows, ours with buffaloe; yours with hog, ours with bear; yours with sheep, ours with deer. He has, indeed, given you an advantage in this, that your cattle are tame and domestic while ours are wild and demand not only a larger space for range, but art to hunt and kill them; they are, nevertheless, as much our property as other animals are yours. . . .

—Onitositah (Corn Tassel), *Cherokee*

Daniel Boone: Appeal for the Intertribal Hunting Grounds (1769)

In 1769 Daniel Boone is a pioneer hero. He has forged a trail into the wilderness and calls the land Kentucky. But on the other side of the Appalachians, Indian nations think differently of Boone's exploits. The trail he has followed across the Cumberland Gap is an Indian road, and the Kentucky "wilderness" is a clearly defined intertribal hunting ground, shared equally by the Cherokee, Chickasaw, Yuchi, Lenape, Shawnee, Wyandot, and Hodenosaunee. In little more than a decade, ten thousand pioneers will swarm onto these lands in direct violation of prior treaties.

In 1776 delegates from the Shawnee, Lenape, Odawa, Hodenosaunee, and Nanticoke nations arrive at the Cherokee capital of Echota. The implication of such encroachment is staggering; without the Kentucky grounds, they will starve. And there are other abuses: hunting parties are waylaid by frontiersmen, vigilantes murder innocent civilians, Indian leaders are forced into humiliating land cessions. Everyone has a story.

When we passed through the country between Pittsburgh and our nations, lately Shawnee and Delaware hunting grounds, where we could once see nothing but deer and buffalo, we found the country thickly inhabited and the people under arms. We were compelled to make a detour of three hundred miles on the other side of the Ohio to avoid being discovered. We saw large numbers of white men in forts; and fortifications around salt springs and buffalo grounds.
— Shawnee, Lenape, Odawa, Hodenosaunee, and Nanticoke delegation

In a few years, the Shawnees, from being a great Nation, have been reduced to a handful. They once possessed land almost to the seashore, but now have hardly enough ground to stand upon. The lands where the Shawnees have but lately hunted are covered with forts and armed men. When a fort appears, you may depend upon it there will soon be towns and settlements of white men. It is plain that the white people intend to extirpate the Indians. It is better for [us] to die like warriors than to diminish away by inches. The cause of the red men is just, and I hope that the [Creator] who governs everything will favor us. —Cornstalk, *Shawnee*

I pity the white people, but the white people do not pity me. . . . The Great Being above is very good, and provides for everybody. It is He that made fire, bread, and the rivers to run. He gave us this land, but the white people seem to want to drive us from it. —Attakullakulla, *Cherokee*

We must inform you that we look upon the white people that live in the new State, very deceitful; we have experienced them, and are much afraid of them; we are now obliged to keep spies out continually on the frontiers, fearing they will return and do us an injury as they did before.
—Little Turkey, *Cherokee*

. . . but what is the reason Congress has not moved those people from off our lands before now? . . . We well remember, whenever we are invited into a treaty . . . and bounds are fixed, that the white people settle much faster on our lands than they did before. —Cherokee Council

... I am surprised you should write me, "That the citizens of the United States are daily encroaching and building on your lands." I deny, positively, that a single house, or settlement, of any kind, has been made. . . .

—William Blount, *North Carolina governor*

Rise of the Chickamauga   (1777)

Demoralized by American attacks and the indiscriminate slaughter of both men and women that have laid waste more than fifty Cherokee towns, many of the older chiefs are cowed into peace. A treaty council to end hostility is proposed for July 1777 at Long island on the Holston River, where they will sign away tracts of Cherokee land as the price of peace. In fury, Dragging Canoe secedes from the nation and removes to Chickamauga, along the Tennessee River. In contempt, he refers to the treaty Cherokee as "Virginians." His name for his own followers is Ani Yunwiya, the Real People—the Cherokee.

Thousands defect to join Dragging Canoe's freedom fighters, including Upper Creek, and Lenape from the north. Entire Cherokee towns follow: Settico, Great Island, Tellico, Toquo, and Chilhowee; and the names of Willenawah, the Bloody Fellow, Hanging Maw, Judd's Friend, Kitegiska, and John Watts become renowned along the Cherokee frontier.

I have certain accounts that some designing men on the Indian lands have assembled . . . and call themselves a convention of the people . . . to raise men by subscription to defend themselves . . . on the Indian lands. . . . A certain Alexander Outlaw . . . collected a party of men and went into an Indian town called Citico, where he found a few helpless women and children, which he inhumanly murdered, exposing their private parts in the most shameful manner, leaving a young child, with both its arms broke, alive, at the breast of its dead mother. . . . So great the thirst for Indian lands prevails, that every method will be taken by a party of people to prevent a treaty with the Indians.

—Joseph Martin, *United States Indian agent*

Our Nation was alone and surrounded. . . . After we had lost some of our best warriors, we were forced to leave our towns and corn to be burned by them, and now we live in the grass as you see us. But we are not yet conquered. . . .

—Tsiyu Gansini (Dragging Canoe), *Cherokee*

We are neither birds nor fish; we can neither fly in the air, nor live under water; therefore we hope pity will be extended towards us.

—Tickagiska King, *Cherokee*

We had hoped the white men would not be willing to travel beyond the mountains; now that hope is gone. They have passed the mountains, and have settled upon Cherokee land. . . . Finally, the whole country, which the Cherokees and their fathers have so long occupied, will be demanded, and the remnant of the Ani Yunwiya, "The Real People," once so great and formidable, will be compelled to seek refuge in some distant wilderness. There, they will be permitted to stay only a short while, until they again behold the advancing banners of the same greedy host. . . . Should we not therefore run all risks, and incur all consequences, rather than submit to further laceration of our country? Such treaties may be all right for men who are too old to hunt or fight. As for me, I have my young warriors about me. We will have our lands.

—Tsiyu Gansini (Dragging Canoe), *Cherokee*

The encroachments on this side of the line have entirely deprived us of our hunting grounds. . . . When any of my young men are hunting on their own grounds, and meet the white people, they, the white people, order them off and claim our deer.   —Unsuckanail, *Cherokee*

Formerly, when I had peace talks, the first thing the white people expressed, was a desire for our lands.
                                   —Chescoenwhee, *Cherokee*

I am still among my people, living in gores of blood.
                                   —Doublehead, *Cherokee*

. . . [I am] encouraged to lay before you a brief account of the present unhappy and distressed situation of the Cherokee Indians . . . [and of] their hardships and sufferings, from the unrighteous and cruel war lately waged against them. . . .

They thought that they had a well grounded hope, that they might quietly and peaceably have enjoyed all their lands within the boundary lines established by the treaty of Hopewell, in the year 1785; but, to their great mortification and distress, the white people, chiefly from North Carolina, have made daily encroachments upon them; and there are now upwards of three thousand families settled within those boundary lines. After receiving reiterated insults and injuries from some of those settlers, a few of the young warriors killed a family of white people within those boundaries, and soon after, the nation in general experienced the most dreadful calamities that refined cruelty could devise, or the vindictive arm of vengeance inflict. Their flourishing fields of corn and pulse were destroyed and laid waste; some of their wives and children were burnt alive in their town houses, with the most unrelenting barbarity; and to fill up the measure of deception and cruelty, some of their chiefs, who were ever disposed to peace with the white people, were decoyed, unarmed, into their camp, by the hoisting a white flag, and by repeated declarations of friendship and kindness, and there massacred in cold blood. Among these, were the old Tassel and his son. . . .

When [I] came to French Broad river, in January last, [I] found that part of the country in great confusion, and the war carried on with all its horrors, between a party of the North Carolinians and the Cherokees; the former, as it would appear, were determined to extirpate the Indians, and to claim the sole property in their lands. . . . If [I] can be, but in a small degree, instrumental in obtaining for those unfortunate people . . . the inestimable blessings of peace, liberty, and safety, [I] will feel [myself] one of the happiest of mankind.
—Bennet Ballew, *agent for the Cherokee nation*

War among the Creek (1783–1786)

A series of dubious treaties made between 1783 and 1786 at Augusta, Galphinton, and Shoulderbone drive the Creek nation from their lands in Georgia. The Creek claim all three invalid; at Oconee, chiefs of two towns only—Cusseta and Tallassee—were forced to sign without the knowledge of the entire nation. With ninety-eight towns not even consulted, Georgia nevertheless allows settlers into the contested territory. By prior treaty, the Creek nation retains the sovereign right to remove the squatters forcibly. Georgia responds by declaring war. Creek hostages are seized to ensure that a boundary line, beneficial to Georgia, is run.

. . . a general convention was held at the Teickibatiks town, when those two chiefs were severally censured for their conduct, and the chiefs of ninety-eight towns agreed upon a talk to be sent to Savannah, disapproving, in the strongest manner, of the demand made upon their nation, and denied the right of any two of their country, to making any cession of land . . . we warned the Georgians of the dangerous consequences that would certainly attend the settling of the lands in question. Our just remonstrances were treated with contempt, and those lands were soon filled with settlers. . . . we made another effort to awaken in them a sense of justice and equity; but, we found from experience, that entreaty could not prevail, and parties of warriors were sent out to drive off all intruders, but to shed no blood, only where self preservation made it necessary.

—Alexander McGillivray, *Creek*

If the Creeks . . . should obstinately refuse to confirm the [cessions] to Georgia, then you are to inform them that the arms of the Union will be called forth for the protection of Georgia. . . . Should . . . the result of your investigation be unfavorable to the claims of Georgia, it would be highly embarrassing to that State to relinquish the said lands to the Creeks. . . . The disputed lands being entirely despoiled of their game by the settlements, are therefore no longer valuable to the Creeks as hunting grounds.

—Instructions to commissioners for treating with the Creek nation

We are told that those lands are of no service to us, but still . . . if we can hold our lands, there will always be a turkey or a deer, or, in the streams of water, a fish to be found, for our young generation that will come after us. We are afraid that, if we part with any more of our lands, that at last the white people will not suffer us to keep as much as will be sufficient to bury our dead.   —Creek delegation

...we were invited, by commissioners of the State of Georgia, to meet them, in conference, at the Oconee, professing a sincere desire for an amicable adjustment of our disputes.... [At the Oconee we] were surprised to find an armed body of men ... professing hostile intentions, than peaceable commissioners. Apprehensions for personal safety, induced those chiefs to subscribe to every demand that was asked by the army and its commissioners; lands were again demanded, and the lives of some of our chiefs were required, as well as some innocent traders, as a sacrifice to appease their anger. Assassins have been employed to effect some part of their atrocious purposes. If I fall by the hand of such, I shall fall a victim in the noblest of causes—that of falling in maintaining the just rights of my country.
                     —Alexander McGillivray, *Creek*

As for talking any more about the land, it is needless to talk any more.   —Alexander Cornell, *Creek*

...we recommended to you the sale of some of your lands, which are of little use to your nation, and are much wanted by your white brethren.... In making this proposition to you, your father, the President, is actuated by a sincere desire ... to secure to his red children a permanent income, more valuable to them than hunting and trapping ... to promote their domestic manufactures, and extend their agricultural pursuits.... In short, to make them useful to themselves and to mankind....   —United States commissioners

. . . I must inform you that our [Creek] friend Chewocleymicho, and his companions, the hostages, are in good health and spirits. I have sent down to request they may be brought up, that it may not appear hard to keep our friends too long from their relations. . . . All we have to request is, that you go and receive your presents, and attend at running the [boundary] line, according to your agreement at the treaty.

—Georgia commissioners

[The hostages] are very happy here, they have as much as they can eat and drink, and live as well as I do. . . . I am sorry to inform you, that . . . one of the men named Sullapaye . . . cut his own throat with his knife, and died in a few minutes. His brother . . . and all the rest, were sleeping along side of him on the same floor, and knew nothing of it, until it was done. . . . He was well used, had every thing he wanted, and no white person was in the house, or near him, when he did it. I am sorry he should be such a fool. . . .

—James Seagrove, *United States Indian agent*

. . . these last strides tell us they never mean to let their foot rest; our lands are our life and breath; if we part with them, we part with our blood. We must fight for them.

—Hallowing King, *Coweta Creek*

The thing that was asked us to part with, was like asking us to cut ourselves in two. . . .

—Efau Harjo (Mad Dog), *Tukabahchee Creek*

. . . and, if, after every peaceable mode of obtaining a redress of grievances having proved fruitless, the having recourse to arms to obtain it, be marks of the savage, and not of the soldier, what savages must the Americans be. . . . If war names had been necessary to distinguish . . . [your heroes], the man-killer, the great destroyer, &c. would have been the proper appellations.   —Alexander McGillivray, *Creek*

You well know, the cause of the discontent with us has ever been, the limits of our country; consider that we have retreated from the plains to the woods, from thence to the mountains; but no limits, established by nature or by compact, have stayed the ambitious, or satisfied your people. It is our determination to adhere to a line fairly agreed on, but such agreement must be by the legislative body of the nation, and not a clandestine bargain, with a few chiefs, that have no manner of right to dispose of any lands; such transactions only regenerate in fraud—always lead to animosities and bloodshed. You well know that no sovereignty was ceded to you at the peace of 1763. . . .

[W]e are now, as we always have been, an independent and free people; knowing this, and our abilities to maintain our independence, we view with astonishment the steps taken by the United States to rob us of our rights. We actually see our whole country laid out into districts, without considering us to have any kind of claim or right, which nature has bestowed on us, and of which oppression or prejudice alone can attempt to rob us.

. . . I have given strict orders to our warriors, to commit no hostilities on the other side of the Oconee; and shall expect that you will give out the same to your people; but, should your intentions be dishonest, know that we have still warriors sufficient to stain your land with blood, and it is our determination to sell our lives with our country.   —Creek Council

The Killing of Lower Creek (1787)

Georgia troops eagerly cross the Oconee River into disputed territory. Along a footpath, a Creek hunting party is returning to their homes in the Cusseta town. The soldiers know this; in fact, they know the people well. The hunters recognize them and walk forward in friendship; the soldiers raise their guns and fire. Twelve Cusseta hunters lie dead. The Lower Creek towns, including Cusseta, are friendly to the English. It is the remote Upper Towns, plagued by encroachment, who have forcibly removed settlers from their borders. Georgia avows that it cannot distinguish between the Lower and Upper Creek. The Cusseta have paid with their lives. The soldiers grin; they have deliberately set the Creek one against another.

[You] yourselves must be fully convinced that our people have not been the aggressors in this instance . . . our warriors crossed the river, and unfortunately fell in with your people. It was impossible then to distinguish whether you were our friends or enemies . . . had we not received your talk, a large army would have been sent into your nation. What consequences would have attended this, you are capable of judging. . . . We really regret the loss of your innocent people who have lately been killed. It is your duty as men and warriors to do yourselves justice, by taking satisfaction of the persons who were the cause of it. . . . It is our wish to see you and the Upper Creeks one people; but should they continue to create differences between you and us . . . we will, as all friends and brothers ought to do, be ever ready to give any assistance you may require.   —Georgia Commission

On what principle can you demand satisfaction? Your warriors were killed for the murder of our innocent inhabitants, committed by your nation. . . . Did you not . . . murder two of our people on the Oconee? . . . Have you complied with a single article of the treaties of Augusta, Galphinton, and Shoulderbone? No! . . . Your conduct towards us long since has authorized our putting flames to your towns, and indiscriminately killing your people. . . .

—Georgia State Assembly

We minded nothing but our hunting. . . . You always promised that the innocent should not suffer for the guilty. You certainly knew us; we were always among the houses; we did not know of the Upper Towns doing any mischief, nor did we think that our friends would kill us for what other bad people did. . . . and we don't think but you must have known that we were your friends, or we should not have been among you a-hunting; and hope you will send us an answer, and tell us the reason that you have killed your friends for what other people did. . . . We look upon all white people as one, and suppose you look upon all Indians as one, is the reason you have killed your friends. . . .

—Hallowing King, *Coweta,* and The Fat King, *Cusseta*

. . . in the late affairs 'tis you that have been rash: for when the injury was done to you, you did not wait but for a little while and look around you to find out from whence the blow came, but fell directly upon our people . . . who were daily among your houses, and whose persons you well knew, and some that were taken, declared themselves and towns to you, which you disregarded. . . . You must give us immediate satisfaction, life for life, an equal number for twelve of our people destroyed by you. . . . then the tears of the relations of the dead will be dried up, and our hearts not continue hot against you: for it is in vain that you call us friends and brothers, and don't consider and treat us as such. . . .

—The Fat King, *Cusseta*

Redstick Movement   (1812)

The Creek turn against each other. The Upper Towns rally behind Creek freedom fighters known as Redsticks, influenced equally by Dragging Canoe's Chickamauga resistance, the Shawnee prophet Tenskwatawa, and prophets within their own nation who demand a return to traditional ways before the world comes to an end.

Soldier Davy Crockett battles a force of Redsticks at the Upper Town of Tallushatchee. A putrid smoke curls among the trees as forty-six bodies burn within a Redstick house. Later, the troops make a meal on potatoes found in the cellar, baked by the smoldering ruins and basted by drippings of human fat. The barbarity that has marked the entire campaign receives its final epitaph at the Battle of Horseshoe Bend, where the Redsticks are defeated by Andrew Jackson's forces. From the skin of the slain, Jackson's men make leather belts.

I hear you are preparing yourselves for war; I hear you have taken part with the prophets. . . . You may frighten one another with the power of your prophets to make thunder, earthquakes, and to sink the earth. These things cannot frighten the American soldiers. . . . The thunder of their cannon, their rifles, and their swords, will be more terrible than the works of your prophets . . . and war with the white people will be your ruin.

—Benjamin Hawkins, *United States Indian agent*

Our enemies are not sufficiently humbled—they do not sue for peace. . . . Buried in ignorance, and seduced by the false pretences of their prophets, they have the weakness to believe they will still be able to make a decided stand against us. They must be undeceived, and made to atone their obstinacy and their crimes, by still further suffering.

—General Andrew Jackson, *United States Army*

[The Creator] says that the Cherokees are adopting the customs of the white people . . . this is not good. . . . The nation must return to the customs of their fathers. . . . You must discard all the fashions of the whites . . . and give up their mills, their houses, and all the arts learned from the white people. If you believe and obey, then will game abound, the white man will disappear, and God will love his people.

—Tsali, *Cherokee*

I am in your power—do with me as you please. I am a soldier. I have done the white people all the harm I could; I have fought them, and fought them bravely: if I had an army, I would yet fight, and contend to the last: but I have none; my people are all gone. I can now do no more than weep over the misfortunes of my nation. . . . Once I could animate my warriors to battle; but I cannot animate the dead. My warriors can no longer hear my voice: their bones are at Talladega, Tallushatchee, Emuckfaw, and Tohopeka. I have not surrendered myself thoughtlessly. Whilst there were chances of success, I never left my post, nor supplicated peace. But my people are gone, and I now ask it for my nation, and for myself.

On the miseries and misfortunes brought upon my country, I look back with the deepest sorrow, and wish to avert still greater calamities. If I had been left to contend with the Georgia army, I would have raised my corn on one bank of the river, and have fought them on the other; but your people have destroyed my nation.

—Red Eagle (William Weatherford), *Creek*

Choctaw and Chickasaw (1792)

You have been told that we want, and will ask you for, land; we shall not; we wish you to enjoy your lands and be as happy as we ourselves are; nor do we want the land of any red people; the United States have land enough.

—William Blount, *North Carolina governor*

Could I once see the day that whites and reds were all friends, it would be like getting new eye-sight.

—Piamingo, *Chickasaw*

I must explain the truth; I was somewhat suspicious you wanted land; I am glad you did not; and if ever the President calls us together again, I request that land may never more be mentioned to us.   —Wolf's Friend, *Chickasaw*

The Americans have hard shoes, and if we permit them to establish that post, they will tread upon our toes.

—Wolf's Friend, *Chickasaw*

The whites, I am told, are very powerful. . . . I am told you have a different way of fighting—[you] can make ditches for your defence, and it may be, you can make it reach my country.　　—Tunnahthoomah (Red Enemy), *Choctaw*

Removal　(1830)

The government lies. At the Treaty of Dancing Rabbit Creek, September 27, 1830, the Choctaw are forced away from their last acre of land in Mississippi. They are the first nation to be removed to the new Indian Territory on the southern plains. By the United States Removal Act of 1830, President Andrew Jackson orders the deportation of eastern nations to lands across the Mississippi. Many will not leave, but willingly risk their lives to defend their homelands. Although destined to remain the darkest era in their history, the removals of the 1830s also produce unsurpassed heroes.

Brother, when you were young, we were strong; we fought by your side; but our arms are now broken. You have grown large; my people have become small. Brother, my voice is weak; you can scarcely hear me; it is not the shout of a warrior, but the wail of an infant. I have lost it in mourning over the misfortunes of my people. These are their graves, and in those aged pines the ghosts of the departed. Their ashes are here, and we have been left to protect them. Our warriors are nearly all gone to the far country west; but here are our dead. Shall we go too, and give their bones to the wolves? . . . Every warrior that you see here was opposed to the Treaty. If the dead could have been counted, it could never have been made. . . . Their tears came in the rain drops, and their voices in the wailing winds, but the pale faces knew it not, and our land was taken away.　　—Colonel Webb, *Choctaw*

We were hedged in by two evils, and we chose that which we thought least. . . . Although the legislature of the state were qualified to make laws for their own citizens, that did not qualify them to become law makers to a people who were so dissimilar in manners and customs as the Choctaws are to the Mississippians. . . . We as Choctaws rather chose to suffer and be free, than live under the degrading influence of laws, where our voice could not be heard in their formation. . . . I could cheerfully hope that those of another age and generation may not feel the effects of those oppressive measures that have been so illiberally dealt out to us; and that peace and happiness may be their reward. . . . Although your ancestors won freedom on the fields of danger and glory, our ancestors owned it as their birthright, and we have had to purchase it from you as the vilest slaves buy their freedom.

Yet it is said that our present movements are our own voluntary acts—such is not the case. We found ourselves like a benighted stranger . . . surrounded on every side . . . to remain would be utter annihilation. Who would hesitate, or would say that his plunging into the water was his own voluntary act? Painful in the extreme is the mandate of our expulsion. . . . The man who said that he would plant a stake and draw a line around us, that never should be passed, was the first to say he could not guard the lines, and drew up the stake and wiped out all traces of the line. . . . I ask you in the name of justice, for repose for myself and my injured people. Let us alone—we will not harm you, we want rest. We hope, in the name of justice, that another outrage may never be committed against us, and that we may for the future be . . . not driven about as beasts, which are benefitted by a change of pasture.

. . . my attachment to my native land is strong—that cord

is now broken; and we must go forth as wanderers in a strange land! I must go—let me entreat you to regard us with feelings of kindness, and when the hand of oppression is stretched against us, let me hope that every part of the United States, filling the mountains and valleys, will echo and say stop, you have no power, we are the sovereign people. . . . Here is the land of our progenitors, and here are their bones; they left them as a sacred deposit. . . . it is dear to us, yet we cannot stay. —George W. Harkins, *Choctaw*

Though you have a fine situation, I am sorry that you cannot participate in the glories of this gloryous Creek War—Delightful task to collect the savage raskals and pack them off to the Arkansas!—After passing four years of winter at Portsmouth, you will readily conceive what a pleasant time we have had in our marchings and drivings beneath the scorching sun of this region of land speculators and defrauders. —William Wall, *United States Army*

. . . our . . . reason for sending this petition is the one which troubles our minds the most, viz. We can not think of our aged people and children taking so long a journey in the heat of summer, without weeping—we feel certain that should we remove in this season of the year, many of those we love, as the white man loves his parents, and children, would fall to the hands of death, and their bones be left far from the bones of their brethren. Sir, will you not pity us! O pity us, relieve us from our troubles and let us go free in the cool season of the year to the west; and the Great Spirit will reward you for your kindness, to those whom all white men abuse. —Chinnebey, *Creek*

We have gloomy tidings from the poor Creeks in Arkansas 6,000 dead most of starvation. From the bad management of the Commissaries, &c.

—Evan Jones, *United States Army*

Last evening I saw the sun set for the last time, and its light shine upon the tree tops, and the land, and the water, that I am never to look upon again. —Menewa, *Creek*

When he first came over the wide waters, he was but a little man, and wore a red coat. . . . The Muscogees gave the white man land, and kindled him a fire, that he might warm himself. . . . But when the white man had warmed himself before the Indian's fire, and filled himself with their hominy, he became very large. With a step he bestrode the mountains, and his feet covered the plains and the vall[eys]. His hands grasped the eastern and the western sea. . . . Then he became our Great Father. He loved his red children, and he said, "Get a little further, least I tread on thee." With one foot he pushed the red man over the Oconee, and with the other he trampled down the graves of his fathers, and the forests [where] he had so long hunted the deer.—But our Great Father still loved his red children, and he soon made them another talk. He said, "Get a little further; you are too near me." But there were some bad men among the Muscogees then, as there are now. They lingered around the graves of their ancestors, till they were crushed beneath the heavy tread of our Great Father. . . . Yet he continued to love his red children; and when he found them too slow in moving, he sent his great guns before him to sweep his path.

Brothers! I have listened to a great many talks from our great father. But they always began and ended in this—"Get a little further; you are too near me." —Speckled Snake, *Creek*

When Creek leader Menewa was forced with his nation into exile, he gave this portrait of himself to a white friend, with the sad comment, "Great as my regard for you is, I never wish to see you in that new country to which I am going, for my desire is that I may never again see the face of a white man."

. . . in the spirit of reconciliation and loyalty to the United States, we agreed to surrender all the lands east of the Chattahoochy River. . . . Farther concessions cannot be made and after the reasons first assigned, more you cannot well demand. . . . It is ordained by the Great Creator, that we are so reduced as to be dependent on your power and mercy: and if, in the hugeness of Strength, you determine to decide by power and not by right, we shall return to our friends and live there, until you take possession of our country.—Then shall we beg bread from the whites and live the life of vagabonds on the soil of our progenitors. We shall not touch a cent of money for our Lands thus forced from our hands. . . . And as fast as we are knocked in the head—the throats of our wives and children are cut by the first tide of population that know not law, we will then afford the United States a Spectacle of Emigration, which we hope may be to a Country prepared by the Great Spirit for honest and unfortunate Indians.

—Creek delegation

Murder is murder and somebody must answer, somebody must explain the streams of blood that flowed in the Indian country. . . . Somebody must explain the four thousand silent graves that mark the trail of the Cherokees to their exile.

Let the Historian of a future day tell the sad story with its sighs, its tears and dying groans. Let the Judge of all the earth weigh our actions and reward us according to our work.

—John Burnett, *United States Army*

I fought through the civil war and have seen men shot to pieces and slaughtered by thousands, but the Cherokee removal was the cruelest work I ever knew.
—John Burnett, *United States Army*

They have neither the intelligence, the industry, the moral habits, nor the desire of improvement. . . . Established in the midst of another and superior race . . . they must necessarily yield . . . and ere long disappear.
—General Andrew Jackson, *United States Army*

No State can achieve proper culture, civilization, and progress . . . as long as Indians are permitted to remain.
—Martin Van Buren, *United States*

. . . news come . . . that Cherokees will have to leave and go to new land . . . soon big prison pens is built and all Cherokees what won't get up and leave is put in pens. . . . Seven thousand soldier men with cannons and muskets guard the Cherokees. . . . Long time we travel on way to new land. People feel bad. . . . Women cry and make sad wails. Children cry and many men cry, and all look sad like when friends die, but they say nothing and just put heads down and keep on go toward west. Many days pass and people die very much. . . . People sometimes say I look like I never smile . . . but no man has laugh left after he's marched over long trail . . . most of time I am keep thinking of Old Nation and wonder how big mountain now looks in springtime, and how the boys and young men used to swim in big river . . . and then there come before picture of march . . . and then my heart feel heavy and sad. Maybeso someday we will understand why Cherokees had to suffer. . . .   —(Name not given), *Cherokee*

But I am still in the midst of efforts to prevail on the United States Government to turn aside, as far as may now be possible, the ruin they are bringing upon my native Country; yes, Gentlemen, the ruin—and for what? Have we done any wrong? We are not charged with any. We have a Country which others covet. This is the only offense we have ever yet been charged with.   —John Ross, *Cherokee*

... We have been made to drink of the bitter cup of humiliation; treated like dogs; our lives, our liberties, the sport of the Whiteman; our country and the graves of our Fathers torn from us, in cruel succession until ... we find ourselves fugitives, vagrants, and strangers in our own country. ...
    —John Ross, *Cherokee*

We are deprived of membership in the human family! We have neither land nor home, nor resting place that can be called our home ... our hearts are sickened, our utterance is paralized when we reflect on the condition in which we are placed, by the audacious practices of unprincipled men ... we are not ignorant of our condition; we are not insensible to our sufferings. We feel them! We groan under their pressure! And anticipation crowds our breasts with sorrows yet to come.   —Cherokee Council

... notwithstanding the cries of our people, and protestation of our innocence and peace, the lowest classes of the white people are flogging the Cherokees with cowhides, hickories, and clubs. We are not safe in our houses—our people are

assailed by day and night by the rabble. . . . This barbarous treatment is not confined to men, but the women are stripped also and whipped without law or mercy. . . .

—John Ridge, *Cherokee*

Of late years, however, much solicitude was occasioned among our people by the claims of Georgia. This solicitude arose from an apprehension that by extreme importunity, threats, and other undue influence, a treaty would be made, which should cede the territory, and thus compel the inhabitants to remove. But it never occurred to us for a moment, that without any new treaty, without any assent of our rulers and people, without even a pretended compact, and against our vehement and unanimous protestations, we should be delivered over to the discretion of those, who had declared by a legislative act, that they wanted the Cherokee lands and would have them.   —Cherokee Council

Florida

I will willingly receive the heads of these Castilians . . . but I want to hear nothing more of their names and words.
                    —*Hirrihigua*, Tocobaga

Spanish "discovery" of Florida was not an act of genius. Lucayan slaves from the Bahamas were quite familiar with the Florida coast, a land they called "Cautió." Armed with this information, and noting that Lucayan slaves were dying at an alarming rate, the Spaniards were excited by the possibility of a populated region located just to the north. Unfortunately, the date of first Spanish contact with Florida is unrecorded; slave expeditions reached there before licensed conquistadors were given official sanction by the king. In 1512 Puerto Rican governor Juan Ponce de León was granted the right of conquest of Florida. He would search for three things: the Fountain of Youth, gold, and slaves.

In the fourteenth century, stories began to circulate in Europe of a rejuvenating fountain in Asia, whose magical waters could make old men young. Although the Spaniards eventually discovered that Hispaniola was not part of the kingdom of the Grand Khan, the legend persisted, and when Caribbean Taíno spoke of curative waters lying toward Florida, the Spaniards accepted it as proof of the mythical Fountain of Youth. With syphilis raging in the Spanish settlements, interest in the curative waters was profound.

But the Spaniards were not the only interested party. Cuban Taíno seized upon the story in the desperate hope of reclaiming their shattered world. The desire to reach the waters that would restore a past free of sickness, slavery, and Spaniards grew so great that a body of Taíno traveled by canoe to the Florida Gulf coast.

When Ponce arrived on the same west Florida shore, in the country of the Calusa, he was greeted by an Indian man in a canoe who spoke Spanish and presumably was Taíno. For their part, the Calusa wasted no time in assailing the ship in battle formation and cutting the cables in an effort to send the Spaniards on their way.

Returning to Puerto Rico, Ponce was at no loss for employment. The king extended the original stipulation of one year to settle the lands of Florida and blessed him with a royal commission to subdue remaining indigenous resistance in the Caribbean. Ponce's fighting dog Becerrillo achieved fame in the Indies as a slayer of Taíno and was paid a soldier's wages in gold. Occupied with these less-than-glorious pursuits, Ponce did not return to Florida until 1521, when he promptly was killed by the Calusa. Although this fact is told routinely in every recounting of Florida history, Spanish chronicles are far less specific detailing the number of Calusa who suffered at Spanish hands or were forcibly torn from their land to die as slaves in the West Indies.

In Cuba, a conversation with a Calusa slave led to the misunderstanding that there was gold in Florida. In 1539 Hernando de Soto was granted right of conquest, and he put down on the west Florida coast with a force of 600 soldiers, 100 servants, 200 horses, and packs of attack dogs.

De Soto's army snaked north through the Timucua country in an invasion that arched westward through scores of nations even to the faraway Bidai in Texas. Native villages were entered in battle formation and ravaged. Citizens were bound by neck collars and strung together in chains of thirty to serve as burden bearers, carrying away sacks of plundered food and precious grave goods. When one fell from exhaustion, de Soto severed his head rather than pause to remove him from the chain. As he slashed his way through village after village, attack dogs tore into people who fled, while lancers gored those who dared to fight back. Local leaders were seized and held hostage, and gory battles waged to free them. Nation after nation attempted to stop him. At Mobile, the fighting was so violent that every man in de Soto's company was injured, and the army lay wounded and bleeding on the ground, only slowly to regenerate and move forward again.

De Soto's route fell across the powerful chiefdoms of the South, polities that boasted of rich agricultural fields, temple mounds, plazas, and charismatic rulers carried in state upon litters accompanied by thronging crowds. After de Soto's march, much of this landscape would be unrecognizable. Villages collapsed to disease and starvation. Seed grain stores lay empty. Local wars raged as regional tribute systems faltered, and many of the great chiefdoms of the Southeast fell in the turmoil.

In 1565 Pedro Menéndez de Avilés became the first governor of Florida and established the capital of Saint Augustine on the lands of the Timucua. The mission field quickly followed, and ultimately established a chain of forty missions, crosscutting the nations of the Apalachee, Timucua, and Guale. Bitter revolts were attempted by all three nations. Epidemics and the slaving activities of the Goose Creek Men preyed upon the sedentary missions. By the eighteenth century, only a few hundred survivors were reported of the many hundreds of thousands that once existed. In 1763 Spanish Florida was ceded to Britain, and the last of the missions was withdrawn.

De Soto (1540)

Mastiffs run beneath the dripping Spanish beard, each swing of their heads spewing flecks of foam onto the broad-leafed palmetto. They are paid the wages of soldiers. And better soldiers there never were; faster and faster they run, on an Indian scent. Sharp fangs pierce a belly—out flow the intestines; and on they run. They are trained for this, and they are good.

The cavaliers and lancers sit proudly, bedecked in chain mail, their weapons gleaming; they thrill to the same chase, but the kill cannot be as immediate as what the dogs experience. And thinking men cannot feel the same glory as a mindless dog, when the victims are unarmed and fleeing Indian men, women, and children.

Burden bearers groan as iron manacles eat into their flesh. They stagger under the heavy bundles of food they are forced to carry away from their own villages. What must be their anguish to know that without this corn, loved ones will starve? But still they must do it. Their lives are not their own.

In the villages, death makes its home. Smallpox boils burst and ooze across dying bodies. Women are raped. There is no food to plant; the seed corn is stolen. The leaders are bound in chains and, like the corn, are carried away. Were they not invincible? The temple mounds crumble and fall; grass overgrows them. And what of the monster de Soto? This is not a man, but a demon; for no man except the criminally insane can act as he does. His presence indelibly marks the land; he leaves an evil imprint as palpable as a strong odor. His deeds inflict permanent scars. Something wrong will always hover over the South; it is de Soto's legacy. Yet something else hangs over the land; it is the imprint of the valiant leaders who dare to defy him. They are his nemesis; the conscience he never has. They, too, leave a shadow that never can be erased. The South is stuck with it, it will not go away. Who now can walk over the red clay soils of Georgia and not think of the blood spilled in the defense of freedom? And who can look at the furrowed hills and not think of the evil creature who once spread horror and pestilence across them?

I have long since learned who you Castilians are through others of you who came years ago to my land; and I already know very well what your customs and behavior are like. To me you are professional vagabonds who wander from place to place, gaining your livelihood by robbing, sacking, and murdering people who have given you no offense. I want no manner of friendship or peace with people such as you, but instead prefer mortal and perpetual enmity. . . . I therefore notify and advise you to protect yourselves and act cautiously with me and my people. . . . I am king in my land, and it is unnecessary for me to become the subject of a person who has no more vassals than I. I regard those men as vile and contemptible who subject themselves to the yoke of someone else when they can live as free men. Accordingly, I and all of my people have vowed to die a hundred deaths to maintain the freedom of our land. This is our answer, both for the present and forevermore. —Acuera, *Timucua*

The bondage in which you have placed yourselves and the vile and cowardly spirit that you have assumed in the brief time since giving yourselves up to serve as slaves of Spaniards make you talk like women, praising as you do people whom you ought to vituperate and abhor. Do you not see that since these Christians are of the same government and race as those who perpetrated so many cruelties among us in the past, they can be no better? You take no note of their treason and perfidies. If you were men of good judgment you would perceive that their very lives and deeds reveal them to be sons of the devil . . . they go from land to land killing, robbing, and sacking whatever they find. . . . They are not content to colonize and establish a site on some of the land that they see and tread upon because they take great pleasure in being vagabonds and maintaining themselves by the labor and sweat of others. If, as you say, they were men of virtue, they would not

Sixteenth-century engraving of Timucua leader Utina, murdered
by Hernando de Soto's men while imprisoned inside his own
statehouse—but not before dealing de Soto a crippling blow.

have left their own country, for there they could have employed their strength in sowing the land and raising cattle to sustain their lives without damage to others and without increasing their own infamy. But they have made highwaymen, adulterers, and murderers of themselves without shame of men or fear of any god. Warn them, therefore, not to enter my land, for I promise that no matter how valiant they may be, if they put foot upon it, they shall never leave it, since I shall destroy them all.   —Vitachuco, *Timucua*

The Guale Revolt   (1597)

The Franciscan mission field stretches north along the Georgia coast and intertwines among the Sea Islands in the country of the Guale. The people have not asked for priests, nor do they want them. The Franciscans complain that the Guale cannot be converted as long as they leave their towns during part of the year to gather acorns. Therefore, they struggle to detain them; then attempt to eradicate their culture. On paper it sounds simple, innocent almost. But in reality, the most terrible mind-altering games play out. The Guale are told again and again that they are no good; that their practices are evil; that they are intractable and dirty and disruptive and heathens lost in sin. And, slowly, the Guale come to believe it. The United States will later practice this technique in the boarding schools to deprive other Indian nations of their language and traditions.

The friar is dead. He would not have been killed had he let us live as we did before we became Christians. Let us return to our ancient customs and prepare to defend ourselves against the retribution the governor of Florida will attempt against us. If he has his way, on account of this friar, it will be as severe as if we had done away with all of them. . . . Well, then, if the retribution inflicted for one will not be less than for all of them, let us take back the liberty these friars steal from us with their promises of treasures they have never seen—in expectation of which they assume that those of us who call ourselves Christian will put up with this mischief and grief now.

They take away our women . . . they prevent our dancing, banquets, feasts, celebrations, games, and warfare, so that by disuse we shall lose our ancient courage and skill inherited from our ancestors. They persecute our old folks, calling them witches. Even our work annoys them and they want us to cease on certain days. When we are disposed to do all they ask, still they are not satisfied. It is all a matter of scolding us, abusing us, oppressing us, preaching to us, calling us bad Christians, and taking away from us all the joy that our fore-fathers got for themselves—all in the hope that we will attain heaven. But these are delusions, to subjugate us by having us disposed to their ends. What can we hope for, unless to be slaves? If we kill them all now, we shake off the heavy yoke from that moment.   —Juanillo, *Guale*

If you are not going to give me clothing and food, it is no good to become a Christian, and no one will want to become one.
                              —The young chief, *Calusa*

. . . just as the Christians cannot cease to be Christians and live without the rosary, neither can we abandon our law and become Christians.   —The young chief, *Calusa*

. . . when I told them that my God was more powerful than their Holy One, they told me not to jest and that I should take care how I proceeded.   —Fray Feliciano López, *Spain*

☷

... the young [chief] sent them a message ... telling them
that there was no point to their tiring themselves preaching to
them; that they did not wish to become Christians. ... And
the said [chief] told the priests on repeated occasions that
they would end up going.   —Juan Estéva, *Spain*

Seminole Wars   (1817–1818, 1835–1842)

Andrew Jackson knows that he did not defeat the Redsticks; he
only won a battle. To break the spirit of a man who fights for freedom is not easy when that man has the strength of tradition behind him. As long as there is one Redstick remaining, Jackson
knows he has been defeated; he is obsessed with Redstick defiance. After the Battle of Horseshoe Bend, many Redsticks flee to
the refuge of Florida. There they join the "Cimarron" Indian nations—the "wild ones" whom the Spanish never missionized, and
who themselves removed to Florida to escape the frontier. The
English call them Seminole. Under the auspices of the Removal
Act, Jackson will try to force them to Indian Territory, or he will
destroy them.

The American public protests that the Seminole Wars in
Florida are unnecessary. Few Americans wish to live there;
there is no need to expend time and money to eradicate refugee
Indian nations living peacefully in lands too wild for Americans
to covet. No, the war is Andrew Jackson's personal vendetta. Despite public protest, it is fought anyway, and without integrity.
Quite possibly, no war is ever waged on North American soil
in which so many truces are broken, so many white flags treacherously violated, than the American campaign against the
Seminole.

But if the Redstick war has not convinced Jackson that extin-
guishing a people's spirit is no easy task, then the Seminole Wars

certainly will. Opposing him is Osceola, from the Redstick town of Tallassee. Strong, defiant, confident in the justness of his fight, Osceola's victories mount. Unlike Jackson, his men never mutilate the dead; never touch an American soldier who has fallen. He might have taught Jackson much about honor.

His defiance threatens Jackson's endeavors; Osceola will be eliminated. Captured under a flag of truce, he is confined as a prisoner of war inside the cold walls of Fort Marion, the former Spanish fortress of San Marcos. There, he will die. But Jackson never wins; Osceola is not broken. The spirit of freedom never dies.

I have done nothing to be ashamed of; it is for those to feel shame who entrapped me.   —Osceola, *Seminole*

I have never made a treaty and never will; I and my people will fight it out forever.   —Arpeika, *Miccosukee*

I have no intention to remove.
                              —Micanopee, *Miccosukee*

You have guns and so have we; you have powder and lead and so have we; you have men and so have we; your men will fight, and so will ours until the last drop of the Seminoles' blood has moistened the dust of his hunting-grounds.
                              —Osceola, *Seminole*

We learn from the *Madisonian,* that an officer of the army, just arrived in Washington from St. Augustine, reports that a vessel with thirty-three blood-hounds, from Cuba, had entered one of the ports. . . . They are to be employed in hunt-

Osceola, the Seminole leader who defied President Andrew Jackson by defending his land in Florida, was taken captive while under a flag of truce.

ing down the miserable remnant of the Seminoles in Florida. We have never read anything more strikingly illustrative of the inhumanity and injustice of this war than these remarks of Mr. Poinsett. It is then, for a country benign to the Indians, but deadly to the whites, that we are contending! Of what advantage can it be when we obtain it? . . .

A great, powerful, and magnanimous nation of fifteen millions of freemen, hunting down with blood-hounds a wretched squad of Indians, dwelling in a country which no white man can inhabit after it is conquered! A war which will complete the solitude of a desert, by destroying the remnant of life that remains in it! . . . With what degree of condemnation will the good and wise of every country and age regard the attempt of our Government to extirpate, by means so terrible . . . the poor remains of a once great and powerful tribe, who, in the unintentionally pathetic language of the Secretary of War, are "hemmed in by the sea, and must defend themselves to the uttermost."

—Editorial, New York *New World*

We have been unable to persuade ourselves that the Government had become so utterly insane and degraded as to think of prosecuting its wanton and inglorious war in Florida with BLOOD-HOUNDS! But we are startled by a report that a "detachment" of these brute "allies" have actually arrived! Still we doubt. For the honour of the Republic—for the honour of civilization—for the honour of human nature, we hope that our cup of national infamy may not be filled to overflowing. Enough of dishonour already attaches to this sanguinary war. . . . We commenced the war without cause, other than the desire to rob the Indians of their lands . . . with no purpose, it would seem, but to allow an army of speculators to "pick and steal," and to sink the nation deeper in its ignominy.   —Editorial, Albany *Argus*

The Miccosukee   (1835–1842)

Far to the south, in the Everglades, the Miccosukee defy Jackson's forces. They have entered a watery mire where Americans have never been. They fight hard. Their bravery is frightening. Soldiers dread entering their country; rumors spread that those who do so never return.

In October 1837, Osceola, Coacoochee, Micanopy, Cloud, Alligator, and other leading men of the Seminole and Miccosukee nations advance under a flag of truce to negotiate a peace to secure the release of Miccosukee prisoners. At a prearranged signal, the soldiers seize the unarmed delegation, along with 116 men and 82 women and children. Bound in chains and forced to march before the army to Saint Augustine, they are thrown inside the stone cells of Fortress San Marcos.

In one corner of the cell wall, near the top, is a tiny breathing space nine inches wide by eighteen inches long. The guards stare in amazement; Coacoochee's cell is empty. He has squeezed through the tiny hole; the skin on his back and chest now hangs in shreds. The other leaders quickly are transferred to a prison on an island at Fort Moultrie, South Carolina. There, Osceola dies. Days later, the body is exhumed and decapitated. The head is placed on display at Stuyvesant Institute, New York City.

I shall never forget that day, nor the sad, disappointed face of Chief Osceola and the other Indians. I thought it too unjust for anything.

—Captain John S. Masters, *United States Army*

. . . he sometimes talked . . . with great spirit and even with fiery indignation, about the base manner in which he had been betrayed; nor did he cease to regret his inability to continue to fight in defense of his country.

—Charles Coe, *United States*

Never was a more disgraceful piece of villainy perpetrated in a civilized land. —Dr. Andrew Welch, *England*

When I was taken prisoner, my band was inclined to leave the country, but upon my return, they said, let us all die in Florida. This caused great suffering among our women and children. I was in hopes I should be killed in battle, but a bullet would never touch me. I had rather be killed by a white man in Florida, than die in Arkansas.

—Coacoochee (Wildcat), *Miccosukee*

I was once a boy, then I saw the white man afar off . . . he came upon me; horses, cattle, and fields, he took from me. He said he was my friend; he abused our women and children, and told us to go from the land. Still he gave me his hand in friendship; we took it; whilst taking it, he had a snake in the other; his tongue was forked; he lied, and stung us. I asked but for a small piece of these lands, enough to plant and to live upon, far south, a spot where I could place the ashes of my kindred, a spot only sufficient upon which I could lay my wife and child. This was not granted me. I was put in prison; I escaped. I have been again taken; you have brought me back; I am here; I feel the irons in my heart.

—Coacoochee (Wildcat), *Miccosukee*

If Coacooche is to die, he can die like a man. It is not my heart that shakes; no, it never trembles; but I feel for those now in the woods, pursued night and day by the soldiers; for those who fought with us, until we were weak.

—Coacoochee (Wildcat), *Miccosukee*

We have listened to the great father at Washington. The Great Spirit wishes no change in his red children. If you teach our children the knowledge of the white people, they will cease to be Indians. To know how to read and write is very good for white men, but very bad for red men. Long time ago, some of our fathers wrote upon a little piece of paper without the nation knowing anything about it. When the agent called the Indians together he told them the little paper was a treaty which their brethren had made with the great father at Washington, and lo! they found that their brethren by knowing how to write, had sold their lands and the graves of their fathers to the white race. Tell our great father at Washington that we want no schools, neither books, for reading and writing makes very bad Indians. We are satisfied. Let us alone.

—Seminole Council

The Ohio Valley

[The Creator] has not given the right to any one nation to say to another, this land is not yours, it belongs to me.
—*Red Pole*, Shawnee

At the close of the Revolutionary War, Britain ceded a part of her North American holdings to the United States. This included territory in the Great Lakes, much of the Ohio Valley, and former French-held lands along the Mississippi, Illinois, and Wabash rivers. In this transaction, both England and the United States failed to recognize the sovereignty of the many Indian nations who lived within the disputed territory. Excluded from the British-American peace talks, no treaties of relinquishment were made with any of the nations.

Americans eased their way around the problem by harking back to the 1768 Treaty of Fort Stanwix, which guaranteed Hodenosaunee rights to the Ohio Valley north of the Ohio River as a refugee area for protectorate nations. Since individuals among the Hodenosaunee sided with the British, as did the Ohio Valley nations themselves, the Americans reasoned that the territory belonged to them by virtue of British defeat. However, by the same logic, the Treaty of Fort Stanwix also forever guaranteed that the Ohio River would be the international boundary line between Indian nations and white settlements. Even if the United States could argue right of possession to the Ohio Valley, it had no right of occupation.

Finally, in 1784, the United States entered into the second Treaty of Fort Stanwix, which was supposed to have ended the war between the Hodenosaunee and the United States. Although the act upheld Hodenosaunee sovereignty as a nation, the treaty did little more than force the alienation of more land by demanding that the Hodenosaunee officially relinquish their claim to the Ohio Valley—without ever once consulting the nations who actually lived there. Hodenosaunee leaders condemned the manner in which the treaty was conducted and insisted that the voice of the Ohio Valley nations be considered. It was not until the 1794 Treaty of Canandaigua that the Hodenosaunee achieved victory by forcing the United States officially to recognize a termination of the war on terms acceptable to both sides.

From the point of view of the United States, however, the second Treaty of Fort Stanwix still stood, and the Ohio lands were theirs to keep. Just as the British had moved into the area more rapidly than the French before them, the American colonists beat them all for speed of occupation. In 1787 an ordinance created the Northwest Territory and opened wide the Ohio Valley, lands that were already thickly settled by the Lenape, Shawnee, Wyandot, and Miami. Along the confluence of the Auglaize and Maumee rivers, Indian settlements appeared like one continuous village, stretching for miles along both banks, and surrounded by cornfields more extensive than any in the colonies. Fantastic numbers of settlers spilled into the Ohio Valley, running directly into the same Indian nations that had been dispossessed from the East in the years before the war.

At the same time, political movements were afoot within the nations. A Seneca prophet received a Divine message that predicted disaster for the Hodenosaunee unless definite steps were taken to eradicate European influence. Everywhere, there was a great awakening to traditional Indian values. Postwar messages within the nations were clear.

During this time, a young Shawnee man by the name of Tecumseh became acquainted with the Chickamauga leader Dragging Canoe. Tecumseh was very impressed with Dragging Canoe's spirit of resistance and noted that his fight for freedom was attracting many followers.

Soon after this, Tecumseh's brother Lalawethika received a Divine warning that urged the Shawnee to return to their traditions. So powerful was the message that Lalawethika became known as Tenskwatawa, the Prophet. Together, the brothers spread their message of political and cultural resistance. Families flocked to their village at Prophetstown (Indiana), settling in camps that spread three miles along the river. Lenape, Wyandot, Miami, Wabash, Wea, Potawatomi, Sauk, Mesquakie, Winnebago, Creek, Chickamauga, Cherokee, Kickapoo, and Seminole were profoundly influenced by the message. The War of 1812 between the British and Americans was also a war of a determined Indian alliance to drive American settlers from their lands once and for all.

I have killed many an Indian, but I always did it with real regret. The necessities of the times . . . is the justification that I and my fellow pioneers have to offer for our conduct. It seemed to us, that so fine, so magnificent a country as the mighty West, was never designed by a kind Providence for the permanent abode of a vagabond race, but rather for the home of civilization.　　—Simon Kenton, *United States*

To the various tribes of the Piankeshaws and all the nations of Red People, lying on the waters of the Wabash river:

The sovereign council of the thirteen United States have long patiently borne your depredations against their settlements on this side of the great mountains, in the hope that you would see your error, and correct it. . . . The United States have no desire to destroy the red people, although they have the power; but, should you decline this invitation, and pursue your unprovoked hostilities, their strength will again be exerted against you; your warriors will be slaughtered, your towns and villages ransacked and destroyed, your wives and children carried into captivity, and you may be assured that those who escape the fury of our mighty chiefs, shall find no resting place on this side [of] the great lakes . . . should you foolishly persist in your warfare, the sons of war will be let loose against you, and the hatchet will never be buried until your country is desolated, and your people humbled to the dust.

—Brigadier General Charles Scott, *United States Army*

Father, do you ask how we possess this land? It is well known that 4,000 years have passed since the [Creator] first placed us here. . . . From the time that our ancestors thus obtained it, it has been truly deemed ours only. This land where lie the bones of our ancestors, is ours. We have never sold it, nor has it been taken from us by conquest, or by any other means.

When the white man came here a stranger from beyond the great salt lake, and found this portion of the world peopled, he saw that the furs worn by our nations were valuable, and he showed to our ancestors many goods which he had brought with him over the big water, and these were very tempting to our old ancestors. The white man said, "Will you not sell the skins of your animals for the goods I bring?" Our ancestors replied, "We will buy your goods, and you will buy our furs." The whites proposed nothing more; our ancestors acceded to nothing else."   —Peau de Chat, *Ojibway*

. . . you have caught me: like a wild Horse is caught with a Lick of Salt you have Hobled me—that I can no longer range the woods as I please. [Y]ou must now [get] a Bell and put on my neck when I shall always be in your Hearing you must also put Bells on the necks of two of my war chiefs [and] this will [enable] you to know at all times where the warriors of the west are and what they are about—

—Main Poc, *Potawatomi*

Gnadenhutten Massacre   (1782)

In the uncertain atmosphere following the Revolutionary War, there is widespread mistrust. Suspicious of the recent movement of Christian Lenape behind the British lines, two hundred militia led by Colonel David Williamson descend on the Lenape mission settlement of Gnadenhutten. After a pleasant day engaged in theological discussion, Williamson's men suddenly seize the ninety-six innocent mission inhabitants, more than half of whom are women and children. They are locked inside the church buildings, women and children separated from the men. They are told that they will die.

In the morning, the first two men are killed inside the cooper shop, where they are beaten to death with hammers. Within the church, the Lenape raise their voice in hymns, and one by one are bludgeoned with axes and scalped. The corpses lie in heaps upon the floor. A boy crouches undetected in a cellar beneath the building where the women and children are murdered. Blood cascades through the floorboards, flowing in dark streams between the cracks. The boy stares at his hands in horror; they are covered, like his hair, head, and shoulders, with running blood. Non-Christian Lenape capture Colonel William Crawford, a member of Williamson's party, and execute him for the crime.

[There is] a class of people, generally known to us, by the name of "backwoods men," many of whom acting up to a pretended belief, that "an Indian has no more soul than a buffalo"; and that to kill either, is the same thing; have from time to time, by their conduct, brought great trouble and bloodshed on the country.

—Rev. John Heckewelder, *Moravian*

Colonel Crawford! you have placed yourself in a situation which puts it out of my power . . . to do anything for you. . . . By joining yourself to that execrable man, Williamson and his party; the man who . . . murdered such a number of the Moravian Indians, knowing them to be friends; knowing that he ran no risk in murdering a people who would not fight, and whose only business was praying. . . .

We told them that there was no faith to be placed in what the white men said; that their fair promises were only intended to allure us, that they might the more easily kill us, as they have done many Indians before. . . . The blood of the innocent Moravians, more than half of them women and children, cruelly and wantonly murdered calls aloud for *revenge*. The relatives of the slain, who are among us, cry out and stand ready for *revenge*. The nation to which they belonged will have *revenge* . . . the offence is become national, and the nation itself is bound to take REVENGE!

Yes, Colonel!—I am sorry for it; but cannot do anything for you. Had you attended to the Indian principle, that as good and evil cannot dwell together in the same heart, so a good man ought not to go into evil company; you would not be in this lamentable situation.　　　　—Wingenund, *Lenape*

Treaty of Fort McIntosh　(1785)

At Fort McIntosh, thirty miles below Fort Pitt, delegates from the Wyandot, Lenape, Ojibway, and Odawa touch pen to paper and sign away thirty million acres of Ohio land. The treaty is made with only a few leaders and at the total exclusion of some nations altogether.

In the course of our councils, we imagined we hit upon an expedient that would promote a lasting peace between us. . . . the first step towards which should, in our opinion, be, that all treaties carried on with the United States . . . should be with the general voice of the whole confederacy, and carried on in the most open manner . . . we hold it indispensably necessary that any cession of our lands should be made in the most public manner, and by the united voice of the confederacy. . . .

We think it is owing to you that the tranquility . . . has not lasted. . . . Let us have a treaty with you early in the spring; let us pursue reasonable steps; let us meet half way . . . and let us pursue such steps as become upright and honest men. We beg that you will prevent your surveyors and other people from coming upon our side [of] the Ohio river. We have told you before, we wished to pursue just steps, and we are determined they shall appear just and reasonable in the eyes of the world.　　—Leaders of the Hodenosaunee, Huron, Odawa, Miami, Shawnee, Ojibway, Cherokee, Lenape, Potawatomi, and Wabash Confederates

The Clark and Harmar Expeditions　(1786–1790)

The nations refuse to relinquish their lands. On the Ohio River, the Shawnee man a flat-bottomed "Kentucky Boat" used to haul emigrants' baggage into the interior. The boat is outfitted with a hundred guns and, like a pirate ship, blocks the emigrant path up the Ohio.

. . . I was induced to endeavor to break up a nest of vagabond Indians, who had infested the river, and seemed to make it an object to establish themselves near the mouth of the Scioto, in order to interrupt the navigation of the Ohio. . . .
　　—Brigadier General Josiah Harmar, *United States Army*

The Americans respond by sending eighteen hundred soldiers under the command of General George Rogers Clark to lay waste Ohio. Among those brutally killed is the ninety-four-year-old leader of a Shawnee town where a young man named Tecumseh lives. The stinging attacks are followed by a force of fifteen hundred men led by General Harmar. But here the contest ends. Harmar's forces suffer humiliating defeat at the hands of an Indian force under Miami leader Little Turtle.

The President of the United States entertains the opinion, that the war which exists is founded in error and mistake on your parts. That you believe the United States want to deprive you of your lands and drive you out of the country. Be assured this is not so; on the contrary, that we should be greatly gratified with the opportunity of imparting to you all the blessings of civilized life, of teaching you to cultivate the earth, and raise corn; to raise . . . domestic animals; to build comfortable houses, and to educate your children, so as ever to dwell upon the land.

—George Washington, *United States*

. . . we are sensible that no one dare pluck a feather from your body; if they do, the fifteen speared arrows in your claws, will display in every direction. . . . Did you not, in the last war between you and the British divide the country? He gave one part to you, and the other part he reserved for himself . . . make out the boundaries that shall divide the lands between our nations, as we, the Wyandots, Delawares, and Shawanese, wish to know if we are entitled to any part of it.

—Wyandot, Mingo, Lenape, Shawnee,
and Odawa delegation

I admit that there are good white men, but they bear no proportion to the bad; the bad must be the strongest, for they rule. They do what they please. They enslave those who are not of their color, although created by the same Great Spirit who created them. They would make slaves of us if they could; but as they cannot do it, they kill us. There is no faith to be placed in their words. They are not like the Indians. . . .

—Pachgantschihilas, *Lenape*

We desire you to consider, brothers, that our only demand is the peaceable possession of a small part of our once great country. Look back and review the lands from whence we have been driven to this spot. We can retreat no farther, because the country behind hardly affords food for its present inhabitants, and we have therefore resolved to leave our bones in this small space to which we are now confined.

—Lenape delegation

Brothers: now we will relate what took place last fall, in our country. General Washington sent an army into our country, which fell into our hands. . . . The President of the United States must well know why the blood is so deep in our paths. . . . We have been informed, the President of the United States thinks himself the greatest man on this Island. We had this country long in peace, before we saw any person of a white skin. . . .

—Council between Hodenosaunee and
nations of the Ohio

You mentioned the treaties of fort Stanwix, Beaver creek, and other places; those treaties were not complete. There were but a few chiefs who treated with you. You have not bought our lands; they belong to us. You tried to draw off some of us. . . . Many years ago, we all know, that the Ohio was made the boundary. . . . This side is ours; we look upon it as our property . . . you have your houses and people on our land; you say you cannot move them off; and we cannot give up our land. . . . We are sorry we cannot come to an agreement; the line has been fixed long ago.   —Sawaghdawunk, *Wyandot*

Battle of Fallen Timbers   (1794)

The defeat of General Harmar by Little Turtle prompts Washington to firmer action. In the fall of 1791, General Arthur St. Clair marches twenty-three hundred men into Ohio. Tecumseh's spies report their movements, and a force of twelve hundred under the joint command of Little Turtle of the Miami, Blue Jacket of the Shawnee, and Pachgantschihilas of the Lenape deal a crushing blow. Nearly six hundred soldiers are killed; the rest break rank and flee in panic, leaving their arms strewn for miles along the road.

General "Mad" Anthony Wayne is the next weapon unleashed against the Ohio Valley nations. Methodical and deadly, he struck terror in the hearts of the British during the Revolutionary War. With three thousand troops behind him, and in sight of the powerful Miami villages, he very deliberately erects a fort called Defiance. Nearby, the British pledge support of the Indian forces entrenched at Presque Isle in a fortification built of fallen timbers. But when the first violent attack forces a retreat to the British fort, the gates close against them. The Indian troops are gunned down without mercy, but they will take 130 of Wayne's men with them. The Wyandot suffer greatly; all of their national leaders are killed.

We have beaten the enemy twice under separate commanders. We cannot expect the same good fortune always to attend us. The Americans are now led by a chief who never sleeps: the night and the day are alike to him. And during all the time that he has been marching upon our villages, notwithstanding the watchfulness of our young men, we have never been able to surprise him. Think well of it. There is something whispers me, it would be prudent to listen to his offers of peace.   —Mishikinakwa (Little Turtle), *Miami*

You were the first shedders of blood. . . . Listen! My warriors never crossed your line, or your boundary, to kill your people.
—Captain Charley, *Eel River*

Money to us is of no value, and to most of us unknown; and as no consideration whatever can induce us to sell the lands on which we get sustenance for our women and children, we hope we may be allowed to point out a mode by which your settlers may be easily removed, and peace thereby obtained.

We know that these settlers are poor, or they would never have ventured to live in a country which has been in continual trouble ever since they crossed the Ohio. Divide, therefore, this large sum of money which you have offered us among these people; give to each, also, a proportion of what you say you would give to us annually, over and above this very large sum of money, and we are persuaded they would most readily accept of it in lieu of the lands you sold them. If you add, also, the great sums you must expend in raising and paying armies with a view to force us to yield you our country, you will certainly have more than sufficient for the purpose of repaying these settlers. . . .

You have talked to us about concessions. It appears strange that you should expect any from us, who have only been defending our just rights against your invasions. We want peace. Restore to us our country, and we shall be enemies no longer. . . . You make one concession by offering to us your money, and another by having agreed to do us justice . . . in the acknowledgement you have now made that the King of England never did, nor ever had a right to give you our country by the treaty of peace. And [yet] you . . . seem to expect that, because you have at last acknowledged our independence, we should for such a favor surrender to you our country.
—Wabash Council

Treaty of Greenville   (1795)

"A treaty of peace between the United States of America and the tribes of Indians called the Wyandots, Delawares, Shawanese, Ottawas, Chippewas, Pattawatamies, Miamies, Eel Rivers, Weas, Kickapoos, Piankeshaws, and Kaskaskias. To put an end to a destructive war, to settle all controversies, and to restore harmony and friendly intercourse between the said United States and Indian tribes. . . ."

So begins the Treaty of Greenville, July 1795. A fraudulent treaty made earlier at Muskingum and rejected by the Ohio Valley nations forms its basis. Hundreds of thousands of acres in Ohio and Indiana are relinquished, driving the nations farther west. Treaty Article Three runs like a roster, detailing forts and posts that will be built on Indian lands. General Wayne explains that these linked tracts are necessary to form a thoroughfare between American settlements. There is no redress for Indian people. The treaties are a farce.

Fireworks, stored for the upcoming Fourth of July celebration, explode in the middle of the proceedings, sending the soldiers flying to their posts. General Wayne apologizes to the astonished Indian delegation for "what yesterday might have had a strange appearance."

. . . all the people of the Fifteen Fires, with shouts of joy, and peals of artillery, will celebrate the period which gave them freedom. Nineteen times have the United States, already, hailed the return of that auspicious morn . . . to-morrow, all the people within these lines will rejoice; you, my brothers, shall also rejoice, and in your respective encampments.
      —General Anthony Wayne, *United States Army*

... our hearts are sorry and afflicted, at seeing the graves of our brothers, who died here last winter.

—New Corn, *Potawatomi*

The New Corn has observed that your hearts were troubled for the loss of your brothers, who died here last winter; grief is unavailing, and ought not to be indulged.

—General Anthony Wayne, *United States Army*

When you yesterday read to us the treaty of Muskingum, I understood you clearly: at that treaty we had not good interpreters, and we were left partly unacquainted with many particulars of it. ... I always thought that we, The Ottawas, Chippewas, and Pattawatamies, were the true owners of those lands, but now I find that new masters have undertaken to dispose of them ... ever since that treaty, we have become objects of pity; and our fires have been retiring from this country.

—Masass, *Ojibway*

I now take the opportunity to inform my brothers of the United States ... that there are men of sense and understanding among my people, as well as among theirs, and that these lands were disposed of without our knowledge or consent. I was yesterday surprised, when I heard ... that these lands had been ceded by the British to the Americans, when the former were beaten by, and made peace with, the latter. ...

—Mishikinakwa (Little Turtle), *Miami*

You have pointed out to us the boundary line between the Indians and the United States, but I now take the liberty to inform you, that that line cuts off from the Indians a large portion of country, which has been enjoyed by my forefathers [since] time immemorial, without molestation or dispute. The print of my ancestors' houses are every where to be seen in this portion. . . . I have now informed you of the boundaries of the Miami nation, where the [Creator] placed my forefather a long time ago, and charged him not to sell or part with his lands, but to preserve them for his posterity. . . . I was much surprised to find that my other brothers differed so much from me on this subject: for their conduct would lead one to suppose that the [Creator] and their forefathers had not given them the same charge that was give[n] to me, but, on the contrary, had directed them to sell their lands to any white man who wore a hat, as soon as he should ask it of them.   —Mishikinakwa (Little Turtle), *Miami*

Here are papers which have been given to me by General Washington, the great chief of the United States. He told me they should protect us in the possession of our lands, and that no white person should interrupt us in the enjoyment of our hunting grounds, or be permitted to purchase any of our towns or lands from us. . . . I wish you to examine these papers. . . . You have asked for a reservation at the Ouiatanon. . . . I can't give you any lands there, brother; I will lend you some as long as you want it.   —Little Beaver, *Wea*

You know we have all buried the hatchet. . . . Why, therefore, do you wish to detain hostages from among us? You may depend on our sincerity. We cannot but be sincere, as your forts will be planted thick among us. . . . Do not view my freedom with displeasure.   —Ausimethe, *Potawatomi*

The heavens and earth are my heart, the rising sun my mouth
. . . I dare not tell a lie. Now, my friend . . . do not deceive us
in the manner that the French, the British, and Spaniards,
have heretofore done. The English abused us much . . . they
have proved to us how little they have ever had our happiness
at heart; and we have severely suffered for placing our dependence on so faithless a people. Be you strong, and preserve
your word inviolate. . . . My friend, I am old, but I shall never
die. I shall always live in my children, and children's children.
—New Corn, *Potawatomi*

The Prophet (1805)

In times of crisis, it is hard to muster the strength to survive.
People, in despair, look everywhere for guidance . . . and then the
Creator sends a message. It comes to the Shawnee prophet
Tenskwatawa. The message is simple but powerful. The strength
to survive comes from traditions. To be Shawnee is to survive. And
to be Shawnee demands the renunciation of alcohol and a return
to customs tested by time that have helped countless generations
of Shawnee through periods of trouble. Culture is a map, a template for living, and it will give the Shawnee the strength to survive
another day.

The Prophet and his brother Tecumseh deliberately move
their village to Greenville, Ohio, onto lands relinquished by the
Treaty of Greenville. President Thomas Jefferson immediately
orders their removal to the Indian side of the line. Tecumseh refuses, and declares that God alone—not the United States—
owns the land.

These lands are ours. No one has a right to remove us, because we were the first owners; the [Creator] above us has appointed this place for us, on which to light our fires, and here we will remain. As to boundaries, the [Creator] above knows no boundaries, nor will [we] acknowledge any.

—Tecumseh, *Shawnee*

I created the first man . . . and it is through him, whom I have awaked from his long sleep, that I now address you. *But the Americans I did not make. They are not my children, but the children of the evil spirit.* They grew from the scum of the great water . . . and the froth was driven into the woods by a strong east wind. They are numerous, but I hate them. . . . I am now on the earth, sent by the [Creator] to instruct you. . . . The bearer of this talk will point out to you the path to my [door]. I could not come myself to Abre Croche, because the world is changed from what it was.

—Extract of Tenskwatawa's speech delivered by Le Maiquois (the Trout) at Le Maiouitinong, Lake Michigan

Prophetstown (1808)

Having made their point by settling on Treaty of Greenville lands, the Prophet and Tecumseh relocate to the Tippecanoe River. There, they build Prophetstown, a mecca for traditional people of all nations inspired by the words of cultural renaissance and resistance.

The prophet has selected a spot on the upper part of the Wabash, for his future and permanent residence, and has engaged a considerable number of Pattawatamies, Ottawas,

Chippewas, and other Northern Indians, to settle there, under his auspices . . . they are constantly engaged in what they term religious duties; but . . . their prayers are always succeeded by, or intermixed with, warlike sports.

—Letter to War Department

. . . unless we support one another with our collective and united forces; unless every tribe unanimously combines to give a check to the ambition and avarice of the whites, they will soon conquer us apart and disunited, and we will be driven away from our native country and scattered as autumnal leaves before the wind. —Tecumseh, *Shawnee*

We thought the land we resided upon was our own . . . our old chiefs, who are now dead and gone, made a great promise to the [Creator] above, that they never would move from the land we, their children, now live upon and occupy. . . . You informed us that the land we occupy belonged to you. . . . It surprises us . . . that . . . the President of the United States, should take as much upon himself as the [Creator] above, as he wants all the land on this island. Father, we think he takes the word out of the mouth of the [Creator]; he does not consider that He is Master . . . he does not think of the [Creator] above, that He is omnipotent, and master of us all, and every thing in this world. —Wyandot delegation

Once there were no white men in all this country; then it belonged to the red men, children of the same parents, placed on it by the [Creator] to keep it, to travel over it, to eat its fruits. . . . [We were] once a happy race, but now made miserable by the white people, who are never contented, but always encroaching. They have driven us from the great salt water, forced us over the mountains, and would shortly push us into the lakes—but we are determined to go no farther. The only way to stop this evil is for all [of us] to unite in claiming a common and equal right in the land, as it was at first, and should be now. . . . No tribe has a right to sell, even to each other, much less to strangers, who demand all and will take no less. The white people have no right to take the land from the Indians, who had it first; it is theirs. . . . Any sale not made by all is not good. The late sale is bad—it was made by a part only. Part do not know how to sell. It requires all to make a bargain for all.   —Tecumseh, *Shawnee*

I have made myself what I am, and I [wish] that I could make the red people as great as the conceptions of my mind, when I think of the [Creator] that rules over all. I would not then come to see Governor [William Henry] Harrison to ask him to tear the treaty, but I would say to him, Brother, you have liberty to return to your own country.

—Tecumseh, *Shawnee*

Tecumseh   (1810–1811)

His eyes flash with the power of oration. Those who hear him speak are overwhelmed by his presence. No less powerful are his words: they are Truth. For the nations to survive, they must join together to defend their homelands. They must form an unbroken chain along the frontier and stem the tide of emigration. He glances toward his brother Tenskwatawa. Their traditions must be their passion. The wisdom of the past will make them indomitable.

Tecumseh's War Embassy, mounted on black horses, wheels and plunges, stirring up the dust before the gathered multitudes. Methodically, they build allies. The electrifying message and the spirit of its delivery ignite the villages with its fire.

More than half the Creek nation flock to his side. But the town of Tukabahchee doubts. Tecumseh whirls his horse around: he is headed north, and when he arrives he will stamp his foot upon the ground to awaken the earth and shake down every house in Tukabahchee. The days pass anxiously, and Tukabahchee waits. Suddenly, rumbling fills the air. The earth reels, the houses fall to the ground. Tecumseh has arrived. An earthquake lays Tukabahchee low.

The implicit obedience and respect which the followers of Tecumseh pay him are really astonishing and more than any other circumstance bespeak him one of those uncommon geniuses which spring up occasionally to produce revolutions and overturn the existing order of things. If it were not for the vicinity of the United States, he would be the founder of an empire that would rival in glory Mexico or Peru. For years he has been in constant motion. You see him to-day on the Wabash and in a short time hear of him on the shores of Lake Michigan or the banks of the Mississippi, and wherever he goes, he makes an impression favorable to his purpose.

—William Henry Harrison, *Indiana governor*

Where to-day is the Pequo[t]? Where [are] the Narragansetts, the Mohawks, Pocanokets, and many other once powerful tribes of our race? They have vanished before the avarice and oppression of the white men, as snow before a summer sun. In the vain hope of alone defending their ancient possessions, they have fallen in the wars with the white men. Look abroad over their once beautiful country, and what see you now? Naught but the ravages of the pale-face destroyers meet[s] our eyes. So it will be with you. . . . Soon your mighty forest trees, under the shade of whose wide spreading branches you have played in infancy, sported in boyhood, and now rest your wearied limbs after the fatigue of the chase, will be cut down to fence in the land which the white intruders dare to call their own. Soon their broad roads will pass over the grave of your fathers, and the place of their rest will be blotted out forever. The annihilation of our race is at hand. . . . Your people, too, will soon be as falling leaves and scattering clouds before their blighting breath. You, too, will be driven away from your native land and ancient domains as leaves are driven before the wintry storms. . . . Our broad domains are fast escaping from our grasp. Every year our white intruders become more greedy, exacting, oppressive and overbearing. Every year contentions spring up between them and our people and when blood is shed we have to make atonement whether right or wrong, at the cost of the lives of our greatest chiefs, and the yielding up of large tracts of our lands. Before the palefaces came among us, we enjoyed the happiness of unbounded freedom, and were acquainted with neither riches, wants nor oppression. How is it now? . . .

Will we not soon be driven from our respective countries and the graves of our ancestors? Will not the bones of our dead be plowed up, and their graves be turned into fields? Shall we calmly wait until they become so numerous that we will no longer be able to resist oppression? Will we wait to be destroyed in our turn, without making an effort worthy [of] our race? Shall we give up our homes, our country, bequeathed to us by the [Creator], the graves of our dead, and everything that is dear and sacred to us, without a struggle? I know you will cry with me, Never! Never! . . . Let us form one body, one heart, and defend to the last warrior our country, our homes, our liberty, and the graves of our fathers.

—Tecumseh, *Shawnee*

War Department Correspondence: Miscellaneous Sources (1807–1811)

I have received information from various sources . . . that the Prophet is organizing a most extensive combination against the United States. The person who had charge of the boat sent up the river with the annuity of salt . . . reports that the Prophet and the Kickapoos who were with him refused to receive [it] . . . he was ordered by the Prophet to leave the salt on the bank of the river . . . as they were determined to have nothing to do with it.

. . . as we have learnt that some tribes are already expressing intentions hostile to the United States, we think it proper to apprise them of the ground on which they now stand . . . if ever we are constrained to lift the hatchet against any tribe, we will never lay it down till that tribe is exterminated, or driven beyond the Mississippi.

—President Thomas Jefferson, *United States*

There appears to be a very general and extensive movement among the savages in . . . [Machilimackinac]. Belts of wampum are rapidly circulating from one tribe to another, and a spirit is prevailing, by no means pacific . . . there can be no doubt, in my mind, but that the object of this great Manitou, or second Adam, under the pretense of restoring to the aborigines their former independence . . . is, in reality, to induce a general effort to *rally,* and to strike, somewhere, a desperate blow.

From the Ioways, I learn that the Sacs and Foxes have actually received the tomahawk, and are ready to strike whenever the Prophet gives the signal.

Winemac assured me that the Prophet . . . proposed to the young men to murder the principal chiefs of all the tribes; observing that . . . these were the men who had sold their lands, and who would prevent them from opposing the encroachments of the white people.

From the hostile appearance of the Indians towards the lakes and about the head of the Wabash river, I have thought it a duty to keep out spies, and have at this time spies among those tribes. I enclose you a talk from the *Ioways*. . . . "I tell you this, although death is threatened against those who discover it: The time is drawing nigh when the murder is to begin, and all the Indians who will not join are to die with the whites."

. . . [At the Prophet's town] there are about six hundred men and . . . Tecumseh is daily expected, with a considerable reinforcement, from the lakes.

All the information received from the Indian country, confirms the rooted enmity of the Prophet to the United States, and his determination to commence hostilities as soon as he thinks himself sufficiently strong. His party is increasing. . . .

The Shawanee chief, Tecumseh, has made a visit to [Vincennes] with about three hundred Indians, though he promised to bring but a few attendants; *his intentions hostile*. . . . The spies say, his object in coming with so many, was to demand a retrocession of the late purchase.

. . . the [Great Lakes] Sioux [are] supposed to have joined the hostile confederacy. . . .

. . . the major part of the Winnebago tribe are at Tippecanoe, with the Prophet and Tecumseh; small bands from the Illinois river and the east of Lake Michigan. . . . The Governor also says there are, at this time, nearly eight hundred warriors embodied at Peoria. . . .

Brothers—We are friends; we must assist each other to bear our burdens. The blood of many of our fathers and brothers has run like water on the ground, to satisfy the avarice of the white men. We, ourselves, are threatened with a great evil; nothing will pacify them but the destruction of all the red men. *Brothers*—When the white men first set foot on our grounds, they were hungry; they had no place on which to spread their blankets, or to kindle their fires. They were feeble; they could do nothing for themselves. Our fathers commiserated their distress, and shared freely with them whatever the [Creator] had given his red children. They gave them food when hungry, medicine when sick, spread skins for them to sleep on, and gave them grounds, that they might hunt and raise corn.

Brothers—the white people are like poisonous serpents: when chilled, they are feeble and harmless; but invigorate them with warmth, and they sting their benefactors to death.

The white people came among us feeble; and now we have made them strong, they wish to kill us, or drive us back, as they would wolves and panthers.

Brothers—the white men are not friends to the Indians: at first, they only asked for land sufficient for a wigwam; now, nothing will satisfy them but the whole of our hunting grounds, from the rising to the setting sun . . . the white men want more than our hunting grounds; they wish to kill our warriors; they would even kill our old men, women, and little ones.

Brothers—many winters ago, there was no land; the sun did not rise and set: all was darkness. The [Creator] made all things. He gave the white people a home beyond the great waters. He supplied these grounds with game, and gave them to his red children; and he gave them strength and courage to defend them.

Brothers—my people wish for peace; the red men all wish for peace; but where the white people are, there is no peace for them. . . .

Brothers—the white men despise and cheat the Indians; they abuse and insult them; they do not think the red men sufficiently good to live. The red men have borne many and great injuries; they ought to suffer them no longer. My people will not. . . .   —Tecumseh, *Shawnee*

Problems Continue   (1812)

The Treaty of Greenville is soon disregarded by citizens of the very country that has stipulated its demands. When fighting erupts during the War of 1812, Americans blame the British for inciting Indian nations to violence. Yet the real reason is obvious enough. Treaties offer little land and fewer rights; and what the treaties grudgingly give, the settlers take away.

. . . in consequence of a species of persecution raised against them under plausible pretexts, it is possible that religion and civilization may become extinct, and the [Wyandot] nation itself entirely exterminated. As they possess a rich, beautiful, and extensive tract of land, surrounded by white settlers; such a fertile spot is an object of desire to avaricious white men. Hence the whites ardently desire to see the Wyandot reservation exposed to sale. . . .

The governor of Ohio has used all his official and personal influence to induce them to sell. Agents and officers of every description press the subject by every means in their power. The white people have impoverished them much by stealing almost all their horses. Thus they are beset by importunate and interested persons, so as to produce divisions among themselves. If they stay where they are they are robbed and harassed.   —Rev. Charles Elliott, *United States*

Several black robes have come to our villages, to preach the religion of white people; they told us the religion of the whites consisted in a few words; that was, to do unto others as we wish that others should do unto us . . . we wish you to put the above Christian rule in practice. . . . If you really want to ameliorate our condition, let us have the land given to us . . . this pretence of bettering our situation, it appears, is only for a temporary purpose . . . we shall have forgot how to hunt, in which practice we are now very expert, and then you'll turn us out of doors, a poor, pitiful, helpless set of wretches.

—Wyandot delegation

We know that some of your wise men, who do not know our customs, will look into your book of treaties, and they will find that at Muskingum, fort Harmar, Greenville, and at the treaty of Detroit, this piece of land has been conveyed to the

United States, by all the nations. . . . We can assure you in sincerity and truth, how the thing is conducted at all treaties. When the United States want a particular piece of land, all our nations are assembled; a large sum of money is offered; the land is occupied probably by one nation only; nine-tenths have no actual interest in the land wanted; if the particular nation interested refuses to sell, they are generally threatened by the others, who want the money or goods offered, to buy whiskey. Fathers, this is the way in which this small spot, which we so much value, has been so often torn from us. We, the Wyandotts, are now a small nation. Unless you have charity for us, we will soon be forgot. . . .

—Wyandot delegation

Missionaries

I feel myself called upon to defend the religion of my fathers, which the [Creator] has given to his red children to regulate their faith, and which we shall not abandon as soon as you might wish. . . . Cast your eyes abroad over the world, and see how many different systems of religion there are in it, almost as many as there are nations—and is not this the work of the Lord? No, my friend, your declaiming so violently against our modes of worshipping the [Creator], in my opinion, is not calculated to benefit us as a nation. We are willing to receive good advice from you; but we are not willing to have the customs and institutions which have been kept sacred by our fathers, and handed down to us, thus assailed and abused. —John Hicks, *Wyandot*

I doubt not but that you state faithfully what your book says; but let me correct an error into which you appear to have run, which is, your belief that the [Creator] designed that his red children should be instructed out of it. This is a mistake; as He never intended that we should be instructed from a book which properly belongs only to those who made it. . . . Ours is a religion that suits us . . . and we intend to preserve it sacred among us, believing that the [Creator] gave it to our grandfathers in ancient days.　　—Mononcue, *Wyandot*

Why does your religion produce contention among us, not only between your side and ours, at large, but even among families, when some of them leave the old religion and go over to you?　　—Warpole, *Wyandot*

Battle of the Thames　(1813)

The War of 1812 erupts. Tecumseh's allies strike heavy blows against the Americans. In these exciting times, hope fills every heart. But by the following year, American victories against Tecumseh mount. General Harrison's troops force a demoralizing British and Indian retreat down the Thames River. Tecumseh has a premonition of his death, and resolves to make a stand. On October 5, the morning of the battle, he carefully dresses in Shawnee clothing, discarding the British military jacket he often wears. He hands a friend his favorite sword, asking him to save it for his son, and to explain to him why he has chosen to give his life for his country. Tecumseh's spirits rise; from horseback, he charges up and down the lines, urging his men to victory. He will face Harrison without fear. In the first moments of the battle, Tecumseh is killed . . . but Harrison has seen the dream in his eyes.

If there be one here to-night who believes that his rights will not, sooner or later, be taken from him by the avaricious American[s] . . . his ignorance ought to excite pity, for he knows little of the character of our common foe.

—Tecumseh, *Shawnee*

My cause will not die, when I am dead.

—Tecumseh, *Shawnee*

Have [you] not heard at evening, and sometimes in the dead of night, those mournful sounds that steal through the deep valleys and along the mountain sides? These are the wailings of those spirits whose bones have been turned up by the plow of the white man, and left to the mercy of the rain and wind. . . . The eastern tribes have long since disappeared—even the forests that sheltered them are laid low; and scarcely a trace of our nation remains, except here and there the Indian name of a stream, or a village. And such, sooner or later, will be the fate of the other tribes. . . . They will vanish like a vapour from the face of the earth: their very history will be lost in forgetfulness, and the places that now know them will know them no more. We are driven back until we can retreat no farther . . . a little longer and the white man will cease to persecute us, for we shall cease to exist!   —Tenskwatawa, *Shawnee*

The Aftermath

But a few years ago, less than my age, the Menominee people occupied much of the rich valley of the Wolf and Fox rivers. We were prosperous and happy. Twenty-five years ago we numbered near 4,000 warriors—to-day, where are we? Within the limits of these few barren gameless townships of land, our numbers growing less with every year, until our pay roll now numbers less than 1,400 souls. Ten years hence the Menominees will only be known as a people that once lived.   —Keshena, *Menominee*

The only time the Americans shook hands was when they wanted another piece of Menominee land.

—Oshkosh, *Menominee*

We see your Council House—it is large and beautiful. But the Council House of the Red Man is yet larger. The earth is the floor—the clear sky is the roof—a blazing fire is the chair of the Chief orator, and the green grass is the seats of our Chiefs. You speak by papers, and record your words in books; but we speak from our hearts, and memory records our words in the hearts of our people. . . .

—Grizzly Bear, *Menominee*

. . . It takes time to wear away attachment to old customs, habits, and superstitions. They cannot be got rid of in a day. . . .   —Hole-in-the-Day, *Ojibway*

The [Creator], although he made the Indian and the white man of a different color, gave each a dialect by which they could understand each other. The Master of Life gave us a faculty of using our tongues, and we should use words enough to make ourselves understood. Take the white man, with all his wisdom, and he is not infallible to faults. Your words strike us in this way. They are very short. "I want to buy your land."

—Hole-in-the-Day, *Ojibway*

Our people must have faith in somebody, or they cannot trust anybody. If not, they could do nothing. Flattery is not my habit; but I must thank the Commissioner for his unusual frankness. It is the first time a person about to do business with us has, in advance, put us on our guard. . . .

—Hole-in-the-Day, *Ojibway*

. . . You must remember . . . that, although we are red and you white, there is One above to whom we all have to give an account, and who will not permit acts of injustice to be done without visiting them with his displeasure.

—Buffalo, *Ojibway*

. . . I know what my people want . . . give them time to reflect. Those who have had experience know that all they can do is to bow down their heads. . . . When we look upon these cities, these fine buildings, and the numbers and wealth of the whites, and reflect upon what the Indians have been, and upon what the whites have come to, we must have time to reflect, for meditation is everything with an Indian. When we view the past, and reflect upon the fact that the Indians once owned the land covered with these cities—when we think of our former treaties and past transactions with you—we understand what was your object in sending for us, and what you intend to do with us.

Under these circumstances, we are compelled to reflect. . . . We look at everything. We are not near[ly] as ignorant as white men think us to be.

—Hole-in-the-Day, *Ojibway*

My father, restrain your feelings, and hear calmly what I shall say. I shall say it plainly. I shall not speak with fear and trembling. I have never injured you, and innocence can feel no fear. . . . I have nothing now to say here in your councils, except to repeat what I said before. . . . You heard it, and no doubt remember it. It was simply this. My lands can never be surrendered; I was cheated, and basely cheated, in the contract. I will not surrender my country but with my life.

—Mackkatananamakee (Black Thunder), *Mesquakie*

How smooth must be the language of the whites, when they can make right look like wrong, and wrong like right. . . .

I was . . . puzzled to find out how the white people reasoned; and began to doubt whether they had any standard of right and wrong!

—Makataimeshekiakiak (Black Hawk), *Sauk*

You know the cause of our making war. It is known to all White men. They ought to be ashamed of it. The White men despise the Indians and drive them from their homes. But the Indians are not deceitful. The White men speak bad of the Indian, and look at him spitefully. But the Indian does not tell lies; Indians do not steal. . . . We told them to let us alone, and keep away from us; but they followed on and beset our

paths, and they coiled themselves among us like the snake. They poisoned us by their touch. We were not safe. . . .
—Makataimeshekiakiak (Black Hawk), *Sauk*

Our people once owned the lead mines in Southwestern Wisconsin. . . . They made lead-mining their regular work. Every fall and spring hunters would go down to the mines and get a stock of lead for bullets, sometimes giving goods for it and sometimes furs. When the whites began to come among the mines, the Big Father said to his Winnebago children: "I want this land and will have my own people to work it, and whenever you go out hunting come by this way, and you will be supplied with lead." But this agreement was never carried out. . . . Never was a bar of lead or a bag of shot presented to us. This was a very great sorrow to our people. For many years there was much sorrowful talk among the Winnebagoes, at the manner in which the Big Father had treated them, with regard to the mines. No, we never saw any of our lead again, except what we paid dearly for; and we never will have any given to us, unless it be fired at us out of white men's guns, to kill us off.   —Spoon Decorah, *Winnebago*

The Grasslands

. . . a brave man dies but once—cowards are always dying.
—*Moanahonga*, Ioway

At the close of the French and Indian War in 1760, French posts and garrisons fell into British hands. This included not only the Ohio Valley, but also French holdings along the Mississippi, Illinois, Kaskaskia, and Wabash rivers, which linked the French domain in Canada to the territory of Louisiana. Few new settlements were made under the British administration, and when the Treaty of Paris assigned these same lands to the United States in 1783, it did so with most Americans knowing little about the region. In 1803, as a result of the Louisiana Purchase, the United States obtained the remainder of the Mississippi and Missouri River valleys. The Kaskaskia, Tamaroa, Cahokia, Konze, Osage, Missouria, Michigamea, Piankashaw, and many other sovereign Indian nations once again were not consulted in this transaction of their homelands.

American explorers Meriwether Lewis, George Rogers Clark, and Zebulon Pike stopped briefly among the nations on the prairies, but returned less than favorable reports about the rolling grasslands. It was determined that the prairies were fit only for wild animals and Indian tribes. Consequently, when the United States initiated its malevolent plan of forcibly removing eastern nations from their homelands, it was to the undesirable grasslands of Kansas and the new Indian Territory of Oklahoma that they were sent.

The opening of the Santa Fe Trail, in 1821, for the first time provided direct access to the famed silver bullion of Mexico. This circumstance, followed by the 1849 California gold rush, dramatically changed Americans' attitude toward the prairies. Suddenly, the wild no-man's-land was transformed into a glittering road to fortune. Almost overnight, Saint Louis grew from a small frontier outpost into a bustling terminus for trails west; and the old Allegheny frontier became only a memory. For Indian nations, Horace Greeley's injunction to "go west, young man" was a sobering reality.

In 1834 United States dragoons were sent onto the southern Plains to establish diplomatic relations with the Kiowa, Kiowa-Apache, Comanche, and Wichita nations. The artist George Catlin accompanied the expedition and transmitted glowing reports to the American public of the southern Plains nations, their leaders, and unrivaled feats of horsemanship. Catlin's enthusiasm was shared. A later observer described an equestrian exercise nothing short of remarkable.

. . . thousands of mounted warriors could be seen concentrating and forming themselves into a wedge shaped mass. . . . When within a mile of the army troops, the wedge, without a hitch or break, quickly threw itself into the shape of a huge ring or wheel, without hub or spokes, whose rim consisted of five lines of . . . horsemen. This ring, winding around and around with the regularity and precision of well-oiled machinery, came nearer and nearer with every revolution. Reaching within a hundred yards of the troops at breakneck speed, the giant wheel or ring ceased to turn and suddenly came to a standstill.   —Alfred A. Taylor, *United States*

Catlin's journeys eventually led him to the northern Plains, where he sketched and described similar wonders, which shortly thereafter were confirmed by the artistic expedition of Prince Maximilian of Wied and Karl Bodmer along the upper Missouri River. Plains culture was gripping the heart of the American public, a circumstance furthered by the advent of photography. But the prosperity exhibited among the Plains nations during Catlin's visits in the early part of the century were destined to change. Gold in California, the Civil War, and shifting U.S. policy assured that life never again would be the same.

The 1848 discovery of gold in California vastly accelerated the process of western migration. Almost overnight, soldiers, prospectors, Mormons, wagon trains, and stagecoaches swarmed across the Oregon Trail on what became the most traveled thoroughfare in the country. In a single year alone, one hundred thousand emigrants raced across valuable hunting grounds, giving the Plains nations real cause for alarm. The situation became so critical on the northern Plains that the Treaty of Fort Laramie was concluded in 1851 between the Lakota and neighboring nations. Under the terms of the treaty, the government obtained the right-of-way to the emigrant road and in return forever guaranteed to the Indian nations the area north of the Platte River. That guarantee was dashed, however, in 1861, when gold was discovered in Montana. In 1874 George Armstrong Custer illegally led troops onto Lakota lands and proclaimed the presence of gold in the sacred Black Hills "from the grass roots down." The gold rush was on, and with it rose the cry for a reduction of the existing reservations.

The second great tragedy for the Plains nations was the United States Civil War. After the surrender at Appomattox, hundreds of ex-soldiers found themselves emotionally unable to return to civilian life. The unstructured western frontier attracted these men, who became notorious as outlaws, renegades, and Indian fighters. United States troops battled Indian nations under experienced Civil War generals such as Philip Henry Sheridan and William Tecumseh Sherman. West Point, which had taught military men to fight Confederates, now churned out soldiers especially trained for Indian combat. And so war continued; only the external surroundings changed.

A second result of the Civil War was the effect that it had on United States Indian policy. Giddy from Confederate defeat and convinced of its own strength and moral right, the United States dramatically shifted its policy toward Indian nations to a much more aggressive stance. Gone were the days of negotiation with Indian nations regarded as formidable equals. Under the direction of the War Department, Plains Indian nations never really had a chance.

On the other hand, the United States grossly underestimated both the sophistication of the nations and the strength of their determination to be free. All too frequently, U.S. representatives were outwitted diplomatically and their forces challenged militarily. To accomplish their goals, Indian commissioners shamelessly resorted to trickery. Indian men were rewarded for their allegiance to the United States by being made "paper chiefs" and, without legal sanction from their own nations, signed the treaties relinquishing their lands. To this neat trick were added threats, bribery, and at least one case of a forged signature on a treaty document. "Accidents," "suicides," and "hostile intentions" were excuses used to eliminate the most defiant leaders.

Finally, starvation, not United States magnanimity or might, became the determining factor in Indian subjugation, and great lengths were taken to ensure that the vast buffalo herds on the Plains were eradicated. Starvation, force, trickery, bribery, forgery, and the creation of factions—these were the tools of the new aggressive Indian policy. By 1890 the United States had triumphantly fought its last Indian "War." But the victims of these campaigns did the unexpected: they told the truth.

The First Amendment (1836)

News travels fast in Indian country. Osceola's victory over government troops in Florida is greeted enthusiastically on the prairies. Under the shadow of Fort Leavenworth, shouts go up in the Kickapoo nation. In the evening, bonfires burn and there is celebration.

It had, he said, been reported to him, that a dance had lately been held at the Upper Village of the Kickapoos, in celebration of the Massacre of a portion of our Army by the . . . [Seminole] Nation of Indians in Florida, and that the Chiefs and [men] of this Nation had, at that time, between the pauses of the dance, exulted on account of that Victory. And that they then declared that the time was near at hand when the white people would all be subdued, and red men returned again to their Country.

That language like this, used by a Nation of Indians against a Government which had done, and was still doing, so much for its happiness was ungrateful and improper, and . . . should not be suffered to pass with impunity . . . much had been done . . . to better their condition, and . . . it was expected in return that red men would be grateful for these favors.

—Captain Matthew Duncan,
Fort Leavenworth commander

Since we made the treaty with our Red headed father at St. Louis, I have kept what was then said to me in my heart . . . that my people would be protected, against all enemies by the troops at that post. . . . But he then deceived me. . . . He said that my father at this Garrison had very big eyes, and that he would see all my enemies, and defend me against them. But instead of this You, my father, are watching me to see if

208

I do anything wrong. . . . There has been a great deal of fuss about our dance! We do not deny that we had a dance. It is the right of all people to dance—the whites as well as the red men dance—when we had this dance we did not expect any fuss about it. . . . Now I will tell you all about this dance, when we were made, by our Great Maker. He told us what to do. . . . We have now got [a priest] among us, and I intend to listen to him, for he must be very good, but if he goes to change the old customs of my forefathers, I will quit him and listen to him no more. —Patsachi, *Kickapoo*

Smallpox (1837)

In a former Letter I gave some account of Mah-to-toh-pa (the four bears), second chief of the Mandans. . . . This extraordinary man . . . is undoubtedly the first and most popular man in the nation. Free, generous, elegant, and gentlemanly in his deportment—handsome, brave, and valiant. . . .
—George Catlin, *United States*

My friends one and all, listen to what I have to say—Ever since I can remember, I have loved the Whites, I have lived With them ever since I was a Boy, and to the best of my Knowledge, I have never Wronged a White Man, on the Contrary, I have always Protected them from the insults of Others, Which they cannot deny. The 4 Bears never saw a White Man hungry, but what he gave him to eat, Drink, and a Buffaloe skin to sleep on, in time of Need. I was always ready to die for them, Which they cannot deny. I have done everything that a [person] could do for them, and how have they repaid it! With ingratitude! I have Never called a White Man a Dog, but to day, I do Pronounce them to be a set of Black hearted Dogs, they have deceived Me, them that I always considered as Brothers, has turned out to be My Worst enemies. I have been in Many Battles, and often Wounded, but the Wounds of My enemies I exalt in, but to day I am Wounded, and by Whom, by those same White Dogs that I have always Considered, and treated as Brothers. I do not fear Death my friends. You Know it, but to die with my face rotten, that even the Wolves will shrink with horror at seeing Me, and say to themselves, that is the 4 Bears the Friend of the Whites. . . .   —Mahto Topah (Four Bears), *Mandan*

. . . we have . . . the most frightful accounts of the ravages of the small-pox among the Indians. . . . [It] has converted . . . the peaceful settlements of those tribes, into desolate and boundless cemeteries. The number of the victims within a few months is estimated at 30,000, and the pestilence is still spreading . . . the funeral torch, that lights the red man to his dreary grave, has become the auspicious star of the advancing settler. . . . The small-pox was communicated to the Indians by a person who was on board the steam-boat which went, last summer, up to the mouth of the Yellow Stone, to convey both the government presents for the Indians, and the goods for the barter trade of the fur dealers. . . .

The disease first broke out about the 15th day of June, 1837, in the village of the Mandans. . . . The character of the disease was as appalling as the rapidity of the propagation. Among the remotest tribes of the Assiniboins from fifty to one hundred died daily. . . . For many weeks together our workmen did nothing but collect the dead bodies and bury them in large pits; but since the ground is frozen we are obliged to throw them into the river. The ravages of the disorder were the most frightful among the Mandans, where it first broke out. That once powerful tribe, which . . . had already been reduced to 1500 souls, was exterminated, with the exception of thirty persons. . . . The prairie all around is a vast field of death, covered with unburied corpses, and spreading, for miles, pestilence and infection.

—Maximilian, *Prince of Wied*

When the great chief came to visit us a few years ago, he said to us: "My children, be faithful to the whites, obey your Great Father, keep the peace and do not break your word, and the smoke of your fires will go straight up to the sky."

We have done as our Great Father ordered, and, in spite of all, the smoke of our fires instead of rising straight up towards the heavens, is thrown upon the ground and has been chased by all the winds.

—Crow Belly, *Hidatsa*

To Die Within

Our camp on a summer's evening was a cheerful scene. At this hour, fires burned before most of the tepees. . . . Here a family sat eating their evening meal. Yonder, a circle of old men . . . in the firelight, joked and told stories. . . . We had dancing almost every evening in those good days.

But for wee folks bedtime was rather early. In my father's family, it was soon after sunset. My mothers had laid dry grass around the tent wall, and on this had spread buffalo skins for beds. . . . My father often sat and sang me to sleep by the firelight . . . with the moon of Yellow Leaves, we struck tents and went into winter camp. My tribe usually built their winter village down in the thick woods along the Missouri, out of reach of the cold prairie winds. It was of earth lodges, like those of our summer village . . . a second, or "twin lodge," was often built. This was a small lodge with roof peaked like a tepee, but covered with bark and earth. A covered passage led from it to the main lodge. The twin lodge had two uses. In it the grandparents . . . could sit, snug and warm . . . and the children of the household used it as a playhouse. I can just remember playing in our twin lodge, and making little feasts with bits of boiled tongue or dried berries that my mothers gave me.   —Waheenee (Buffalo Bird Woman), *Hidatsa*

I am an old woman now. The buffaloes and black-tail deer are gone, and our Indian ways are almost gone. Sometimes I find it hard to believe that I ever lived them. . . . We no longer live in an earth lodge, but in a house with chimneys; and my son's wife cooks by a stove. But for me, I cannot forget our old ways.

Often in summer I rise at daybreak and steal out to the cornfields; and as I hoe the corn I sing to it, as we did when I was young. No one cares for our corn songs now.

Sometimes at evening I sit, looking out on the big Missouri. The sun sets, and dusk steals over the water. In the shadows I seem again to see our Indian village, with smoke curling upward from the earth lodges; and in the river's roar I hear the yells of the warriors, the laughter of little children as of old. It is but an old woman's dream. Again I see but shadows and hear only the roar of the river; and tears come into my eyes. Our Indian life, I know, is gone forever.

—Waheenee (Buffalo Bird Woman), *Hidatsa*

Catlin's European Tour   (1844–1845)

The artist George Catlin eyes the crowd gathered around the small group from the Ioway nation. They have traveled far together, he and the Ioway, from the rolling prairies to a crowded East Coast harbor and across the ocean on a steamship bound for Europe. To capacity crowds, to kings, to gentlemen and ladies, to people from all walks of life, the Ioway will explain their life and customs. They will learn much about Europe, but Europe will learn much more about them. One evening in England, cornered by a minister and forced into theological discussion in which he is told his religion is wrong, Neumonya proves that he can hold his own by delivering an equally candid view of Christianity. Aghast, the Christian ladies hurriedly distribute Bibles.

THE REVEREND GENTLEMAN: Did it ever occur to you, that the small pox that swept off half of your tribe, and other tribes around you, a few years ago, might have been sent into your country by the [Creator] to punish the Indians for their wickedness and their resistance to his word?

NEUMONYA: . . . If the [Creator] sent the small pox into our country to destroy us, we believe it was to punish us for listening to the false promises of white men. It is [the] white man's disease, and no doubt it was sent amongst white people to punish *them* for their sins. It never came amongst the Indians until we began to listen to the promises of white men, and to follow their ways; it then came amongst us, and we are not sure but the [Creator] then sent it to punish us for our foolishness. . . .

As to the white man's religion which you have explained, we have heard it told to us in the same way, many times, in our own country. . . . We do not think your religion good, unless it is so for white people, and this we don't doubt. The [Creator] has . . . given us our religion, which has taken our fathers to "the beautiful hunting grounds," where we wish to meet them. . . . you speak of the "*good book*" that you have in your hand; we have many of these in our village; we are told that "all your words about the Son of the [Creator] are printed in that book, and if we learn to read it, it will make good people of us." I would now ask why it don't make good people of the pale faces living all around us? . . . In *our* country the white people [have] two faces, and their tongues branch in different ways; we know that this displeases the [Creator], and we do not wish to teach it to our children.

—Neumonya, *Ioway*

Poverty (1844–1845)

Through the misty streets of Dublin come the begging poor. A little child extends a hungry hand and speaks words that Neumonya cannot understand. But he knows poverty. Into the outstretched hand, he places a shining coin. When he is next asked to speak to the crowd, instead of entertaining them with the savage lore they hope to hear, Neumonya speaks to them about humanity.

I am willing to talk with you if it can do any good to the hundreds and thousands of poor and hungry people that we see in your streets every day when we ride out. We see hundreds of little children with their naked feet in the snow, and we pity them, for we know they are hungry, and we give them money every time we pass them . . . we give our money only to children. We are told that the fathers of these children are in the houses where they sell fire-water, and are drunk. . . . You talk about sending *black-coats* among the Indians: now we have no such poor children among us; we have no such drunkards, or people who abuse the [Creator]. . . . Now we think it would be better for your teachers all to stay at home, and go to work right here in your own streets, where all your good work is wanted. This is my advice. I would rather not say any more.

—Neumonya, *Ioway*

The Zoo   (1844–1845)

The enjoyable stroll through the gardens of Paris comes abruptly to an end. At the edge of the walkway, the black iron bars enclosing the stinking cages cause the Ioway delegation to reel back in distress. Of all the things that they have seen in Europe, nothing sickens them more than this.

The ostrich . . . and the kangaroo excited the admiration and lively remarks of the Indians; but when they met the poor distressed and ragged prisoner, the buffalo from their own wild and free prairies, their spirits were overshadowed with an instant gloom. . . . They sighed, and even wept, for this worn veteran, and walked on.

—George Catlin, *United States*

[The Indian delegation] reflect[ed] and comment[ed] upon the cruelty of keeping all those poor and unoffending animals prisoners in such a place, merely to be looked at. They spoke of the doleful looks they all wore in their imprisoned cells, walking to and fro, and looking through the iron bars at every person who came along, as if they wished them to let them out. I was forcibly struck with the truth and fitness of their remarks, having never passed through a menagerie without coming out impressed, even to fatigue, with the sympathy I had felt for the distressed looks and actions of these poor creatures, imprisoned for life, for man's amusement only.

—George Catlin, *United States*

What have all those poor animals and birds done that they
should be shut up to die? They never have murdered anybody—they have not been guilty of stealing, and they
owe no money; why should they be kept so, and there to
die?   —Washkamonya [Fast Dancer], *Ioway*

Sand Creek   (1864)

June 27, 1864—Governor John Evans of the Colorado Territory
issues a circular instructing peaceful Indian nations to relocate
immediately onto reservations. Those who do not comply will be
considered hostile and at war with the United States. In September, Black Kettle of the Cheyenne surrenders to Governor Evans
and Colorado Colonel John Chivington.

Black Kettle's band is conducted south to Fort Lyon, under the
care of Major Edward Wynkoop. Evans testifies that it is his understanding that the Cheyenne are prisoners of war. Wynkoop
understands this also, and the band is issued prisoners' rations.

Black Kettle's surrender cannot have been more untimely. Gov-
ernor Evans already has raised a volunteer army in Denver to fight
Indians. He asks what will become of the volunteers if there is no
Indian menace; they have been trained to fight Indians, and fight
Indians they must. As Black Kettle's nation heads peacefully to
Fort Lyon, Evans circulates stories of Cheyenne "depredations."
Fabricated, but effective, the tales incite the citizens of Denver to
panic and call for immediate action. On September 28, the same
day that the so-called peace conference is held with Black Kettle
in Denver, Colonel Chivington receives a telegraph from Major
General Samuel Curtis of Fort Leavenworth stating: "I want no
peace till the Indians suffer more. . . . No peace must be made
without my directions." There never was a peace conference held
in Denver. It was a sham.

The plan is set in motion and events move rapidly. Kindly Major
Wynkoop is abruptly and mysteriously recalled from duty. He is

A Cheyenne family. After the massacre at Sand Creek,
U.S. troops under George Armstrong Custer attacked the
survivors along the Washita River, yet the Cheyenne still dared
to assert that they were free.

replaced by Major Scott Anthony. Days after his arrival, Anthony withholds the prisoners' rations and instructs the Cheyenne to remove to nearby Sand Creek to hunt. Once they are out of sight, Anthony telegraphs Denver requesting troops to assist against hostile Cheyenne in the area.

Chivington marches south with seven hundred mounted Denver Volunteers. Roads are sealed and all communication to Fort Lyon cut off; every effort is made to conceal the army's approach. At the fort, Anthony's troops join the Volunteers, and together they march against the unsuspecting Cheyenne along Sand Creek.

I heard shouts and the noise of people running about the camp. I jumped up and ran out of my lodge. From down the creek a large body of troops was advancing at a rapid trot, some to the east of the camps, and others on the opposite side of the creek, to the west. . . . I looked toward the chief's lodge and saw Black Kettle had a large American flag tied to the end of a long lodgepole and was standing in front of his lodge holding the pole. . . . I heard him call to the people not to be afraid, that the soldiers would not hurt them; then the troops opened fire. . . . The women and children were screaming and wailing, the men running to the lodges for their arms and shouting advice and directions to one another. . . . Many of the people had preceded us up the creek, and the dry bed of the stream was now a terrible sight: men, women, and children lying thickly scattered on the sand. . . . We . . . came to a place where the banks were very high and steep . . . and the older men and the women had dug holes or pits under the banks, in which the people were now hiding. . . . Most of us . . . had been wounded before we could reach this shelter; and there we lay all that bitter cold day from early in the morning until almost dark, with the soldiers all around us, keeping up a heavy fire most of the time. . . .

That night will never be forgotten as long as any of us who went through it are alive. . . . Many who had lost wives, husbands and children, or friends, went back down the creek and crept over the battleground among the naked and mutilated bodies of the dead. Few were found alive, for the soldiers had done their work thoroughly. . . .
—George Bent, *Southern Cheyenne*

The Cheyennes will have to be soundly whipped before they will be quiet. If any of them are caught in your vicinity kill them, as that is the only way.
—Colonel John Chivington, *United States Army*

On sight of your circular of June 27, 1864, I took hold of the matter, and have now come to talk to you about it. . . . All we ask is that we may have peace with the whites. . . . We want to take good tidings home to our people, that they may sleep in peace. I want you to give all the chiefs of the soldiers here to understand that we are for peace, and that we have made peace, that we may not be mistaken by them for enemies.
—Motavato (Black Kettle), *Southern Cheyenne*

I have heard that there are a great many white people in the East who know nothing of the wrongs which have been done to our people. . . . I want you to stop the white men from killing the Indians after this. The Indian loves to live as well as the white men. They are there, and they can't help being there.
—Buffalo Good, *Wichita*

I once thought that I was the only man that persevered to be the friend of the white man, but since they have come and cleaned out our lodges, horses, and everything else, it is hard for me to believe white men any more.

—Motavato (Black Kettle), *Southern Cheyenne*

But what do we want to live for? The white man has taken our country, killed all of our game; was not satisfied with that, but killed our wives and children.

—Southern Cheyenne Council

Trial Testimony

Five hundred Cheyenne are killed along Sand Creek. Two-thirds are women and children. After committing the abominable massacre, the soldiers walk across the killing fields, mutilating bodies and collecting scalps. Back in Denver, more than a hundred Sand Creek scalps are exhibited jubilantly during a theater intermission while the audience cheers and the band plays.

There was one little child, probably three years old, just big enough to walk through the sand. The Indians had gone ahead, and this little child was behind following them. The little fellow was perfectly naked, travelling on the sand. I saw one man get off his horse . . . and draw up his rifle and fire—he missed the child. Another man came up and said, "Let me try the son of a bitch; I can hit him" . . . but he missed him. A third man came up and made a similar remark, and fired, and the little fellow dropped.

—Major Scott Anthony, *United States Army*

. . . I did not see a body of a man, woman, child but was scalped; and in many instances their bodies were mutilated in the most horrible manner, men, women, and children— privates cut out, etc. I heard one man say that he had cut a woman's private parts out and had them for exhibition on a stick; I heard another man say that he had cut the fingers off an Indian to get the rings on the hand. . . . I also heard of numerous instances in which men had cut out the private parts of females, and stretched them over the saddle bows, and wore them over their hats, while riding in the ranks.

—First Lieutenant James Connor, *United States Army*

I never heard Anthony express himself except exultingly over the battle of Sand Creek or the arrival of troops to give battle.

—Harry Richmond, *United States Army*

Congressional Statement

In Washington, the Joint Special Committee of the two houses of Congress conduct an official inquiry into the circumstances of the Sand Creek Massacre. They determine that the crime was premeditated, citing testimony of "the fiendish malignity and cruelty of the officers who had so sedulously and carefully plotted the massacre." Yet none of the guilty were ever convicted.

It is difficult to believe that beings in the form of men, and disgracing the uniforms of United States soldiers and officers, could commit or countenance the commission of such acts of cruelty and barbarity. . . . The hatred of the whites to the Indians would seem to have been inflamed and excited to the utmost. . . . Governor [Evans] in a proclamation calls upon all "either individually or in such parties as they may organize, to kill and destroy as enemies of the country, wherever they may be found, all such hostile Indians." . . . What Indians he would ever term friendly it is impossible to tell. His testimony . . . was characterized by such prevarication and shuffling as has been shown by no witness they have examined during the four years they have been engaged in their investigations. . . .

As to Colonel Chivington, your committee can hardly find fitting terms to describe his conduct. Wearing the uniform of the United States, which should be the emblem of justice and humanity . . . he deliberately planned and executed a foul and dastardly massacre which would have disgraced the veriest savage among those who were the victims of his cruelty. Having full knowledge of their friendly character, having himself been instrumental to some extent in placing them in their position of fancied security, he took advantage of their inapprehension . . . to gratify the worst passions that ever cursed the heart of men . . . the truth is that he surprised and murdered, in cold blood, the unsuspecting men, women, and children on Sand Creek . . . and then returned to Denver and boasted of the brave deeds he and the men under his command had performed.

—Joint Special Committee of United States Congress

Land Greed: *Removal, Reservations, Restriction*

The United States government pursues its plan to relocate Indian nations from coveted lands to Indian Territory. The Konze are robbed of Kansas; the Quapaw forced out of Arkansas. The Kiowa, Comanche, Southern Cheyenne, and Arapaho are forced onto shrunken islands in their former territory, their movement restricted, their freedom curtailed. Of the scores of nations relocated to Indian Territory, few receive more attention than the

Ponca, whose resistance against removal prompts the landmark U.S. court decision of Judge Elmer Dundy that an Indian is indeed a person and therefore guaranteed rights under the law. Yet removals occur anyway. All is effected by treaties, all looks legal. Settlers swarm around remaining Indian lands like sharks with the taste of blood.

Be-che-go, great father, you treat my people like a flock of turkeys. You come into our dwelling places and scare us out. We fly over and alight on another stream, but no sooner do we get well settled than again you come along and drive us farther and farther. . . .   —Allegawahu, *Konze*

The land we now live on, belonged to our forefathers. If we leave it, where shall we go to? . . . Since you have expressed a desire for us to remove, the tears have flowed copiously from my aged eyes. To leave my natal soil, and go among red men who are aliens to our race, is throwing us like outcasts upon the world. . . . Have mercy—send us not there.
                                        —Heckaton, *Quapaw*

When I was a boy, still a little child, the country which the Southern Arapahoes claim as theirs was north of the Arkansas River, from there to the Republican River and back to the Rocky Mountains. That was the country my father lived in. . . . Then the whites came into our country. The whites wronged us; they were the first to commit a wrong, before we had ever injured them. . . . They crowded us out from the country we had been roaming in most, and moved us down toward the heads of the South Platte and the heads of the Republican. Then the white people crowded upon us again, and gave us a reservation in the Purgatoire country, and told us that was to be our home. But afterward we were taken away from there and brought here, and told that this was to be our reservation. . . .　—Powderface, *Southern Arapaho*

. . . [the] chiefs made a treaty with the Government and kept a piece about as big as a hog-pen. . . . I cannot live up in the air, nor in the water; if I go into the water I sink, if I go into the air I fall. I believe [the Otoe] were right when they said we would rather be naked and have our toes sticking out but let us have the land as it is, and have a home as long as there is an Otoe under Heaven . . . we don't like to see our people running after a home like calves running on the prairies.

—Mitchel Deroin, *Otoe*

The soldiers came to the borders of the village and forced us across the Niobrara to the other side, just as one would drive a herd of ponies; and the soldiers pushed us on. . . . And I said, "If I have to go, I'll go to that land. Let the soldiers go away. . . ." . . . We found the land [in Indian Territory] . . . was bad and we were dying one after another, and we said, "What man will take pity on us?"　—White Eagle, *Ponca*

I thought God intended us to live, but I was mistaken. God intends to give our country to the White people, and we are to die. It may be well; it may be well. I do not protest. But let our bones be mingled together in the earth where our forefathers lie, and on which we lived so many years and were happy.

—Machunazha (Standing Bear), *Ponca*

[My] hand is not the color of yours; but if I prick it the blood will flow and I shall feel pain. The blood is the color of yours. God made me, and I am a man. I never committed a crime. . . .

I seem to be standing on the bank of a great river with my wife and little girl by my side. I cannot cross the river, and impassable cliffs rise behind me. I hear the noise of great waters; I look and see a flood coming. The water rises to our feet, and then to our knees. My little girl stretches her hands to me and cries, "Save me!" I stand where no member of my race ever stood before. There is no tradition to guide me. The chiefs who have preceded me knew nothing of the circumstances that surround me. I only hear my little girl say, "Save me!"

In despair, I look toward the cliffs behind me. I seem to see a dim trail that may lead to a way of life; but no Indian ever passed over that trail. It looks to be impassable. I make the attempt. I take my child by the hand, and my wife follows me. Our hands and our feet are torn by the sharp rocks, and our trail is marked by our blood. At last, I see a rift in the rocks. A little way beyond there are green prairies. The Swift Running Water pours down between the green islands. There are the graves of my fathers. There again we will pitch our tepee and build our fires. I see the light of the world just ahead.

But in the center of that path there stands a man. Behind him I see soldiers like the leaves of the trees. If that man gives permission, I may pass on to life and liberty. If he refuses, I must go back and sink forever beneath the raging flood. . . .

You are that man!

—Machunazha (Standing Bear), *Ponca*, to United States District Court Judge Elmer Dundy

Satanta outwitted the U.S. military at every turn, and for this he was eliminated. The Kiowa remember him as a fun-loving and dedicated family man.

I have heard that you intend to settle us on a reservation near the mountains. I don't want to settle. I love to roam over the prairies. There I feel free and happy, but when we settle down we grow pale and die. I have laid aside my lance, bow, and shield, and yet I feel safe in your presence. I have told you the truth. I have no little lies hid about me, but I don't know how it is with the commissioners. Are they as clear as I am? A long time ago this land belonged to our fathers; but when I go up to the river I see camps of soldiers on its banks. These soldiers cut down my timber; they kill my buffalo; and when I see that, my heart feels like bursting. . . .

—Satanta, *Kiowa*

But there are things which you have said to me which I do not like. They are not sweet like sugar, but bitter like gourds. You said that you wanted to put us upon a reservation, to build us houses and make us medicine lodges. I do not want them. I was born upon the prairie, where the wind blew free and there was nothing to break the light of the sun. I was born where there were no enclosures and where everything drew a free breath. I want to die there and not within walls. I know every stream and every wood between the Rio Grande and the Arkansas. I have hunted and lived over that country. I lived like my fathers before me, and, like them, I lived happily. . . . So, why do you ask us to leave the rivers, and the sun, and the wind, and live in houses? . . . Do not speak of it more. . . . But it is too late. The white man has the country which we loved, and we only wish to wander on the prairie until we die.   —Parrawasamen (Ten Bears), *Comanche*

Buffalo Wars (1870)

Just when it is that the United States War Department decides to dispense with negotiation and starve Indian nations into submission is not clear. Perhaps it is a trick learned from the germ warfare practiced during Pontiac's alliance. It is also reminiscent of the destruction of the vast intertribal hunting ground of Kentucky. Whatever the precedent, it is decided that starvation works swiftly and saves the War Department much time and money. In fact, starvation makes money. The demand for buffalo hides soars. Tanners, freighters, and ammunition manufacturers turn a profit hand over fist. In 1870 the powerful Sharps breech-loading buffalo guns add a dramatic touch to the extermination policy. Hunters brag that the Sharps can shoot a buffalo at a distance of five miles. That same year, two million buffalo are killed on the southern Plains.

[The buffalo hunters] have done more . . . to settle the vexed Indian question than the entire regular army. . . . For the sake of lasting peace, let them kill, skin, and sell until the buffalos are exterminated.

— General Philip H. Sheridan, *United States Army*

Kill every buffalo you can. Every buffalo dead is an Indian gone.　　　　— Colonel R. I. Dodge, *United States Army*

Has the white man become a child that he should recklessly kill and not eat? When the red men slay game, they do so that they may live and not starve.　　　　— Satanta, *Kiowa*

Everything the Kiowas had came from the buffalo. Our tipis
were made of buffalo hides, so were our clothes and mocca-
sins. We ate buffalo meat. [Our] containers were made of
hide, or of bladders or stomachs. The buffalo were the life of
the Kiowas.   —Old Lady Horse, *Kiowa*

The Staked Plains   (1871)

As starvation forces southern Plains nations onto reservations,
many continue to resist. Kiowa under the leadership of Lone Wolf
defy the United States government by maintaining their sovereignty and freedom. They will not live in confinement under government supervision. Among them is Satanta, fast gaining a
reputation for outmaneuvering the military. He bugles counter-
commands during U.S. cavalry charges, throwing them into confusion. In full view, he drives off their horses, then delivers the
officers a sweeping bow. His intelligence mocks them. They know
it. They feel it. They burn with it. Satanta will be made to pay. To
the military, he is a scapegoat for every crime committed on the
southern Plains, whether or not he has been anywhere nearby.

Hunger forces Satanta to lead a raid on a mule train in Texas.
He is caught. Satank—whose son was killed by Texans—and
Ădoe'et also are implicated. Crammed into a tiny crawl space beneath the barracks of Fort Sill, they wait in darkness. The air is
suffocating; they are hungry. Hauled out after twelve days to be
taken to Texas for "trial," they stand squinting in the blinding
light of the sun. Prominent military officials recommend hanging. Satank, although an old man, offers so much resistance
that he is separated from the others. As the wagons bearing
them rumble out of Fort Sill, Satank delivers a parting message
to his people. Nearing a tree in the road, he breaks free from his
guard. Moments later, his body riddled with bullets, Satank is
dead. In a few short years, Satanta will join him. The government

claims he has committed suicide by leaping from his prison window. But the Kiowa know better. No one has broken Satanta's spirit.

This is our country. We have always lived in it. We always had plenty to eat because the land was full of buffalo. We were happy. . . . Then you came. First the traders. That is all right for we were in need of blankets and kettles. Then the soldiers came. We can understand that for we are soldiers. Then other men came. They are farmers. They want to work the land. That is not all right. Land doesn't want to be worked. Land gives you what you need if you are smart enough to take it. This is good land but it is our land. We know how to take what it gives us. We don't want these people working this land. You kill the land by taking things out of it. . . . We have to protect ourselves. We have to save our country. We have to fight for what is ours.　　　　　　　　　　—Satanta, *Kiowa*

Yes, I led in that raid. I have repeatedly asked for arms and ammunition, which have not been furnished. I have made many other requests which have not been granted. You do not listen to my talk. The white people are preparing to build a railroad through our country, which will not be permitted. Some years ago they took us by the hair and pulled us here close to Texas where we have to fight them. More recently I was arrested by the soldiers and kept in confinement several days. But that is played out now. There is never to be any more Kiowa Indians arrested. I want you to remember that. On account of these grievances, a short time ago I took about a hundred of my warriors to Texas, whom I wished to teach how to fight.　　　　　　　　　　—Satanta, *Kiowa*

I wish to send a little message by you to my people. Tell my people that I am dead. I died the first day out from Fort Sill. My bones will be lying on the side of the road. I wish my people to gather them up and take them home.

—Satank, *Kiowa*

I think all the old things will soon be dead. There is an end to one kind of living for the Kiowas. Things will never be as before. —Wood Fire, *Kiowa*

Crow Country

The Crow country is a good country. The [Creator] put it exactly in the right place; while you are in it you fare well; whenever you are out of it, whichever way you travel, you fare worse. . . . The Crow country is exactly in the right place. It has snowy mountains and sunny plains; all kinds of climates and good things for every season. When the summer heats scorch the prairies, you can draw up under the mountains, where the air is sweet and cool, the grasses fresh, and the bright streams come tumbling out of the snowbanks. There you can hunt the elk, the deer, and the antelope, when their skins are fit for dressing; there you will find plenty of white bear and mountain sheep. . . . The Crow country is exactly in the right place. —Arapooish, *Absaroka*

They spoke very loudly when they said their laws were made for everybody; but we soon learned that although they expected us to keep them, they thought nothing of breaking them themselves. They told us not to drink whisky, yet they

Nineteenth-century photograph of a Crow woman,
taken by Edward Curtis.

made it themselves and traded it to us for furs and robes until both were nearly gone. Their Wise Ones said we might have their religion . . . we saw that the white man did not take his religion any more seriously than he did his laws, and that he kept both of them just behind him, like Helpers, to use when they might do him good. . . . These were not our ways. We kept the laws we made and lived our religion. We have never been able to understand the white man, who fools nobody but himself.

—Aleekchea-ahoosh (Plenty Coups), *Absaroka*

The Great Father in Washington sent you here about this land. The soil you see is not ordinary soil—it is the dust of the blood, the flesh, and bones of our ancestors. We fought and bled and died to keep other Indians from taking it, and we fought and bled and died helping the whites. You will have to dig down through the surface before you can find nature's earth, as the upper portion is Crow. The land, as it is, is my blood and my dead; it is consecrated, and I do not want to give up any portion of it.   —Curly, *Absaroka*

The Blackfeet

. . . what the Blackrobe tells us is the truth? How is it that he tells the truth when the truth has never come from the mouth of a single white man?   —Seen-From-Afar, *Blood*

We are going after the buffalo. The whites must be stronger than we are to turn us back and if that happens, then we will camp along the boundary line and steal every horse and drive off every head of stock that crosses until the whites allow us in the country which belongs to us.   —One Spot, *Blood*

Our land is more valuable than your money. It will last forever. It will not even perish by the flames of fire. As long as the sun shines and the waters flow, this land will be here to give life to men and animals. We cannot sell the lives of men and animals. It was put here for us by the Great Spirit and we cannot sell it because it does not belong to us. You can count your money and burn it within the nod of a buffalo's head, but only the Great Spirit can count the grains of sand and the blades of grass on the plains. As a present to you, we will give you anything we have that you can take with you; but the land, never.   —Crowfoot, *Blackfoot*

The Agency issued rations, but not nearly enough to keep a person alive. Each week they gave out a little flour and sugar and sometimes a small piece of meat. On Friday they would butcher maybe two or three cows from the Agency herd. . . . But when you divide a couple of beeves up amongst about three thousand people, nobody gets very much. Thursday we called Nothing-Happens-Day, because by then all the people would be starving and just sitting around waiting for the next rations. Every day people died of starvation, and a lot of others died because they were too weak to resist pneumonia and other diseases.   —White Calf, *Piegan*

Smoky Hill and Powder River Roads   (1866)

. . . three years will see the alternative of war eliminated from the Indian question, and the most powerful and hostile bands of to-day thrown in entire helplessness on the mercy of the Government. Indeed, the progress of two years more, if not of another summer, on the Northern Pacific Railroad will of itself completely solve the great Sioux problem, and leave the ninety thousand Indians ranging between the two trans-continental lines as incapable of resisting the Government as are the Indians of New York or Massachusetts. Columns moving north from the Union Pacific, and south from the Northern Pacific, would crush the Sioux and their confederates as between the upper and the nether mill-stone; while the rapid movement of troops along the northern line would prevent the escape of the savages. . . .
—Report of the commissioners of Indian Affairs

By these my people have suffered. We have been brought up to live on wild game, I and my brothers. When the iron roads came they scared away the game. All we want is to have this stopped [in the Platte and Smoky Hill]. . . . If the whites would let the game alone we can all live.
—Man-Who-Walks-Under-The-Ground, *Oglala*

[Washington should] open up the entire region so long dedicated to the sloth and sterility of Indian worthlessness, and break down the barriers which have barred industry and civilization. It would hasten the inevitable day when the Indian shall be driven utterly from the rich heritage which he neither uses or improves himself, nor allows others better than him to use.   —Editorial, *Battle River Pilot*

In 1866, Red Cloud succeeded in forcing the United States to remove
all of its forts along the Bozeman Trail in Lakota territory, vowing
that he would rather die fighting than of starvation.

The white men have crowded the Indians back year by year until we are forced to live in a small country north of the Platte, and now our last hunting grounds, the home of the People, is to be taken from us. Our women and children will starve, but for my part I prefer to die fighting than by starvation. —Mahpiua Luta (Red Cloud), *Oglala*

Whose voice was first heard in this land? It was the red people.... The Great Father has sent his people out there and left me nothing but an island.... The white people have sprinkled blood on the blades of grass about the line of fort Fetterman. Tell the Great Father to remove that fort, then we will be peaceful and there will be no more trouble. I have got two mountains in that country—Black Hills and Big Horn—I want no roads there. There have been stakes driven in that country, and I want them removed. I have told these things three times, and I now have come here to tell them for the fourth time.

—Mahpiua Luta (Red Cloud), *Oglala*

I am an Oglalla chief. We are few in number, but have no bad habits.... The cause of all the trouble at the north is the Powder River road, and at the south the Smoky Hill. These roads run off what little game we have left. We want these roads stopped and the soldiers kept out. Let there be peace.... —Pawnee Killer, *Oglala*

There is no fun in the subject about which we are to speak. You commissioners have not come for nothing.... We will tell you of our troubles, and the cause. The great grandfather has made roads North and South. To the roads on the rivers we have no objection. War came from making the roads through the country. These roads scare away all the game. . . . We look to the game; it is all we care for, and we wish to live on it as long as there is any in the country.

—Sinte Gleshka (Spotted Tail), *Sichangu*

Treaty Councils

Treaty councils are interesting entertainment for the callous-hearted. Polished performances are delivered by an accomplished cast of characters: smooth-talking commissioners; slick politicians; military officers; interpreters with little compunction to translate correctly; "paper chiefs" and "yes men"—given medals and certificates of leadership by the government as reward for their fidelity; "squaw men" and traders and contractors and Indian agents who circle hungrily, looking for profit; newspaper reporters; missionaries; and eastern philanthropists who guarantee Indian rights by destroying their culture. The so-called "hostile" bands do not sign treaties. This isn't their style of politics. But the poor and the starving have learned the proper words to say to receive the little food that will keep them from dying. Cajolery, endless demands, bribery, and even forgery mark the treaty sessions. The show always ends the same: the papers are signed, the commissioners exit with a bow. And as the curtain falls, the Indian nations know that again they have been robbed.

SENATOR: What particular part of your country do you wish to give?

LITTLE CHIEF (Assiniboin): The [Creator] brought, and made, and placed us in this country; we always lived between here and the Yellowstone. . . . I understand that the committee wants to put us on a new reservation.

SENATOR: Your reservation is too large, and you must learn to live by farming. . . . The best thing you can do is to get rid of so many ponies and get cattle for them—it is better to have more cattle and less ponies.

LITTLE CHIEF: Good plan.

SENATOR: . . . Do you think it is better for your people to have each a farm or to roam over the reservation as you do to-day? . . . Would you like a separate reservation?

LITTLE CHIEF: We want to live with the [Atsina].

SENATOR: The [Atsina] have told us where they want to live, now tell us where you want to live.

LITTLE CHIEF: Assinaboines want [the] reservation to extend east to [the] mouth of Milk River.

SENATOR: Your reservation is too large.

LITTLE CHIEF: Our reservation is not very great, just enough to live on. . . . We don't like to leave our country. . . . I am talking for our home.

SENATOR: We do not want to take your home from you; only want to give you a smaller home and pay you for the land you give us. . . . We want to give you a title for your homes, a deed, like the white man has. . . .

When I went to Washington last winter, the Great Father showed me my reservation . . . and I told him then it was not right. [Rev. Samuel] Hinman came here again and asked some more people to sign this paper, and told them how big the reservation was, and that he had put it down in writing. . . . Hinman lies, and we want to take the names of all the men who signed the paper off of it. The Great Father has given me a map of this country which I have, and I don't want to sell any portion of it at all. . . .

The young ones know they have to live here, and he forced them to sign the paper. That is the reason I said they were crying. . . . Mr. Hinman told the Indians that if they did not sign they would not receive any rations or annuities, and, furthermore, they would send them to the Indian Territory; and if I did not sign it I would go to the guard-house.

—Mahpiua Luta (Red Cloud), *Oglala*

What is it they want of us at this time? They want us to give up another chunk of our tribal land. This is not the first time nor the last time. They will try to gain possession of the last piece of ground we possess . . . the Great Father's representatives have again brought with them a well-worded paper, containing just what they want but ignoring our wishes in the matter . . . we who realize that our children and grandchildren may live a little longer must necessarily look ahead and flatly reject the proposition. I, for one, am bitterly opposed to it.   —Tatanka Yotanka (Sitting Bull), *Hunkpapa*

Tell the Grandfather at Washington not to let white men come into our country. That is what they promised in their treaty. . . . If you think you are buying the right to go through our country with your annuities, keep them, we do not want them. What good are they, anyway?

—Bear Ribs, *Hunkpapa*

JOHN GLASS (Hunkpapa): We talked with them about the land they wanted, and they said they would give us cows. . . . I wanted . . . to keep [the] land. When I was talking to them the Indians all at once rushed up from behind me and signed the paper, and everything was so mixed up, I didn't know what I was doing until after I had signed the paper.

Q. Did you expect to have the land and the cows both?

A. No; we wanted nothing but our land.

Q. You did not want the cows at all?

A. Of course we preferred to keep our land. . . .

Q. Which would you rather have, the 25,000 cows or the land?

A. We prefer the land.

Q. What made the Indians behind you rush up to sign the paper if they did not want to give up the land for the cows?

A. The white men talked in a threatening way and the crowd of Indians behind me got frightened and rushed up and signed the paper. . . . Bishop Marty . . . stood before us and told us if we did not sign it we might as well take a knife and stab ourselves; the consequences would be equally as bad. That is what frightened the Indians. . . . All these men present know that was the reason they went up and signed that paper.

Q. What did the commissioners say to frighten the Indians?

A. They told us they could send us away from here to a different country if they wished to do it. . . .

Q. Would any of the Indians like to take their names off of the paper if they could?

A. Yes, sir.

Q. Would you not be willing to let the United States have some of your land if you could get pay enough for it?

A. We have not offered our land for sale. . . .

Q. Do you think it would be better to let the United States Government have some of it, and take a good many cows for it?

To Washington (1870)

In protest of the violation of their sovereign rights, defined by the second Treaty of Fort Laramie, Red Cloud of the Oglala nation travels to Washington to meet with President Ulysses S. Grant. But Grant's reception is cool, and the Oglala leader is horrified to learn that sections of the 1868 Fort Laramie treaty were never interpreted correctly.

Red Cloud's delegation asks to be returned to their nation immediately. Instead, the government forces them into boxcars bound for New York City, hoping that the bustling crowds and overwhelming proof of American civilization will awe them into submission. The attempt fails. Before capacity crowds at Cooper Union, Red Cloud delivers an impassioned address for justice.

Nevertheless, on December 6, 1875, all Teton nations are ordered onto specially designated reservations, away from the gold-rich areas of the Black Hills. Those who do not comply are considered hostile and at war with the United States.

The Great Father that made us both wishes peace to be kept; we want to keep peace. Will you help us? In 1868 men came out and brought papers. We could not read them, and they did not tell us what was in them. We thought the treaty was to remove the forts, and that we should then cease from fighting. . . . When I reached Washington, the Great Father explained to me what the treaty was, and showed me that the interpreters had deceived me. All I want is right and justice. I have tried to get from the Great Father what is right and just. I have not altogether succeeded. I want you to help me get what is right and just. . . . Look at me, I am poor and naked, but I am the Chief of the nation. We do not want riches but we do want to train our children right. Riches

would do us no good. We could not take them with us to the other world. We do not want riches, we want peace and love.
—Mahpiua Luta (Red Cloud), *Oglala*

Tell them at Washington if they have one man who speaks the truth to send him to me, and I will listen to what he has to say. —Tatanka Yotanka (Sitting Bull), *Hunkpapa*

Now my friends this land belongs to me, and you have land of your own that belongs to you; that you can keep, and can do anything you wish on that land, because it belongs to you. Suppose I come on your land and tell you to do this and that way; you would not like me to come there to your place and tell you any such thing as that. Now look at me, this land here belongs to me and to my people, and I want to keep them on that land, and help them to live there the best way I know how. . . . The Great Father sends men out here, and of course there are a great many rascals between the Great Father and the Indians, who try to take this land from us, but I have no land to spare. —White Thunder, *Sichangu*

This war did not spring up here in our land. It was brought upon us by the children of the Great Father, who came to take our land from us without [a] price, and who do a great many evil things. The Great Father and his children are to blame for this trouble. . . . It has been our wish to live here [in our country] peaceably, but the Great Father has filled it with soldiers who think only of our death. Some of our people who have gone from here in order that they may have a change, and others who have gone north to hunt, have been attacked by the soldiers from other directions; and now, when they are willing to come back, the soldiers stand between them and keep them from coming home. It seems to me there is a better way than this. When people come to trouble, it is better for both parties to come together without arms and talk it over and find some peaceful way to settle [it].　　—Sinte Gleshka (Spotted Tail), *Sichangu*

Black Hills Gold　(1875)

Isn't Black Hills gold pretty? Don't the eastern ladies love to wear it! Does its value increase with the agony it produces? . . . because it tears a people's heart out to see it mined? . . . because it scars the lands they hold sacred?

One does not sell the earth upon which the people walk.
　　　　　　　—Tashunka Witko (Crazy Horse), *Oglala*

Our tribe were to have a permanent home in our favorite Black Hills country. We were promised that all white people would be kept away from us there. But after we had been there a few years, General Custer and his soldiers came there and found gold. Many white people crowded in, wanting to get the gold. . . . Soldiers came and told us we would have to move to another part of the country and let the white people have this land where was the gold.
　　　　　　　　　　　—Iron Teeth, *Northern Cheyenne*

The land known as the Black Hills is considered by the Indians as the center of their land. The ten nations of Sioux are looking toward that as the center of their land.
　　　　　　—Tatoke Inyanke (Running Antelope), *Hunkpapa*

You have driven away our game and our means of livelihood out of the country, until now we have nothing left that is valuable except the hills that you ask us to give up . . . and when we give these up to the Great Father we know that we give up the last thing that is valuable either to us or the white people. . . .

—Wanigi Ska (White Ghost), *Lower Yanktonai*

Look at me, and look at the earth. Which is the oldest, do you think? The earth, and I was born on it. . . . It does not belong to us alone: it was our fathers', and should be our children's after us. When I received it, it was all in one piece, and so I hold it. If the white men take my country, where can I go? I have nowhere to go. I cannot spare it, and I love it very much. Let us alone. That is what they promised in their treaty—to let us alone. What is this white soldier doing here? What did he come for? To spy out the land, and to find a good place for a fort and a road, and to dig out gold.

—Tatanka Yotanka (Sitting Bull), *Hunkpapa*

Custer Battle   (1876)

Hunkpapa leader Sitting Bull and his allies do not sign treaties; they do not sell their lands; they do not move onto reservations. Defectors from the agencies join them; their numbers grow by the thousands. Gall, Crazy Horse, and Two Moons join Sitting Bull. The combined encampment stretches three miles along the Bighorn River. They are marked by the government; they are the "hostiles" though they have committed no crime. They are strong, but they wish to live in peace. They do not deserve the wrath of the Seventh Cavalry marching against them under General George Armstrong Custer. After Custer's death, Sitting Bull is maligned by the world; but those who knew him agreed they knew greatness.

I knew this man; knew him in relation to his high office among his people and in his elements as a man. As to his office or rank I honored him. He filled a station older than human records, as a man I admired him. He represented in person, in manners, in mind and in the heroism of his spirit the highest type of a race which in many and rare virtues stands peer among the noblest races of the world.

—Rev. W. H. Murray, *United States*

Yet hear me, people, we have now to deal with another race— small and feeble when our fathers first met them, but now great and overbearing. . . .

They claim this mother of ours, the earth, for their own, and fence their neighbors away; they deface her with their buildings and their refuse. That nation is like a spring freshet that overruns its banks and destroys all who are in its path. We cannot dwell side by side.

. . . My brothers, shall we submit or shall we say to them: "First kill me before you take possession of my Fatherland. . . ."   —Tatanka Yotanka (Sitting Bull), *Hunkpapa*

. . . we all went over the divide and camped in the valley of [the] Little Horn. Everybody thought, "Now we are out of the white man's country. He can live there, we will live here." . . . I went to water my horses at the creek, and washed them off with cool water, then took a swim myself. I came back to the camp afoot. When I got near my lodge, I looked up the Little

Horn towards Sitting Bull's camp. I saw a great dust rising. It looked like a whirlwind. . . . I saw flags come up over the hill to the east. . . . Then the soldiers rose all at once . . . the Sioux rode up the ridge on all sides, riding very fast. The Cheyennes went up the left way. Then the shooting was quick, quick. . . . We circled all round . . . swirling like water round a stone. . . . Soldiers in line drop, but one man rides up and down the line—all the time shouting. He rode a sorrel horse with white face and white fore-legs. I don't know who he was. He was a brave man. . . .

All the soldiers were now killed, and . . . were left where they fell. We had no dance that night. We were sorrowful.

—Two Moons, *Northern Cheyenne*

Removal of the Northern Cheyenne (1877)

The Northern Cheyenne are allies of the Teton Lakota. They, too, oppose the Smoky Hill and Powder River roads, which drive away the game from the northern Plains. They, too, defended themselves along the Little Bighorn River against General Custer. They were there when Custer died. And they will pay. In the winter of 1876, Dull Knife's camp is attacked by the United States Army. The following year, the Northern Cheyenne are removed to a reservation in Oklahoma. But the agency is infested with malaria, and the promised food supplies are never issued. The Cheyenne starve.

Our men did not want to fight. They wanted to be left alone so they might get food and skins to provide for their families. . . . But we were not allowed to live in quiet. When the snow had fallen deep, a great band of soldiers came. They rode right into our camp and shot women and children as well as men. . . . We who could do so ran away . . . my hus-

band and our older son kept behind and fought off the soldiers. . . . I saw him fall, and his horse went away from him.
I wanted to go back to him, but my two sons made me go on
away with my three daughters. From the hilltops we Cheyennes looked back and saw all of our lodges and everything in
them being burned into nothing but smoke and ashes. . . . I
was afraid of all white men soldiers. It seemed to me they
represented the most extreme cruelty. They had just killed
my husband and had burned our whole village. There was in
my mind a clear recollection of a time . . . when they had
killed and scalped many of our women and children in a
peaceable camp [at Sand Creek]. . . . At that time I had seen
a friend of mine, a woman, crawling along on the ground,
shot, scalped, crazy, but not yet dead. After that, I always
thought of her when I saw white men soldiers.

—Iron Teeth, *Northern Cheyenne*

We were *always* hungry; we *never* had enough. When they
that were sick once in a while felt as though they could eat
something, we had nothing to give them. . . . When winter
came we went out on a buffalo hunt and nearly starved; we
could not find any game . . . the children died of a disease we
never knew anything about before; they broke out in blotches
and dots all over, their noses would bleed and their heads
split open. . . .   —Wild Hog, *Northern Cheyenne*

Exodus (1878)

The Cheyenne are told that if they do not like Indian Territory,
they can return to their old homes. This is only rhetoric. No Cheyenne is allowed off of the reservation boundary—not even to
hunt—without permission.

A hot September wind gusts across the southern Plains. The Cheyenne have decided how they will die; the agent will be robbed of the glory. A slow train of several hundred sick and weakened Cheyenne under Little Wolf and Dull Knife head resolutely north, preferring death by the soldiers who will follow, than the slow agony of sickness and starvation. Thirteen hundred soldiers and civilians swarm after them, and America is electrified with the news that the Northern Cheyenne have "broken out." They are on the run. The Cheyenne drop from soldiers' bullets; the chase ends with surrender at Fort Robinson, Nebraska. But still the Cheyenne refuse to return to Indian Territory.

In a tiny prison cell thirty feet square are the Northern Cheyenne—forty-three men, twenty-nine women, and twenty children. Daily the harsh question, "Will you return south?" Daily the quiet answer, "No." Food is cut off. Then water. For eleven days, the Cheyenne do not eat. For three days, they do not drink. There is nothing to do but sit, huddled on the cold prison floor, in dignity.

All we ask is to be allowed to live, and to live in peace. . . . We bowed to the will of the Great Father and went far into the south where he told us to go. There we found a Cheyenne cannot live. Sickness came among us that made mourning in every lodge. Then the treaty promises were broken and our rations were short. . . . To stay there meant that all of us would die . . . [so] we thought it better to die fighting to regain our old homes than to perish of sickness. Then our march was begun. The rest you know. . . . You may kill me here; but you cannot make me go back. We will not go. The only way to get us there is to come in here with clubs and knock us on the head, and drag us out and take us down there dead.

—Tahmelapashme (Dull Knife), *Northern Cheyenne*

Breakout (1879)

Wild Hog, Old Crow, and Left Hand return the stare of the commanding officer at Fort Robinson. They say if they return to Indian Territory, it will not be in the winter. They will do so only in the spring. They have inadequate clothing—they will freeze. They have no food—they will starve. The interrogation is over. Wild Hog, Old Crow, and Left Hand are hauled away in irons.

From the motions of the soldiers I thought they were going to kill me; then I concluded I would stab myself. I thought I would rather kill myself than be killed by anybody else. Then the soldiers sprang at me and grabbed my arm . . . when I and these other men were called out and ironed and taken away they thought we were to be killed, and not only we, but those who remained behind; and if they were to die anyway, they determined to sell their lives as dearly as possible.

—Wild Hog, *Northern Cheyenne*

The men decided to break out of this jail. The women were willing. It was considered that some of us, perhaps many of us, would be killed. But it was hoped that many would escape and get away to join other Indians somewhere. . . . Four of my women friends were shot to death the night we broke out. I do not know how many men and children were killed. Some of the people were never seen again after that night. . . .

—Iron Teeth, *Northern Cheyenne*

From the actions of the soldiers outside who had captured the others, we who were inside thought they were getting ready to commence shooting us down. Some soldiers came to the door and said, "We want your women and children to come out"; but the young men surrounded their women and children, and would not allow them to go out. Then we all consulted together and decided that, rather than be shot down in there, we would break out. Just as soon as we broke out, the first shot was fired by the soldiers. When we broke out, it was not with the intention of doing harm to anybody, but to try to get away. The soldiers fired on us, and then it was just like shooting cattle. . . .

—Tangled Hair, *Northern Cheyenne*

The Assassination of Sitting Bull   (1890)

The land grabbers wanted the Indian lands. The lying, thieving Indian agents wanted silence touching past thefts and immunity to continue their thieving. The renegades from their people among the Indian police wanted an opportunity to show their power over a man who despised them as renegades, and whom, therefore, they hated. The public opinion of the frontier—the outgrowth of ignorance, credulity and selfish greed—more than assented to a plan to rid the country of one who while he lived, so great was he in fame and in fact, must forever stand as a reminder of wars passed and a threat of war to come. Out of all these and other causes peculiar to the condition of things there localized . . . was born, as Milton's Death was born, from Satan to Sin, the plot to kill him.

—Rev. W. H. Murray, *United States*

I read that the great Sioux [leader] was dead, that he was set upon in the midst of his family, with his wives and children and relatives around him, that he had committed no overt act of war . . . [by] a company of Indians—yclept Indian police—many of them despised renegades from his own tribe and enemies of his under cover of the United States cavalry . . . they went to kill—had killed him, and I said—understanding the conditions and circumstances better than some—I said: "That is murder." And then I read in a great journal that "everybody is well satisfied with his death." And I cried out against the saying as I had against the deed.

I read that they have buried his body like a dog's—without funeral rites. . . . That is the deed of to-day. That is the best that this generation has to give to this noble historic character, this man who in his person ends the line of aboriginal sanctities older than the religion of Christian or Jew. Very Well. So let it stand for the present. But there is a generation coming that shall reverse this judgment of ours. Our children shall build monuments to those whom we stoned, and the great aboriginals whom we killed will be counted by the future American as among the historic characters of the Continent . . . for as the Lord liveth and my soul liveth a monument shall be builded on that spot before many years—if I live—inscribed to the memory of the last great Prophet of the Sioux. . . .

—Fletcher Johnson, *United States*

I wish all to know that I do not propose to sell any part of my country, nor will I have the whites cutting our timber along the rivers, more especially the oak. I am particularly fond of the little groves of oak trees. I love to look at them, because they endure the wintry storm and the summer's heat and—not unlike ourselves—seem to flourish by them.

—Tatanka Yotanka (Sitting Bull), *Hunkpapa*

The wise and respected Hunkpapa leader Sitting Bull was feared
by the U.S. military, who had him murdered by Indian police;
however, they could not prevent his memory from inspiring
countless generations of Lakota people.

When I was a boy the Sioux owned the world. The sun rose and set in their lands. They sent 10,000 men to battle. Where are the warriors to-day? Who slew them? Where are our lands? Who owns them? What white man can say I ever stole his lands or a penny of his money? Yet, they say I am a thief. . . . What white man has ever seen me drunk? . . . Who has ever seen me beat my wives or abuse my children? What law have I broken? Is it wrong for me to love my own? Is it wicked for me because my skin is red? Because I am a Sioux; because I was born where my fathers lived; because I would die for my people and my country?

—Tatanka Yotanka (Sitting Bull), *Hunkpapa*

To Understand America

The white man does not understand the Indian for the reason that he does not understand America. He is too far removed. . . . The roots of the tree of his life have not yet grasped the rock and soil. The white man is still troubled with primitive fears; he still has in his consciousness the perils of this frontier continent, some of its vastness not yet having yielded to his questing footsteps and inquiring eyes. . . . The man from Europe is still a foreigner and an alien. And he still hates the man who questioned his path across the continent. But in the Indian the spirit of the land is still vested; it will be until other men are able to divine and meet its rhythm. Men must be born and reborn to belong. Their bodies must be formed of the dust of their forefathers' bones.

—Standing Bear, *Oglala*

As yet I know of no species of plant, bird, or animal that were exterminated until the coming of the white man. For some years after the buffalo disappeared there still remained huge herds of antelope, but the hunter's work was no sooner done in the destruction of the buffalo than his attention was attracted toward the deer. . . . The white man considered natural animal life just as he did the natural man life upon this continent, as "pests." Plants which the Indian found beneficial were also "pests." There is no word in the Lakota vocabulary with the English meaning of this word . . . [the Indian] was . . . kin to all living things and he gave to all creatures equal rights with himself. Everything of earth was loved and reverenced. . . . [To the white man] the worth and right to live were his, thus he heartlessly destroyed. Forests were mowed down, the buffalo exterminated, the beaver driven to extinction and his wonderfully constructed dams dynamited, allowing flood waters to wreak further havoc, and the very birds of the air silenced. Great grassy plains that sweetened the air have been upturned; springs, streams, and lakes that lived no longer ago than my boyhood have dried, and a whole people harassed to degradation and death. The white man has come to be the symbol of extinction for all things natural to this continent. Between him and the animal there is no rapport and they have learned to flee from his approach, for they cannot live on the same ground.

—Standing Bear, *Oglala*

Ghost Dance (1890)

A dance appears among the Teton. Crowded on reservation concentration camps, the dance brings a flood of hope to many, but the white people begrudge them even this. They fear it, because they do not understand. That is sad, for they will never experience the euphoria of reliving life as it was, of seeing loved ones return, of feeling the earth renewed. All this the dance brings, but the white people do not know it.

The Indians must be killed as fast as they make an appearance and before they can do any damage. It is better to kill an innocent Indian occasionally than to take chances on goodness. To exterminate them it will be necessary to employ first class killers, regardless of expense. . . . The Indians continue to dance and defy the soldiers, and even to defy them to fight, and declare that they will continue to dance to their heart's content. And what does the government do? Send back for more ammunition and report that if the Indians will only stay on the agency that they are masters of the situation. . . . In the name of all that is sensible, why were these soldiers moved from all quarters of this continent if not to subdue this insolence of a savage race, to take their arms from them, to stop their infernal ghost dancing . . . ?

—Editorial, *Black Hills Daily Times*

You say, "If the United States army would kill a thousand or so of the dancing Indians there would be no more trouble." . . . The Indians have never taken kindly to the Christian religion as preached and practiced by the whites. Do you know why this is the case? Because the Good Father of all has given us a better religion—a religion . . . that is adapted to our wants. . . . You are anxious to get hold of our Messiah, so you can put him in irons. This you may do—in fact, you may crucify him as you did that other one, but you cannot convert the Indians to the Christian religion. . . . The white man's heaven is repulsive to the Indian nature, and if the white man's hell suits you, why, you keep it. I think there will be white rogues enough to fill it.

—Masse Hadjo, *Oglala*

There was no hope on earth, and God seemed to have forgotten us. Some one had . . . been talking of the Son of God, and said He had come.

The people did not know; they did not care. They snatched at the hope. They screamed like crazy men to Him for mercy. They caught at the promise they heard He had made.

The white men were frightened and called for soldiers. We had begged for life, and the white men thought we wanted theirs. We heard that soldiers were coming. We did not fear. We hoped that we could tell them our troubles and get help. A white man said the soldiers meant to kill us. We did not believe it. . . .   —Mahpiua Luta (Red Cloud), *Oglala*

. . . You whites assumed we were savages. You didn't understand our prayers. You didn't try to understand. When we sang our praises to the sun or moon or wind, you said we were worshipping idols. Without understanding, you condemned us as lost souls just because our form of worship was different from yours.   —Tatanga Mani (Walking Buffalo), *Assiniboin*

Wounded Knee   (1890)

Using the Ghost Dance as a pretext, government soldiers massacre a band of the Hokwozhu nation under the leadership of Big Foot, who is sick with pneumonia. Everyone knows that the Ghost Dance is only an excuse for murder. By 1890 killing Indians has become a national pastime.

Suddenly I heard a single shot from the direction of the troops—then three or four—a few more—and immediately a volley. At once came a general rattle of rifle firing. Then the Hotchkiss guns.

. . . the Hotchkiss guns . . . opened fire on the little central band of Indians—106 men . . . and 252 women and children. Every warrior, including Big Foot himself, who was ill in his tent with pneumonia, was killed or seriously wounded. . . . Indian women and children fled . . . some of them on up out . . . across the prairie, but soldiers followed them and shot them down mercilessly. . . . The boom of the Hotchkiss guns and rattle of the rifles . . . satisfied me that hardly an Indian would be left alive. . . . I had known definitely that not one single leading man among all the Sioux bands intended or wanted to fight. . . .   —Thomas Tibbles, *United States*

The men were separated, as has already been said, from the women, and they were surrounded by the soldiers . . . and then they turned their guns, Hotchkiss guns, etc., upon the women who were in the lodges standing there under a flag of truce, and of course as soon as they were fired upon they fled, the men fleeing in one direction and the women running in two different directions. . . . There was a woman with an infant in her arms who was killed as she almost touched the flag of truce, and the women and children of course were strewn all along the circular village until they were dispatched. Right near the flag of truce a mother was shot down with her infant; the child not knowing that its mother was dead was still nursing, and that especially was a very sad sight. The women as they were fleeing with their babies were killed together, shot right through, and the women who were very heavy with child were also killed . . . and after most all of them had been killed a cry was made that all those who were not killed or wounded should come forth and they would be safe. Little boys who were not wounded came out of their places of refuge, and as soon as they came in sight a number of soldiers surrounded them and butchered them there.

—American Horse, *Oglala*

It was a good winter day when all this happened. The sun was shining. But after the soldiers marched away from their dirty work, a heavy snow began to fall. The wind came up in the night. There was a big blizzard, and it grew very cold. The snow drifted deep in the crooked gulch, and it was one long grave of butchered women and children and babies, who had never done any harm and were only trying to run away.

—Black Elk, *Oglala*

Talk not of grief till thou hast seen the tears of warlike men.

—Maskepetoon (Crooked Arm), *Cree*

The Southwest

Every struggle, whether won or lost, strengthens us for the next to come. It is not good for people to have an easy life. They become weak and inefficient when they cease to struggle. Some need a series of defeats before developing the strength and courage to win a victory.

—*Victorio*, Chienne

T he overthrow of the Aztec Empire in 1521 found Spain in possession of the Valley of Mexico. Conquests rapidly enlarged her holdings into a vast territory checked in the north only by the forbidding Sonoran desert. In Mexico City, Indian traders from across this arid expanse spoke in glowing terms of nations whose cities lined the Rio Grande. In the markets of Mexico, the Sonoran traders unloaded the turquoise, buffalo hides, finely woven blankets, and exquisite pottery they had obtained there; and rumors circulated freely that the citizens of these nations lived in multistoried houses, ornamented their doors with turquoise, and drank from golden vessels. Spain was aroused by visions of wealth, and promptly outfitted an expedition; in 1540, Francisco Vásques de Coronado marched north toward the Rio Grande.

The Coronado entourage rivaled that of his contemporary Hernando de Soto, who at that moment was plundering his way across the Southeast. For a brief moment on the Plains, the two armies nearly met, neither aware of the presence of the other, but the Indian nations in the region knowing all too well of both.

Coronado's army reached the Zuñi town of Hawikuh in July 1540 and, after a full-scale assault upon the town in the name of the patron saint Santiago, wintered in the country of the Tiwa. Coronado established headquarters in a Tiwa village, forcing its residents out into the cold and at the same time demanding precious blankets and corn as tribute. The rape of a Tiwa woman was the final insult in a long list of atrocities committed by the Spanish that led to the "Tiwa War" of 1541. To ensure the submission of other towns, leaders from the neighboring pueblo of Pecos were chained in the plaza and forced to watch as two hundred Tiwa burned at the stake. Many fled into the snowy Sangre de Cristo (Blood of Christ) Mountains, preferring to starve or freeze to death rather than fall into the hands of the Spaniards. Others continued to fight from the fortified town of Moho, augmenting the death toll by many hundreds.

The following summer, Coronado made his way to the Plains, killed numerous innocent citizens of the Wichita nation, and took a woman captive. Marching back toward the Rio Grande, this woman hurled herself down a shallow ravine and fled across the Plains into Texas—unluckily running straight into the arms of de Soto's army, en route from the Bidai country to the Mississippi.

In 1542 Coronado returned to Mexico with his hands empty of gold but stained with the blood of many innocent victims. In 1598 Spain established the first permanent colony in New Mexico at San Juan. Governor Juan de Oñate set out immediately to subdue the Rio Grande nations and demand their submission. Although Oñate established peace with the Acoma, soldiers who followed his detachment abused an old woman in the mesa village of A'ku. The Acoma exacted swift justice. In the melee that followed, thirteen soldiers lost their lives.

Having secured the blessing of the Catholic church to punish the Acoma as enemies of the state, Oñate's men battled their way to the top of A'ku in January 1599, and fired cannon into the houses. Eight hundred Acoma lay dead in streets awash with blood; 580 survivors were rounded up and dragged to the Spanish presidio at Santo Domingo to face an inquisition. Punishment was severe. Children were deported to Mexico or consigned as indentured servants. Women were indentured for twenty years. Adult males were tortured by having one foot hacked off on a large chopping block set up in the plazas; hobbled, they were sentenced to twenty years of service. Two visiting Hopi suffered similar mutilation. Each had a hand cut off, and were returned to their nation as a warning of what would befall those who did not submit to Spain.

In 1680 the Spanish Inquisition's violent suppression of native religion, combined with unjust demands on Indian labor, precipitated the Pueblo Revolt. Spanish friars were put to death. The capital at Santa Fé was destroyed and colonial administrative papers raked into a large bonfire. Victory was complete, and the Rio Grande would be free of Spaniards for twelve years, giving the nations time to rebuild their lives and religions.

To the south, the mobile Apache, Suma, and Jano did their part by defending themselves and keeping a two-hundred-mile-wide stretch of territory, known as the Apache Corridor, free from settlement for many years. This corridor later would form the basis of the southwestern portion of the United States/Mexican border.

Unfortunately, despite these efforts, Spain was in the region to stay. Silver, lead, and gold mines already were opened in Sonora, protected by military presidios. Mirroring the unrest on the Appalachian frontier, the Southwest erupted into chaos—Indian hunting grounds were disturbed, nations fought each other, and clashes with settlers and soldiers increased daily. Many hundreds of Indian people were seized and sold into slavery to work the mines. Sedentary agricultural nations came under the most severe attack. When missionaries entered Sonora, many of these nations flocked to them willingly, using the missions as a refuge from conscripted labor in the mines and as security from soldier and Indian raids.

In 1687 Jesuit father Eusebio Kino furthered Spanish claim by establishing a chain of missions in the O'odham country in the desert to the south of the Grand Canyon. Although adored and beloved by many, his endeavors were not universally accepted. O'odham around the proposed Mission Señora de los Remedios expressed a clear dislike for the Church and Spaniards in general, following a 1689 massacre of several hundred Mututicachi Pima. The mission was built anyway. In 1695, O'odham broke out of the mission at Tubutama and attempted to free neophytes at other missions in Sonora. Father Kino, wishing to avoid bloodshed, arranged for peace talks. The O'odham agreed, but when they arrived at El Tupo to conclude the peace, Spanish soldiers opened fire and a bloody massacre ensued. In 1751 soldiers suppressed yet another revolt led by Luís Oacpicagigua from the O'odham town of Saric.

Arizona and New Mexico were transferred to the United States from Mexico in 1848. Pursuing the same Indian policy begun in the rest of the country, nations were forced onto government reservations. Across the border, Mexico did the same thing but employed tactics considerably more final. In 1857 the Chienne Apache received rations in Sonora, poisoned with arsenic. So many died that initially the malady was misdiagnosed as an epidemic. In 1864 Navajo were forced by United States troops to join the Mescalero on a military prison camp at Fort Sumner called the Bosque Redondo. The Navajo were made to walk from their homes in Arizona across the desert to eastern New Mexico. This march, called the Long Walk, took a heavy toll in human life. But of all the casualties suffered in the last decades of the nineteenth century in the Southwest, the Apache perhaps sustained the heaviest, and would be remembered as the most "hostile" and "warlike" nation on the continent.

Oppression was blind, and hatred obstructed the recognition of Apache defense of their homelands. Rendered outlaws in their own land by individuals who knew neither justice nor mercy, the Apache were condemned simply for the determination of their leadership to remain free. And those who received the fiercest condemnation—men such as Juh, Cochise, and Geronimo—were in reality among the most compassionate and humane leaders of their time.

When Earth was still young
and giants still roamed the
earth, a great sickness came
upon them. All of them died,
except for a small boy. One
day, while he was playing
around, a snake bit him. The
boy cried and cried. The blood
came out, and finally he died.

With his tears our lakes became,
with his blood the red clay became,
with his body our mountains became,
and that was how Earth became.

—Taos tradition

Inquisition (1655)

Juan Cuna smells the sharp odor of turpentine; feels it burn into the bloody cuts on his body. Earlier, in the Hopi town of Shongopovi, Fray Salvador de Guerra entered his home and caught him in possession of a kachina doll. This is idolatry. The Spanish presidio of Santa Fé has ordered an Inquisition to stamp out Indian religion once and for all. Soldiers force their way into the underground kivas and burn and destroy everything within. At a Hopi town, a kiva has been filled with sand and a large Franciscan church built on top using forced Indian labor. The Hopi call it the "slave church." Many have died in the construction of it, hauling timbers across the desert with inadequate food and water. They die in fits and convulsions, but still the church is built.

In the plaza outside the church, Father Guerra viciously whips Juan Cuna into a bloody pulp. The show over, the priest drags the beaten form into the church, and now Juan Cuna feels the sting of turpentine cover his body. Good friar Salvador de Guerra lights a match.

In flames, Juan Cuna staggers from the church toward a water tank. But Salvador de Guerra thinks that he runs toward the governor's house. The friar mounts a horse and charges after him, knocking him to the ground. Back and forth the raving priest rides over Juan Cuna, until he is trampled into the ground. A Hopi delegation travels on foot to Santa Fé where they will tell the governor that Fray Guerra has burned alive other Hopi besides Juan Cuna. Spanish witnesses corroborate the story. Very well. He will be removed. Fray Salvador de Guerra now serves happily as parish priest in Santa Fé.

Always vital to us is the subject of our land. In times far back before your history, we were taught truthful and peaceful living, which remains with us in the traditional life way of the Hopi people. We could not remain here in selfish tenant. In our traditional life we are strong against selfishness and tyranny, and are to be governed in our traditional way so we might have prosperity, happiness, honor and peace, not only for ourselves but for all people including our white brothers.

. . . we have failed to find where you gave us any legal way or rights or title to the land which was ours from times long before you came among us. . . . The Hopi Tusqua [land] is our Love and will always be, and it is the land upon which our leader fixes and tells the dates for our religious life. Our land, our religion, and our life are one. . . . It is from the land that each true Hopi gathers the rocks, the plants, the different woods, roots, and his life, and each in the authority of his rightful obligation brings to our ceremonies proof of our ties to this land. Our footprints mark well the trails to these sacred places. . . .

It is here on this land that we are bringing up our younger generation and through preserving the ceremonies are teaching them proper human behavior and strength of character to make them true citizens among all people.

It is upon this land that we wish to live in peace and harmony with our friends and with our neighbors . . . our way requires us to conduct our lives in friendship and peace, without anger, without greed, without wickedness of any kind among ourselves or in our association with any people. . . . Although we are small in numbers, scarce in money, and without wide knowledge of your ways and your laws, with humble hearts but strong determination, we state the traditional claims of the Hopi people. . . .

—Hopi elders of Shongopovi

Pueblo Revolt (1680)

. . . they say all must fight with the Spaniards to the death. . . .
—Lucas, *Piro*

As night falls, Santa Fé burns under a murky orange sky; the Governor's Palace is under siege. Trapped inside the buildings, the Spaniards scarcely can believe their ears. Christian hymns rise audibly above the roar of burning timber. It is the voice of the Indian army, mocking the Spaniards as the city collapses.

In the Hopi country, the mission church is torn down and the earth dug out of the kiva. Popé, Tewa leader of the revolt, rides swiftly through the nations, instructing the people to destroy everything connected with Spain. There is much work to be done—rejoicing will come later. Under Popé's guidance, they will relearn their traditions. But who will help Christians learn that it is wrong to kill and destroy and force their religion upon others?

The destruction of all the temples, sacred vessels, and vestments, shows the iniquity of those barbarians and the hatred which they feel for our holy faith. These are sufficient reasons for war being waged against them without mercy, and for declaring all those who may be captured, slaves for a period of ten years in the manner which was done formerly. . . . I hold it impossible . . . that that province can be recovered or settled if those captured are not declared slaves. . . . With all this, these barbarians will not receive the just punishment which they deserve.
—Don Bartolomé de Estrada, *governor of El Parral*

On reaching [Santa Fé] . . . I recognized . . . Indians of all nations, and a number of Taos and Pecuries . . . [and they] told me "We are [finished] with the Spaniards and the persons whom we have killed; those of us whom they have killed do not matter, for [the Spaniards] are going, and now we shall live as we like and settle in this [town] and wherever we see fit." —Antonio, *Tewa*

. . . the Indians do not want religious [orders] or Spaniards. —Pedro Nanboa, *Tewa*

. . . the resentment which all the Indians have in their hearts has been so strong, from the time this kingdom was discovered, because the religious and the Spaniards take away our [religion]; we have inherited successively from our old men the things pertaining to our ancient customs; and I have heard this resentment spoken of since I was of an age to understand. —Pedro Nanboa, *Tewa*

Popé came, in company with another native of the pueblo of Taos named Saca, through all the pueblos of the kingdom . . . proclaiming . . . that we should burn all the images and temples, rosaries and cross[es] and that all the people should discard the names given them in holy baptism . . . we were not to mention in any manner the name of God, of the . . . Virgin, or of the Saints . . . [and were] not to teach the Castilian language in any pueblo and to burn the seeds which the Spaniards sowed and to plant only [corn] and beans, which are the crops of our ancestors. —Juan, *Tesuque*

What we say is from our hearts. We speak truths that are based upon our own tradition and religion. . . . The Hopi form of government was established solely upon the religious and traditional grounds. The divine plan of life in this land was laid out for us by our great spirit, Masau'u. This plan cannot be changed. The Hopi life is all set according to the fundamental principles of life of this divine plan. We can not do otherwise but to follow this plan. There is no other way for us. . . . What the Great Spirit made and planned no power on earth can change it. —Hopi delegation

Great Spirit made us to be Hopis, to speak Hopi, to worship Hopi way, to be independent and free on our own land. Are you going to deny us all these? —Hopi delegation

. . . we . . . will not sell our homes, our land, our religion, and our way of life for money. —Hopi elders of Hotevilla

Our tradition and religious training forbid us to harm, kill, and molest anyone. . . . What nation who has taken up arms ever brought peace and happiness to his people? —Hopi delegation

The Hopi people have developed a way of life rooted deep in the traditions and experiences of their ancestors. We look to the wisdom of the past to assist us in those decisions which determine the future of ourselves and our children. To follow another course would be untrue and would bring upon us those troubles which fall upon a people who are not true to themselves and their beliefs.

—Hopi elders of Shongopovi

We, the traditional leaders, want you and the American people to know that we will stand firmly upon our own traditional and religious grounds. And that we will not bind ourselves to any foreign nation. . . . We have met all other rich and powerful nations who [have] come to our shores, from the early Spanish Conquistadors down to the present government of the United States, all of whom have used force in trying to wipe out our existence here in our own home. We want to come to our own destiny in our own way.

—Hopi delegation

Long Walk (1864)

To the American soldiers stationed at Fort Defiance, New Mexico, there is a "Navajo problem." To the Navajo whose lands are being invaded, there is an "American problem." General James Carleton solves his side of the problem by ordering Colonel Kit Carson to kill all "hostile" Navajo men, and to imprison the women and children. Before he has had time to accomplish this massacre, however, the Navajo are spared by a government order that declares war against them. General Carson is obliged to force a surrender and take captives to a prison camp at Bosque Redondo, New Mexico.

The Navajo begin their long walk to the Bosque. They say that those who die along the way are mutilated by the soldiers. Therefore, the Navajo try to hide their dead. Four hundred Mescalero already are interred at the prison camp when the Navajo arrive. What is the United States thinking? There is no food at the Bosque, no shelter, but misery enough for all.

... when we had a way of living of our own, we lived happy. . . .   —Barboncito, *Navajo*

We think we were born to live in our old country. Disease is more prevalent here than there. The water does not suit us here. We think we were not born to live here.

—Ganado Mucho, *Navajo*

Is it American justice that we must give up everything and receive nothing?   —Armijo, *Navajo*

I hope to God you will not ask me to go to any other country except my own.   —Barboncito, *Navajo*

After the Bosque Redondo we returned to the Bonito and camped upstream from the fort. The soldiers did not want us to live there. They did not want us to live anywhere. They had sent us to Fort Sumner to die, and they could not leave us alone in our own land. They killed many, mostly women and children. So again our people slipped away in the night. It was late in the fall and very cold. We left fires burning and took everything we could carry and went silently into the forest. When we camped, we scattered so that when the cavalry followed some might escape. We could not risk fires, so we ate what cold food we had and huddled together for warmth. One old woman who had a blanket took several orphaned children and covered them with it. She had only a very little food but gave each a mouthful; there was none left for her. She got them to sleep and hovered over them as best she could. When the men came at dawn, the children were safe, but she was dead.   —Big Mouth, *Mescalero*

The surest way to kill a race is to kill its religion and its ideals. Can anybody doubt that the white race deliberately attempted to do that? This is to kill the soul of a people. And when the spirit is killed, what remains?

—Frederick Peso, *Mescalero*

Hualapai (1875)

The Hualapai gaze through the shimmering heat toward the outline of the Colorado River and think of the mountains that used to be home. In the East, newspapers proclaim that the Hualapai are subdued. In fine parlors in Boston, the gentlemen and ladies who talk of it as a grand thing probably would not last five minutes on a barren concentration camp in the middle of a desert, but the Hualapai do. However, a scorching prison camp is no place to raise children; it is no place to dream. In 1875, Colonel August Kautz of the Eighth Infantry, Arizona, receives word that the Hualapai nation has broken free and returned to their homeland south of the Grand Canyon. But now their lands are occupied by miners.

In 1867, this Band of Indians consisted of over 1500 people, between 400 and 500 fighting men; they were a wild, capable, implacable foe. . . . They were relentlessly pursued by me for two years, and in 1869, surrendered and asked for peace; several of their prominent men were sent to San Francisco in irons, and remained for months as prisoners on Alcatraz and Angel Islands. . . . They were thoroughly subdued, and . . . sent to the Colorado River Reservation; being Mountain Indians they died there very rapidly; they sent word to General [George] Crook that they did not want to fight, but that they could not live there, and that they would rather die fighting on their native mountains than sicken and die as they were doing on the river bottom.

—Lieutenant Colonel William Price,
United States Army

My people cannot live there; it is very hot; the water is bad, and my people sickened and died. There is no grass, and our horses have nearly all perished. While we were permitted to remain at La Paz, Captain Byrne saw that we got our rations, but when we went up to the Agency they did not get enough to eat, and instead of getting twenty-four beeves per week, my people only got seven. . . . My people would rather die than go back there.   —Sherum, *Hualapai*

. . . in the country over which we used to roam so free, the white men have appropriated all the water; large numbers of cattle have been introduced, and . . . in many places the water is fenced in and locked up, and we are driven from all waters. The Railroad is now coming, which will require more water and will bring more men, who will take up all the small springs remaining; we urge that the following Reservation be set aside for them while there is still time; the land can never be of any great use to the whites; there are no mineral deposits upon it, as it has been thoroughly prospected; there is little or no arable land; the water is in such small quantities, and the country is so rocky and void of grass, that it would not be available for stock-raising.

—Sherum, Sequania, Soskuorema,
and Cowarrow, *Hualapai*

The Colorado River

Behold, to give justice is to punish the bad; but since none of
us is bad, what purpose will [your] justice serve?
                                                                   —(Name not given), *Cocomaricopa*

In the old times we were strong. We used to hunt and fish.
We raised our little crop of corn and melons and ate the mes-
quite beans. Now all is changed. . . . Each day in the old
times in summer and in winter we came down to the river
banks to bathe. This strengthened and toughened our firm
skin. But White settlers were shocked to see the naked Indians, so now we keep away. In old days we wore the breech-
cloth, and aprons made of bark and reeds. We worked all
winter in the wind—bare arms, bare legs, and never felt the
cold. But now, when the wind blows down from the mountains, it makes us cough. Yes—we know that when you come,
we die.   —Chiparopai, *Quechan*

Why not knock us on the head and end it at once, it would be
kinder than the slow agony.   —Chiparopai, *Quechan*

The Bascom Affair   (1861)

An Irish boy named Mickey Free is captured by Apaches, and
Cochise's Chok!onen are falsely accused of the crime. U.S. army
officer George Bascom invites Cochise to talks, but under a flag of
truce, the delegation is seized. Cochise escapes, but members of
his family are hung. When the army finally discovers Mickey Free,
he is clothed like an Apache and living with them in such content-
ment that it is claimed his mind is ruined.

After the Bascom affair, Cochise joins his brother-in-law Mangas Coloradas, leader of the Chienne, and spends the winter defending Apache Pass from further invasion. The army responds by declaring the Apache hostile and at war with the United States.

There is to be no council held with the Indians, nor any talks. The men are to be slain whenever and wherever they can be found. The women and children may be taken prisoners. . . . I trust that these . . . demonstrations will give those Indians a wholesome lesson.
> —General James H. Carleton, *United States Army*

The Indians always tried to live peaceably with the white soldiers and settlers . . . a few days after the attack [on Cochise] at Apache Pass we organized in the mountains and returned to fight the soldiers. There were two tribes—the Bedonkohe and the [Chok!onen] Apaches, both commanded by Cochise. After a few days' skirmishing we attacked a freight train that was coming in with supplies for the Fort. We killed some of the men and captured the others. These prisoners our chief offered to trade for the Indians whom the soldiers had captured at the massacre in the tent. This the officers refused, so we killed our prisoners, disbanded, and went into hiding in the mountains. —Goyathlay (Geronimo), *Bedonkohe*

The Americans are everywhere, and we must live in bad places to shun them. —Cochise, *Chok!onen*

I do not think you will keep the peace. Once again you tell me we can stay in our mountains and our valleys. That is all we wish; we do not want to fight and kill whites, and we do not want the whites to fight and kill us. We want nothing but to live in peace. But I do not believe you will allow us to remain on the lands we love. I warn you, if you try to move us again, war will start once more; it will be a war without end, a war in which every Apache will fight until he is dead. Prove to me that I am wrong; prove to me that this time I can trust you.

—Cochise, *Chok!onen*

When I was young I walked all over this country, east and west, and saw no other people than the Apaches. After many summers I walked again and found another race of people had come to take it. How is it? Why is it that the Apaches wait to die—that they carry their lives on their fingernails? They roam over the hills and plains and want the heavens to fall on them. The Apaches were once a great nation; they are now but a few, and because of this they want to die and so carry their lives on their fingernails.

—Cochise, *Chok!onen*

Mangas Coloradas (1863)

I come into Santa Rita and am told you will decide what country belongs to the United States and what belongs to Mexico. I know all about this, for I have talked with your General [Stephen] Kearny and your Colonel Cooke. . . . This country where we have hunted for all time does not belong to Mexicans. They cannot sell it to the United States. It belongs to Apaches. It is not right for either Americans or Mexicans to take our hunting grounds away from us.

—Mangas Coloradas, *Chienne*

Mangas Coloradas walks alone into a soldiers' camp to talk of peace. The same strategy employed in the Bascom Affair is repeated again. Mangas is seized and bound in irons. In the night, his captors prod him with red-hot bayonets. When Mangas flinches, he is shot for trying to escape. But the barbarity does not end.

He went into their camp under promise of safety. . . . As [his men] had anticipated, Mangas did not leave that place alive. Instead, the soldiers killed him and threw his body out of the camp, dug a shallow ditch, and buried him. That was not the worst: the next day they dug up his body, cut off his head, and boiled his head in a big black kettle. To an Apache, the mutilation of the body is much worse than death, because the body must go through eternity in the mutilated condition. Little did the White Eyes know what they were starting. . . .

—Daklugie, *Nednhi*

His head was severed from his body by a surgeon, and the brain taken out and weighed. The head measured larger than that of Daniel Webster, and the brain was of corresponding weight. The skull was sent to Washington, and is now on exhibition at the Smithsonian Institution.

—Tucson *Arizona Star*

Camp Grant Massacre   (1871)

While living peacefully as prisoners of war at Camp Grant, Arizona, 144 Aravaipa are massacred by a civilian mob from Tucson, aided by O'odham and Mexican fighters. All carry government-issued weapons. The attack occurs just before dawn, while the unarmed Aravaipa sleep securely under the protection of Camp Grant. Newspaper reports try to justify the massacre, but the

majority killed are women and children, their bodies horribly mutilated. Most of the men are unharmed; it is women who will give
birth to more Apache.

If it had not been for the massacre, there would have been a
great many more people here now; but, after that massacre,
who could have stood it? . . . When I made peace with Lieutenant [Royal E.] Whitman my heart was very big and happy.
The people of Tucson and San Xavier must be crazy. They
acted as though they had neither heads nor hearts . . . [they]
must have a thirst for our blood . . . these Tucson people write
for the papers and tell their own story. The Apaches have no
one to tell their story. . . .   —Eskiminzin, *Aravaipa*

I no longer want to live; my women and children have been
killed before my face, and I have been unable to defend them.
Most Indians in my place would take a knife and cut his
throat, but I *will live* to show these people that all they have
done . . . shall not make me break faith. . . .
                              —(Name not given), *Aravaipa*

That evening they began to come in from all directions, singly
and in small parties, so changed in forty-eight hours as to be
hardly recognizable. . . . Many of the men, whose families
had all been killed, when I spoke to them and expressed sympathy for them, were obliged to turn away, unable to
speak. . . . The women whose children had been killed or stolen were convulsed with grief, and looked to me appealingly,
as though I was their last hope on earth. Children who two
days before had been full of fun and frolic kept at a distance,
expressing wondering horror.
            —Lieutenant Royal E. Whitman, *United States Army*

We were once a large people covering these mountains; we lived well; we were at peace. One day my best friend was seized by an officer of the white men and treacherously killed. . . . The worst place of all is Apache Pass. There, five Indians, one my brother, were murdered. Their bodies were hung up and kept there till they were skeletons. . . . Now Americans and Mexicans kill an Apache on sight.

—Cochise, *Chok!onen*

. . . and the story that "the Apaches were treacherous and cruel" went forth into all the land, but nothing of the wrongs they had received. . . . The killing of . . . [Mangas] Colorado . . . by pushing a heated bayonet through the canvas tent in which he was a prisoner, and shooting him when he moved under the pretense that he was trying to escape. The equally treacherous attempt to kill. . . . Cochise, by inviting him in under a flag of truce. . . . And more recently the massacre at Camp Grant. . . . Events like these and many others would seem to be quite sufficient to have made these Apaches the "blood-thirsty and relentless savages" they are now reported to be.   —J. H. Lyman, *United States Indian agent*

The Arizona Citizen . . . published at Tucson, and the Arizona Miner . . . have been excessive in their abuse of Lieut. [Royal E.] Whitman . . . and all other officers . . . who have shown the least sympathy for the Apaches. . . . The editors seem to fear the damaging effect produced on the public mind by the statements made officially by these Army officers of the general good conduct of the Apaches whenever they have been allowed an opportunity to display it. . . .

—United States commissioner of Indian Affairs

Reservations   (1872)

Cochise, old and in failing health, secures a reservation for his Chok!onen in the beloved Apache Pass. It is promised to the Chok!onen forever, but less than two years after Cochise's death and four years following the signing of the agreement, the entire nation is forced to relocate to the desolate San Carlos reservation, where other Apache nations are gathered.

When Cochise dies, his son Naiche assumes his place at the head of the nation, but it is the Bedonkohe leader Geronimo who becomes the real force behind Chok!onen resistance. Together with Nednhi leader Juh, the Bedonkohe, Chok!onen, and Nednhi break away from San Carlos and determine to live—or die—free in the Arizona mountains.

[Juh] told them that he could offer them nothing but hardship and death. . . . As he saw it they must choose between death from heat, starvation, and degradation at San Carlos and a wild, free life in Mexico—short, perhaps, but free. . . . Let them remember that if they took this step they would be hunted like wild animals by the troops of both the United States and Mexico. . . . All of us knew that we were doomed, but some preferred death to slavery and imprisonment.

—Daklugie, *Nednhi*

The Creator did not make San Carlos. It is older than He. . . . He just left it as a sample of the way they did jobs before He came along. . . . Take stones and ashes and thorns and, with some scorpions and rattlesnakes thrown in, dump the outfit on stones, heat the stones red hot, set the United States Army after the Apaches, and you have San Carlos.

—Kaywaykla, *Chienne*

Why shut me up on a reservation? We will make peace. We will keep it faithfully. But let us go around free as Americans do. Let us go wherever we please. . . . You Americans began the fight.   —Cochise, *Chok!onen*

Geronimo

During my [childhood] we had never seen a missionary or a priest. We had never seen a white man. Thus quietly lived the Be-don-ko-he Apaches.

—Goyathlay (Geronimo), *Bedonkohe*

They never explained to the Government when an Indian was wronged, but always reported the misdeeds of the Indians. Much that was done by mean white men was reported at Washington as the deeds of my people.

—Goyathlay (Geronimo), *Bedonkohe*

In the summer of 1858, being at peace with the Mexican towns . . . we went south into Old Mexico to trade. . . . Late one afternoon when returning from town we were met by a few women and children who told us that Mexican troops . . . had attacked our camp . . . when all were counted, I found that my aged mother, my young wife, and my three small children were among the slain. There were no lights in camp, so without being noticed, I silently turned away and stood by the river. How long I stood there I do not know. . . . I stood until all had passed, hardly knowing what I would do—I had

Geronimo's unflinching defense of his homeland made him the
most maligned of all Indian leaders. Ever strong, he once remarked
to U.S. officials, "The papers all over the world say I am a bad
man, but I never do wrong without a cause."

no weapon, nor did I hardly wish to fight, neither did I con-
template recovering the bodies of my loved ones. . . . I did
not pray, nor did I resolve to do anything in particular, for I
had no purpose left. I finally followed the tribe silently, keeping just within hearing distance of the soft noise of the feet of
the retreating Apaches. . . . [Later, I] talked with the other
Indians who had lost in the massacre, but none had lost as I
had, for I had lost all.

Within a few days we arrived at our own settlement. There
were the decorations that [my wife] Alope had made—and
there were the playthings of our little ones. I burned them
all. . . . I was never again contented in our quiet home . . .
and whenever I . . . saw anything to remind me of former
happy days my heart would ache for revenge upon Mexico.

—Goyathlay (Geronimo), *Bedonkohe*

To Live Free (1876–1886)

For ten years, United States troops pursue Geronimo's band until
they are reduced to thirty-seven. Even then, they do not surrender.
Eight thousand United States and Mexican troops track them
across the mountains, swarming after them, never catching them.

We were reckless of our lives, because we felt that every
man's hand was against us. If we returned to the reservation
we would be put in prison and killed; if we stayed in Mexico
they would continue to send soldiers to fight us; so we gave
no quarter to anyone and asked no favors.

—Goyathlay (Geronimo), *Bedonkohe*

. . . now the very rocks have become soft. We cannot put our feet anywhere. We cannot sleep, for if a coyote or fox barks, or a stone moves, we are up—the soldiers have come.

—Delche, *Tonto*

I give myself up to you. Do with me what you please. I surrender. Once I moved about like the wind. Now I surrender to you, and that is all.

—Goyathlay (Geronimo), *Bedonkohe*

At that time Geronimo's band . . . consisted of seventeen men; he had also Lozen . . . known as the Woman warrior. Geronimo was handicapped by the presence, too, of women and children who must be defended and fed. Nobody ever captured Geronimo. I know. I was with him. Anyway, who can capture the wind?   —Kanseah, *Nednhi*

POWs *on American Soil*   (1886–1913)

No one can run forever. Geronimo surrenders to the United States Army on condition that his people will be held for only two years, then returned to their own land. Hauled away to prisons in Alabama, Pensacola, the notorious fortress of San Marcos, Florida—where countless Indian leaders, including Osceola, have languished—and finally to Fort Sill (Indian Territory), they remain prisoners of war for twenty-seven years.

... above all living men I respected Geronimo. He was the embodiment of the Apache spirit, of the fighting Chiricahua. . . . As long as Geronimo lived, he regretted having surrendered. He often said he wished he had died fighting in Mexico.   —Daklugie, *Nednhi*

When I had given up to the Government they put me on the Southern Pacific Railroad and took me to San Antonio, Texas, and held me to be tried by their laws. In forty days they took me from there to Fort Pickens [Pensacola], Florida. . . . For nearly two years we were kept at hard labor in this place and we did not see our families until May, 1897. . . . After this we were sent with our families to Vermont, Alabama, where we stayed five years. . . . I looked in vain for General [Nelson A.] Miles to send me to that land of which he had spoken. . . . During this time one of my warriors, Fun, killed himself and his wife. Another one shot his wife and then shot himself.
                    —Goyathlay (Geronimo), *Bedonkohe*

There is no climate or soil which, to my mind, is equal to that of Arizona . . . that land which the Almighty created for the Apaches. It is my land, my home, my fathers' land, to which I now ask to be allowed to return. I want to spend my last days there, and be buried among those mountains. . . . Could I but see this accomplished, I think I could forget all the wrongs that I have ever received. . . .
                    —Goyathlay (Geronimo), *Bedonkohe*

What is the matter that you don't speak to me? . . . I'd be better satisfied if you would talk to me once in a while. Why don't you look at me and smile at me? I am the same man; I have the same feet, legs, and hands, and the sun looks down on me a complete man. I want you to look and smile at me.

—Goyathlay (Geronimo), *Bedonkohe*,
to General George Crook, *United States Army*

We are vanishing from the earth, yet I cannot think we are useless or Usen would not have created us. . . . For each tribe of men Usen created, He also made a home. In the land created for any particular tribe He placed whatever would be best for the welfare of that tribe. . . . Thus it was in the beginning: the Apaches and their homes each created for the other by Usen himself. When they are taken from these homes they sicken and die. How long will it be until it is said there are no Apaches?

—Goyathlay (Geronimo), *Bedonkohe*

> *Ussen gave us this land,*
> *Through our forefathers*
> *It has come to us.*
> *It was our land*
> *Before the White Eyes came;*
> *It is still our land.*

—Nednhi song

The Grand Canyon

Tourists flock to the Grand Canyon National Park, but few realize that when they descend upon mules to the canyon floor, they descend into Havasupai land. Over the years, cattlemen, miners, and tourists have claimed this country for themselves, assuming that the Havasupai have willingly accepted a few small acres of canyon land in lieu of the country they once held dear.

Our case is clear and undeniable. We are the people of the Grand Canyon. Our legends say the Havasupai were created on these lands of the Grand Canyon's South Rim. . . . prospectors invading our area had hopes of getting rich. . . . Soon we were crowded from all our ancient lands, viewed as intruders. . . . We never agreed to the situation we find ourselves in. . . .   —Havasupai nation

Not too many of you would stand the humiliation we stand every day. We live in a Park Service zoo. . . . We are the only ones who don't seem to matter, and we are human beings who have to support ourselves on this land. And we used to own it.   —Augustine Hanna, *Havasupai*

The Ute

Agreements the Indian makes with the government are like the agreement a buffalo makes with the hunter after it has been pierced by many arrows. All it can do is lie down and give in.   —Ouray, *Ute*

I realize the ultimate destiny of my people. They will be extirpated by the race that overruns, occupies and holds our hunting grounds, whose numbers and force . . . will, in a few years, remove the last trace of our blood that now remains. We shall fall as the leaves from the trees when frost or winter

comes, and the lands which we have roamed over for countless generations will be given over to the miner and the plow-
share . . . and we shall be buried out of sight beneath the
avalanche of the new civilization.　　　　　—Ouray, *Ute*

There is no use of making a long ado about the Indian question, the only solution of the problem is extermination.
　　　　　　　　　　　　　　　　　—Colorado *Banner*

We do not want to sell a foot of our land—that is the opinion
of all.　　　　　　　　　　　　　　　　　—Ouray, *Ute*

The West

*Do you see me! . . . Do you all help me! My words are tied in one
with the great mountains, with the great rocks, with the great
trees, in one with my body and my heart. Do you all help me. . . .
All of you see me one with this world!*
—Anonymous, Yokuts

In 1542 the Spanish crown, still convinced that gold and riches
existed north of the Valley of Mexico, directed Juan Cabrillo to
explore the Alta California coast. England pursued a similar
course, landing Sir Francis Drake in northern California in 1579.
Both nations immediately claimed ownership of the territory. The
situation might have been tense had not English interest waned at
the same time that Spain found it unprofitable to extend her realm
to a region holding as little promise as California. Failing to find
the fabulous gold deposits that awaited later discovery, the nations
of California were granted a lengthy reprieve. In fact, it was not
until eighteenth-century reports of Russian activity along the
North Pacific coast that Spain took renewed interest the area.

In 1769 an unlikely cavalcade made up of Franciscan friars under the direction of Father Junípero Serra and a column of Spanish soldiers led by Captain Gaspar de Portolá set out from the
missions in Baja toward Alta California. In July, Mission San Diego de Alcalá was constructed in the country of the Kumeyaay,

marking the first in a chain of twenty-one missions along the California coast.

Although converts were made, and many Indian people raised within the mission system came to invest a true interest in the affairs of the church, many more suffered under what was, in fact, a severely coercive system. Few neophytes entered the missions of their own free will. Spain continued to operate under the European assumption that non-Christian nations were base and immoral, and the church was obligated to effect conversion. Spain also discovered that the missions were useful tools in regional pacification. Conversion allowed conquest without bloodshed. Produce and products manufactured by the neophytes at self-sufficient missions supplied frontier settlements. For the Spanish, it was a perfect system. For Indian nations, it was slavery.

Separated from family, community, and culture, the neophytes were rounded into the missions, baptized, and indoctrinated with European culture and the Christian faith. Spanish garments replaced traditional clothing, a monotonous diet of gruel and soup replaced native foods, and strict military regimen became a way of life. Unable to leave the missions, Indian nations were deprived of their freedom, their rights, and their dignity.

In 1775, only six years after the founding of Mission San Diego, the Kumeyaay revolted. Troops were called out on a manhunt to recapture the ringleaders, who had fled into the countryside.

That same year, frontier captain Juan Bautista de Anza made the first overland expedition from Arizona to California. Previously, such a route across the Mojave Desert to the Pacific Ocean was thought to be impossible. Alta California remained isolated, reachable only from Baja. Notwithstanding, Quechan and Mohave visitors to the new missions in Arizona reported Serra's movements along the coast, observed with their own eyes. Indian trails crisscrossed the desert, and runners made the trip very easily. Eventually, Anza began to admit of the possibility of such an expedition. He would be remembered as a hero for his discovery.

Anza's troops arrived in California immediately after the San

Diego revolt and, not surprisingly, encountered Indian people in the hills who motioned them away. Anza helped to suppress the revolt, and a priest in his company expressed revulsion at the emaciated condition of the Kumeyaay without ever realizing that their malnutrition very likely was the result of Spanish interference.

In 1834 the California missions were secularized and Indian nations free to leave. But by this time, many of their old homelands had been taken by Mexican landholders. Left with few choices for survival, many ex-neophytes became laborers and servants on these estates and *rancherías*. Others wound up in urban slums, living on the streets, homeless in their own lands. In northern California, Mexican settlers engaged in intensive slave-raiding expeditions, and the mass murder of Indian populations who resisted was common.

In 1848 California became a part of the United States. That year gold was discovered at Sutter's Mill along the American River in the country of the Nisenan. Within three years, more than two hundred thousand people spilled across the Sierras in a frantic rush to reach the goldfields.

California quickly degenerated into a turbulent frontier society of prospectors, bandits, gamblers, and swindlers. If Indian nations had any hope of redress before, it was completely shattered with the onset of the gold rush. Immigrant trails mowed over Indian communities, sending their citizens into hiding. Rumors of Indian depredations flared, though in reality most either were committed by lawless white men, were acts of self-defense, or were completely fabricated. Indian-fighters became heroes, and newspaper reports boasted of native people butchered or kidnapped and sold into slavery.

Two labor laws, passed in 1850 and 1860, effectively legalized the system, allowing for "vagrant" Indian people to be placed in indentured servitude. Suddenly, all Indian nations were vagrant. More than ten thousand California Indian people would fall victim to the acts. In 1855 the Rogue River War erupted when miners opened fire on a sleeping camp of Shasta men, women, and children, and an "Indian War" was announced. As the nations begged for mercy, assassins were paid soldier's wages to gun them down. Such atrocities were repeated among the Chowchilla, Pomo, Achumawi, Yurok, Konkow, Yana, and many others. Women, children, and old people were indiscriminately slaughtered, and reports of soldiers hurling babies into bonfires as villages burned were far too prevalent.

In 1911 Ishi, the last of the Yahi nation, walked alone into the town of Oroville. Settler raids had reduced his people to five. Their last days were spent in hiding along the inaccessible reaches of Mill Creek, where they remained invisible for a quarter century until Ishi, the last survivor, made himself known. Ishi lived the remainder of his life in a room in the Museum of Anthropology in San Francisco; after his death, his brain was deposited in the Smithsonian Institution, where it remains to this day.

Missions (1769–1836)

A bell tolls at the first light of day. Neophytes struggle awake and file into the church sanctuary for mass. Afterward come the studies that will replace their languages with Spanish. The bells toll, signaling a breakfast of watery cornmeal. Bells toll, it is time to attend the trades of washing, weaving, tilemaking, and woodworking. Bells toll, again the prayers and an allowance of hominy soup. They sing in the choirs with enthusiasm, there is blessed release in music. Again the bells toll. Like regimented soldiers, they follow the ringing of the bells.

New converts are captured and brought into the mission by force. The church claims neophytes come voluntarily. Inside a closed room, a novice is held until he is baptized and given a new Christian name. To show defiance is to be whipped, chained, tortured, and even killed.

The meals of hominy soup are not nearly enough. Infrequently, a little meat, a few vegetables are added. In the hills, many Indian people do not eat as well now either; they are too busy keeping clear of the missionaries. White people derisively call them Diggers, and are shocked by their starving condition.

In fine, they are so savage, wild and dirty, disheveled, ugly, small, and timid, that only because they have the human form is it possible to believe that they belong to mankind. . . . [They go about] like Cain, fugitive and wandering, possessed by fear and dread at every step. Indeed, it seems as if they have hanging over them the curse which God put upon Nebuchadnezzar.   —Father Pedro Font, *Spain*

. . . sometimes [the neophytes] come bringing some heathen relative [to the mission] . . . attracted by the pozole. . . . and so these Indians are usually caught by the mouth.

—Father Pedro Font, *Spain*

God is called the Great Spirit. I have studied both sides of religion and I believe the Indians have more real religion than the whites. . . . Spirits are all about us—in a gust of wind, or a light wind whirling around our door, that is a family spirit of our loved ones, wanting to know that we are safe. . . .

—Grant Towendolly, *Wintu*

My grandfather . . . went up to Yolla Bolly Mountain with about six hundred others and stayed [away] three years. . . . Men died every day from starvation. That was in Camp of Dark Canyon in the winter. Women would find a little bunch of grass and eat it and would bring a handful back for their husbands. The women would have to chew it for the men. The man was too weak to swallow it. She would take a mouthful of water and pour it into his mouth. That was the way they saved a lot of them.   —Andrew Freeman, *Nomlaki*

I and two of my relatives went down . . . to the beach . . . to catch clams. . . . we saw two men on horseback coming rapidly toward us; my relatives were immediately afraid and they fled with all speed . . . but already it was too late, because in a moment they overtook me and lassoed and dragged me for a long distance . . . with their horses running. . . . When we arrived at the mission, they locked me in a room for a week . . . telling me that . . . [the Father] would make me a Christian . . . the interpreter, told me that I should do as the father told me, because now I was not going to be set free, and it would go very bad with me if I did not consent to it. . . . I found a way to escape; but I was tracked and they caught me like a fox; there they seized me by lasso as on the first occasion, and they carried me off to the mission torturing me on the road . . . [the Father] ordered that they fasten me to the stake . . . they lashed me until I lost consciousness.

—Janitin, *Kumeyaay*

End of the Missions (1836)

By 1836 the missions are secularized. The padres depart, leaving buildings abandoned, and Indian converts with an uncertain future. Many eagerly seize their freedom and, with a yell, fly to the hills to rejoin their families. Others seek a living working on the Mexican *rancherías* as herders and servants. And still others linger around the old missions either out of love, or for nowhere else to go. Some carry on the old masses and sing the church hymns, others try to reclaim a captured past, only to find that the memory is painful.

On the *rancherías,* it is not uncommon to find Indian people starving, their ribs protruding, worked like dogs and fed next to nothing. Their owners do not care if they starve; there are plenty more Diggers for the taking.

You see . . . how miserable we now are; the Fathers cannot protect us, and those in power rob us . . . to be exposed incessantly, together with our families, to the worst possible treatment and even death itself, is a tragedy! Would we be blamed if we defend ourselves, and returned to our tribes in the Tulares, taking with us all the live stock that could be led away?   —(Name not given), *Luiseno*

Another person who was then living in that abandoned mission was an Indian woman named Ursula. . . . She was a Santa Rosa Islander, and I first saw her when she was living at Jalama Vieja. Once, when I went to see her at her fixed-up mission room, I found her crying and combing her hair. She was thinking of old friends of Santa Rosa Island.

—Kitsepawit (Fernando Librado), *Chumash*

Donociana and Nolberto knew the Indian dances too. . . . I once went over to Donociana's house. . . . I wanted to learn the Swordfish Dance. After the meal I asked her to teach me the old dances, saying, "for you are the only ones left who know the old dances." Donociana began to cry, and I left saying nothing more.

—Kitsepawit (Fernando Librado), *Chumash*

I am very old; my people were once around me as the sands of the shore—many—many. They have all passed away—they have died like the grass—they have gone to the mountains. I do not complain—the antelope falls by the arrow. I had a son—I loved him—when the pale-faces came he went away—I know not where he is. I am a Christian Indian—I am all that is left of my people—I am alone.

—(Name not given), *Miwok-Costanoan*

Gold (1848)

They come crawling, running, slithering, dragging on their bellies after the gold. Swarms of them have collected along the timbered streams and hundreds more wind across the mountains like ants marching toward honey. The earth oozes prospectors, and the yellow rock bleeds from the gouges they make in her sides.

The miners will go to their country, and the question which comes up is, shall the miners be protected and the country be developed, or shall the Indians be suffered to kill them and the nation be deprived of its immense wealth?

—General James H. Carleton, *United States Army*

The majority of tribes are kept in constant fear on account of the indiscriminate and inhuman massacre of their people for real or supposed injuries. They have become alarmed of the increased flood of immigration much spread over their country... I have seldom heard of a single difficulty between the whites and the Indians in which the original cause could not readily be traced to some rash or reckless act of the former. In some instances it has happened that innocent Indians have been shot down for imaginary offenses which did not in fact exist. . . .

—Adam Johnston, *United States Indian agent*

Before the Spanish, they [the Indians] used to have gold and silver. . . . But when the Spanish came, the word got around about that gold and silver and the Indians buried that. . . . They weren't going to give that to nobody. That was used to torture many an Indian to death—just good, honest people— just to find out where some more of that gold is.

—Tom Lucas, *Kumeyaay*

The white people never cared for land or deer or bear. . . . When we dig roots we make little holes. When we build houses, we make little holes. . . . We shake down acorns and pinenuts. We don't chop down the trees. We only use dead wood. But the White people plow up the ground, pull down the trees, kill everything. . . . The spirit of the land hates them. They blast out trees and stir it up to its depths. They saw up the trees. That hurts them. The Indians never hurt anything, but the White people destroy all. They blast rocks and scatter them on the earth. The rock says, "Don't. You are hurting me." But the White people pay no attention. When the Indians use rocks, they take little round ones for their cooking. . . . How can the spirit of the earth like the White man? . . . Everywhere the White man has touched it, it is sore.
—Kate Luckie, *Wintu*

When the present race of the white people made their first appearance upon the American continent, we believed it was the Wa-gas returning, and a hearty welcome was extended to them; and there was great rejoicing among our tribes. But soon the sad mistake was discovered, to our sorrow, when the men began to debauch our women, give whiskey to our men, and claim our land that our forefathers had inhabited for so many thousands of years; yet not a single [white] family has ever been driven from their house on the Klamath River up to this day. We no longer termed them as Wa-gas, but as Ken-e-ahs, which means foreigners, who had no right to the land and could never appreciate our kindness, for they were a very different people from the Wa-gas. They had corrupt morals that brought dissolution upon our people and wrought the horrors of untold havoc.
—Lucy Thompson, *Yurok*

Yosemite (1851)

A line of soldiers pick their way down the torturous path clogged with snow that leads into the Valley of Yosemite. The Mariposa Battalion have come after the Yosemite Miwok, who have joined other nations in a determined effort to drive the miners from their lands. The soldiers bear one message only: you must surrender to be placed on reservations on the plains of the San Joaquin Valley or you will be destroyed. Not one person will be left alive. The Yosemite refuse to surrender; the soldiers pick their way deeper into the canyon. The leader Tenieya desires peace, but only if his people are allowed to remain in the valley he calls Paradise. The thought occurs to one of the officers that perhaps Tenieya has rights. But Major James D. Savage replies that Satan himself once entered Paradise; the Miwok have no rights, the matter is closed.

Tenieya's son is captured along a rocky ledge. In the soldier's camp, a grinning guard allows him to untie the ropes that bind him. When he runs, he is shot in the back. The young soldier who murders him thinks that killing Indians is sport. Days later, Tenieya is captured. On the snowy ground in the soldier's camp he steps across the body of his dead son and says nothing. Only his lip quivers, and his eyes burn hatred.

My people are now ready to begin a war against the white gold diggers. If all the tribes will be as one tribe, and join with us, we will drive all the white men from our mountains.
—José Rey (King Joseph), *Chowchilla*

The white soldiers have killed our great chief; they have killed many of our best warriors; they have burned up our huts and villages and destroyed our supplies, and have tried to drive our people from our territory, and they would have killed our women and children if we did not hide them where they could not be found. . . .

—Tomkit and Frederico, *Chowchilla*

Where can we now go that the Americans will not follow us? . . . Where can we make our homes, that you will not find us?   —(Name not given), *Miwok*

My people do not want anything from the "Great Father" you tell me about. The Great Spirit is our father, and he has always supplied us with all we need. We do not want anything from white men. . . . Go, then; let us remain in the mountains where we were born; where the ashes of our fathers have been given to the winds.

—Tenieya, *Miwok*

Kill me, sir Captain! Yes, kill me, as you killed my son; as you would kill all my race if you had the power. Yes, sir, American, you can now tell your warriors to kill the old chief; you have made me sorrowful, my life dark; you killed the child of my heart, why not kill the father? But wait a little; when I am dead I will call to my people to come to you, I will call louder than you have had me call; that they shall hear me in their sleep, and come to avenge the death of their chief and his son. Yes, sir, American, my spirit will make trouble for you and your people, as you have caused trouble to me and my people. . . . You may kill me, sir, Captain, but you shall not live in peace. I will follow in your foot-steps, I will not leave my home, but be with the spirits among the rocks, the waterfalls, in the rivers and in the winds; wheresoever you go I will be with you. You will not see me, but you will fear the spirit of the old chief, and grow cold. . . . I am done.   —Tenieya, *Miwok*

Reservations   (1853)

Land grabbers and gold speculators flood into California. While there is ore left to mine, panhandlers ravenously snatch up claims and settle lands. Along the coast, rich mission pasturage offers additional prospects for gaining wealth and Indian nations again are regarded as being in the way. Some say they should be pushed west, off the continent entirely, to an island in the Pacific, or at least to Catalina opposite the Southern California coast.

In 1853 the government establishes reservations in California, and Indian nations are forced onto them. Others are simply pushed aside, to areas where it is impossible for a goat to live.

The largest of the reservations of our Californians was Nome Lackee. . . . It had no game, no acorns, no fishery, and no rain, and hence, being useful for nothing else, was eminently fitted for a reservation. . . . Mendocino reservation . . . was an excellent place. There were fish and mussels enough there for all the Indians located there, if it had not been that some white friends of the agency started a saw-mill and filled the river with logs, so that a fish could not get through. Tejon reservation, near the base of the Sierra Nevada . . . in Southern California, was a nice, dry place, where the Indians were never bothered by rain or crops. . . . The management of these reservations was under one of the ablest Indian rings ever known in America.   —J. P. Dunn, *United States*

Derisively called "diggers," Southern California Indian people,
even children such as this Cahuilla girl, were subject to
kidnapping, enslavement, and inhumane labor laws by first the
Mexican, then the American, government.

The Americans are now squatting here, and taking away my land, wood, and water. The man Weber living at San Gorgonio, has our animals killed whenever they go there. We have not land enough to plant; my people are poor and hungry. . . . Some Americans tell us we must go away to the mountains to live; other Americans tell us that we must all live together on some land. We do not understand it; we do not like it. . . . I do not tell lies; I tell the truth. You are an officer of the government—what shall we do?   —Juan Antonio, *Cahuilla*

We thank you for coming here to talk to us in a way we can understand. It is the first time anyone has done so. You ask us to think what place we like next best to this place, where we always lived. You see that graveyard out there? There are our fathers and our grandfathers. You see that Eagle-nest mountain and that Rabbit-hole mountain? When God made them, He gave us this place. We have always been here. We do not care for any other place. . . . If you give us the best place in the world, it is not so good for us as this. . . . This is our home. . . . We cannot live anywhere else. We were born here and our fathers are buried here. . . . We want this place and not any other. . . .

There is no other place for us. We do not want you to buy [us] any other place. If you will not buy this place, we will go into the mountains like quail, and die there, the old people and the women and children. Let the Government be glad and proud. It can kill us. We do not fight. . . . If we cannot live here, we want to go into the mountains and die. We do not want any other home.   —Cecilio Blacktooth, *Cupeño*

. . . a promise was made to the Indian, "You shall have Hoopa Valley for your home," and they have been waiting all these years to have the land set apart. . . . When will the white man give us our land . . . ? . . . Shall we ever get justice done to us? We have waited now thirty years. . . . Many here died, others are suffering now. Is this my treatment at the hands of my white brother for all my good will and deeds toward him?

—Billy Beckwith, *Hupa*

Rogue River War   (1855)

Bullets fly. Vigilante soldiers stumble over corpses and bodies lying bloody upon the ground. A giant bonfire hisses in the center of the field and white hands heap the ceremonial clothing, feathers, and headpieces on top for fuel. Flames illuminate the abalone ornaments as they sizzle and blacken. The wail of babies tossed alive into the pyre is drowned out by the shouts of the soldiers.

Miners along the Rogue River abduct and rape Indian women with impunity. Volunteer armies form against the resistance. Local townspeople, nicknamed "the exterminators," raid villages of the Shasta, Tolowa, Tututni, and Takelma, vowing total extermination. Howitzers and rifles open fire into sleeping Indian camps; two villages are massacred on Christmas Eve. When the Rogue River nations fight back, they fight well; numerically stronger companies sent against them repeatedly are routed.

. . . the only correct method of quieting Indians [is] killing them fast as you can lay hands on them. The Indian nature . . . is devoid of gratitude, and of all . . . humanizing influences. . . . Shoot them down, scourge them with saber and brand till they cringe and beg for their lives—and you . . . may get along with him.   —Editorial, *Humboldt Register*

I promised to give you some of our experience in hunting Indians—a kind of game not often treated of in your journal—and as the sport has become rather universal on this

Tolowa basket maker, Northern California. As an alternative to extermination, the U.S. government once considered moving California Indian people off the continent entirely and impounding them on islands in the Pacific.

coast, every bit of experience will be of service to the amateur or professional hunter. . . . A large herd crossed the mountains last winter. . . . We have caught a great many females or squaws and young, but the bucks have generally made their escape. . . . You must [as a hunter] vow vengeance against every Indian you meet, but never molest any except peaceable Indians, who are unarmed, and expect no danger; this is a very gallant thing, when done in the face of public opinion, law, and order. If an Indian is a prisoner and charged with some offence, you go up to him very fiercely and say, "You d-d scoundrel, why did you steal my pantaloons?" The Indian does not understand a word of English, but thinks it is something terrible, looks scared, and shakes his head. This is proof positive of his guilt, and you haul out your revolver and blow his brains out. He can't help himself, for his feet and hands are tied. You have done a determined thing, and are henceforth a made man. —Editorial, *Porter's Prairie*

Good Haul of Diggers—One White Man Killed—Thirty eight Bucks killed, Forty Squaws and Children Taken.

Good Haul of Diggers—Band Exterminated.
—Editorials, *Humboldt Times*

My grandfather and all of my family—my mother, my father, and we—were around the house and not hurting anyone. Soon . . . some white men came. They killed my grandfather and my mother and my father. I saw them do it. . . . Then they killed my baby sister and cut her heart out and threw it in the brush where I ran and hid. My little sister was a baby, just crawling around. I didn't know what to do. I was so scared that I guess I just hid there a long time with my little sister's heart in my hands. . . . —Sally Bell, *Sinkyone*

Well, soldier come, everybody scatter, run for hills. One family this way, one family other way. Some fighting. My father killed, my mother killed. . . . Well, most like dream, I 'member old grandmother pack me round in basket on her back. All time she cry and holler. I say, "Grandmother, what you do?" "What is it, crying, grandmother?" "I sorry for you, my child. Why I cry. I not sorry myself, I old. You young, maybe somebody find you all right, you live.". . . Pretty soon soldiers come again. That's the time they leave my old grandmother cause she can't walk, maybe she die right there, maybe soldiers kill her. She cry plenty when my uncle take me away. Well, all time going round in woods. After while my uncle get killed. Then I'm alone. Klamath Indian find me, bring me to new reservation.

—John Adams, *Rogue River Shasta*

When those claiming a Christian civilization and calling themselves American citizens can thus designate MEN as "bucks" and treat them worse than brutes, it is time to stop speaking of Indians as "the savages."

—John Beeson, *United States*

Lost River (1852)

The so-called Modoc War begins in 1852, although the army will say that it begins years later, in 1873. Good relations with Americans are scarred by an unprovoked attack by miners, followed by subsequent Modoc retaliation on an immigrant train. In these days of the California gold rush, no Indian nation is safe. Indian-hunters under Ben Wright advance toward the Modoc camp along Lost River, calling for peace talks. The Modoc are glad. On the morning of the proposed conference, Captain Jack's father, leader of the Modoc, walks unarmed into Wright's camp. He is gunned down and the slaughter begins.

᎐

. . . that we, yes, let us meet the disgrace, that we, in the fall of 1852, sought the fathers of these, the living Modoc chiefs; invited them to a "peace" conference; raised the white flag . . . in the selected spot of the lava-beds near (O, strange return!) the place of the death of General [Edward] Canby and Dr. [Eleasar] Thomas; and while conversing as to future peace arrangements, Benjamin Wright, the leader of the American force, raised his pistol, upon a preconcerted signal, and shot down the "Modoc" nearest to him; simultaneously twenty pistol-shots from his men brought eighteen Modocs writhing in their death-agony on the rocks, and our humane "braves" bent over the persons of the expiring Modocs, [and] cut off their scalps. . . .

Was Ben. Wright punished? No; he was rewarded with an Indian agency. A fine specimen of Indian agency was this red-handed assassin. Did our people at Yreka view Ben. Wright and his brother butchers with detestation of their horrid crime? No; they turned out en masse to meet the returning warriors with their bloody trophies, the Modoc scalps. They opened the hotel to entertain the assassin guests; they sang songs, made speeches laudatory of bloody Ben. Wright. . . . Think you that the captured chiefs are ignorant of the fate their fathers met under the "flag of truce?" If General Canby did not know it, he was utterly unfit for the position he held. If he did know it, he knew that retaliation is the art of war. —Mrs. Mary L. Benham, *United States*

᎐

My people, we [were] born in this country; this is our land. God put our fathers and mothers here. We have lived here in peace. . . . Now, my people, I see we cannot get along with the white people. They come along and kill my people for nothing. Not only my men, but they kill our wives and children. I did not give the white men any cause to commit these murders. Now, what shall I do? Shall I run every time I see white people? If I do, they will chase us from valley to mountain, and from mountain to valley, and kill us all. They will hunt us like we hunt the deer and antelope. Shall we defend our wives and our children and our country? I am not afraid to die. If I die in war against the white people, I will die for a good cause.　　　　　—Captain Jack's father, *Modoc*

I am a Combutwaush. I am a leader of my people. My people are only a handful. I have listened to the chosen words of the Modoc Chief. He predicts the truth: we shall all be killed in time by the white men if we run every time we see them. I am not going to run. . . . I will see what they will do when they see their women and children killed, lying around dead, food for the coyotes. . . . My heart bleeds to know that we have been treated bad by the white man.

　　　　　—Legugyakes, *Combutwaush*

Ben Wright . . . told them he would like to hunt Indians . . . so [he] got some men that liked to hunt Indians to go with him. When they all got together they numbered over one hundred men. . . . They all left Yreka . . . to hunt down the Modoc Indians. . . . Wright traveled all through the Klamath Indian country, killing Klamath Indians wherever he could find them. He went through Goose Lake country, killed Paiute Indians wherever he got a chance. . . . On the south bank of Lost River . . . Ben Wright looks along his gun barrel; he turns slowly around to his men and says . . . "Boys, don't spare the squaws; get them all!" . . . The whites shot them down so fast on the south bank, they jumped in the river. . . .

When they got about half way across, the whites on the north bank opened fire on them. Only five escaped. . . . the citizens [of Yreka] gave Wright a big dance. He was . . . the mighty Indian Hunter, Savage Civilizer, Peace Maker, etc.

—Frank Riddle, *Modoc*

The Lava Beds (1873)

From the cinder caves of the lava beds, Captain Jack surveys Canby's army encamped below. His only crime has been to lead his people away from the Klamath Reservation. They have tried to live peacefully at the Yainax agency, but there is no food. The Modoc have chosen to go home.

Their number is swelled by Hooker Jim's band of Modoc, who find refuge with Jack after having murdered settlers in retaliation for the deliberate firing into an unarmed Modoc camp, killing women and babies.

Now Captain Jack is hunted like a deer. He tells General Canby that he can guarantee peace if allowed a home where his people will be protected from the settlements. All he asks is a reservation among the lava beds, where Whites will never want to go. This is denied. His own people urge him to war. When he resists, he is knocked off his feet by a jeering crowd of Modoc and threatened with death unless he makes a stand. Hooker Jim vows to kill any Modoc who surrender to Canby.

At the peace talks, Captain Jack sadly offers Canby a final chance to agree to a reservation in the lava beds. Canby is belligerent; the military offers only ultimatums. There are no negotiations. Again, Jack urges for peaceful resolution, and again Canby offers the Modoc no quarter. Captain Jack draws a revolver, and Canby is dead.

The Modoc escape from the lava beds. Hooker Jim has drawn the entire nation into war. Now he blames Jack for their condition and leaves him. Jack has thirty-seven men; the army coming after him numbers more than a thousand. The same Hooker Jim who has forced Jack to kill Canby now leads the army to Jack's location. In a cell at Fort Klamath, cold shackles around his legs, Captain Jack awaits a "trial" whose verdict has been reached long ago. Hooker Jim testifies against Jack and walks free.

. . . the Indians were compelled to slaughter their horses for food on the Klamath reservation to keep from starving, and when they had no more horses to slaughter they were then forced by hunger to seek their fishing grounds on Lost River, a tract of land set apart and given to them by the Hon. E. Steele, late superintendent of Indian affairs for California. The land is valuable. Land speculators desired it and sought to have the Indians removed. The Indians say there was but one of two deaths left to them, by starvation on the reservation, or a speedier death by the bullet in the lava-beds. They chose the latter.   —J. K. Luttrell, *United States*

Captain Jack   (1873)

The trial begins. The courtroom is filled to capacity, guarded by soldiers with fixed bayonets. Spectators and reporters eagerly watch as six Modoc men in striped prison clothes are hauled into the room. Their ankles are encircled by heavy iron shackles. Captain Jack is asked to make a statement. He looks disdainfully at the chains on his legs, mumbling "I cannot talk dressed in these irons." There is no sympathy in the courtroom. Condemned to die are Captain Jack, John Schonchin, Black Jim, and Boston Charley. The others involved go free. Two days later, fresh graves beneath the swinging gallows are opened. Captain Jack's head is severed from his body and deposited in the Smithsonian Institution, along with those of the other three prisoners. In 1984 the skull was

Modoc leader Captain Jack (at right), shackled and dressed in prison garb prior to the mock trial that would sentence him to death.

returned to Oregon for burial,* but his body remains at the Fort Klamath State Park, a tourist spectacle.

Life is mine only for a short time. You white people conquered me not; my own men did. . . . Some of my men voted to kill the Commissioners. I fought it with all of my might. I begged them not to kill unarmed men. What did they finally do? They threw me down . . . saying . . . "Lie there. You may not take any part in our plot. That's alright, be not afraid that you will die with a soldier's bullet. We will save that trouble for the soldier now." What could I do? My life was at stake no matter which way I might turn, so I agreed to do the coward's act, which the world knows this day. All I wish is that my side of the story may be told. I am not afraid to die, but I must say, I am ashamed to die in the way that I am to die, with my hands tied behind me. Ashamed is not the right expression. I once thought that I would die on the battlefield, defending my rights and home that was mine, given to me by no man. . . .

The very men that drove me to kill Canby, gave themselves up and then run me down. If I had only known what they were doing, you men would not have had me here today with chains on my legs and with satisfied smiles on your faces, for I would have died fighting, but my people lied to me, so I would not shoot them. The men that I speak of are here now free. They fought for their liberty with my life. . . .

I see it is too late to repent now. It is my duty to give some explanation, so that the White Father may know something of

---

* In 1984 Captain Jack's skull was released from the Smithsonian Institution into the custody of his family in Oregon. This historic achievement was accomplished through the efforts of Deborah Riddle, Tony Herrera, and Francis Harjo in Oregon; and Dr. Lawrence Angel, Dr. William Sturtevant, Ed Garner, and the author at the Smithsonian Institution. This was the first act of repatriation of Indian remains made by the Smithsonian, and indeed by any major United States museum, and set a precedent for future repatriation efforts.

what caused me to fall. So I will say again, hoping that at least a few of my words may become known to the white people. I see no crime in my heart although I killed Canby. But why did I do it? Do you understand? I was forced to do it. . . . You white people have driven me from mountain to mountain, from valley to valley, like we do the wounded deer. At last you have got me here. . . .

Why, I am a murderer! Everybody says that. That is so. Do I deny the charge? No, I do not. I did it, but I say again I had to do it. . . . I see in your faces you are tired of listening to me. . . . The government ought to care for my young people. See the good land and the size of my country that is taken away from me and my people. If I wanted to talk more, I could do so and tell you facts and prove by white people that would open the eyes of all of you that are here today, about the way my people have been murdered by the whites. I will say, not one white man was ever punished for their deeds. If the white people that killed our women and children had been tried and punished, I would not have thought so much of myself and companions. Could I? Could I? Please answer. No, you men answer me not. Do we Indians stand any show for justice with you white people, with your own laws? I say no. I know it. You people can shoot any of us Indians any time you want to whether we are in war or in peace. Can any of you tell me where ever any man has been punished in the past for killing a Modoc in cold blood? No, you cannot tell me.

I am on the edge of my grave; my life is in your people's hands. I charge the white people of wholesale murder. Not only once but many times. Think about Ben Wright. What did he do? He killed nearly fifty of my people. Among the killed was my father. He was holding a peace council with them. Was he or any of his men punished? No, not one. Mind you, Ben Wright and his men were civilized white people. The other civilized white people at Yreka, California, made a big hero of him, gave him a fine dinner and a big dance in his honor for murdering innocent Indians. He was praised for his crime. Now here I am. Killed one man, after I had been fooled by him many times and forced to do the act by my own warriors. The law says, hang him. He is nothing but an Indian, anyhow. We can kill them any time for nothing, but this one has done something, so hang him. Why did not the white man's law say that about Ben Wright? So now I do quit talking. In a few days I will be no more. I now bid the world farewell.

—Kintpuash (Captain Jack), *Modoc*

Murder of the Washo (1859)

All along the immigrant route to the goldfields of California, settlements spring up. Mormons have settled in the Carson Valley among the Paiute. Relations continue very peacefully until the year 1859, when two settlers, McMullen and MacWilliams, decide to cross the Sierras for supplies before the snow falls. McMullen is a shopkeeper, and everyone knows he carries a large amount of money with him for supplies.

Two of them, MacWilliams and McMullen, went off the same night, and camped in the mountains. Some one came in the night and killed them both, and after they had shot them with guns or pistols, they placed arrows in the wounds to make it appear as if Indians had killed them. The next day news came in that Indians had killed John McMullen. . . . Major [William] Ormsbey showed the arrows, and asked them if they knew them. The Washoe chief, who is called Jam, said, "You ask me if these are my people's arrows. I say yes. . . . I know my people have not killed the men, because none of my men have been away; we are all at Pine-nut Valley, and I do not know what to think of the sad thing that has happened."   —Sarah Winnemucca, *Paiute*

The Washoe are ordered to surrender the guilty men for execution. Frightened, and not knowing what else to do, they deliver three innocent men to pay for a crime they never committed. The men are handcuffed and a mob forms, pelting them with rocks and calling for a lynching. In the afternoon, thirty-one armed soldiers escort the prisoners outside the jail house. They break free and run. Two drop instantly from a blast of gunfire. The third runs back toward the soldiers with his hands up in surrender. Bullets rip him apart.

Oh, such a scene I never thought I should see! At daybreak all the Washoes ran to where they were killed. The wife of the young man threw herself down on his dead body. Such weeping was enough to make the very mountains weep to see them. They would take the dead bodies in their arms, and they were all bloody themselves. . . . My poor little sister made herself sick she cried so much that day. . . . Some time during the winter the Washoe chief came and told us that the white men who killed McMullen and MacWilliams were caught.   —Sarah Winnemucca, *Paiute*

Pyramid Lake War   (1860)

The Pyramid Lake War holds a place in history as one of the greatest Indian victories in the annals of the West. To the Paiute, this is only small comfort; for the events that have led to it are sad indeed. Blame rests unequivocally on two brothers who have kidnapped and molested two Paiute children. When the victims' father retaliates, troops are sent against the nation. Grossly outnumbered and hotly pursued, the Paiute ambush the army in a canyon. The soldiers call a truce, and the Paiute sign a peace treaty that guarantees them lands around Pyramid Lake forever.

Two little girls about twelve years old went out in the woods to dig roots, and did not come back, and so their parents went in search of them, and not finding them, all my people who were there came to their help, and very thoroughly searched, and found trails which led up to the house of two traders named Williams, on Carson River, near by the Indian camp. But these men said they had not seen the children, and told my people to come into the house and search it; and this they did, as they thought thoroughly. After a few days they sorrowfully gave up all search, and their relations had nearly given them up for dead, when one morning an Indian rode up to the cabin of the Williamses . . . they set their dog upon him. When bitten by the dog he began halloing, and to his surprise he heard children's voices answer him, and he knew at once it was the lost children. . . . [My] brother . . . and others went straight to the cabin of the Williams brothers. The father demanded the children. They denied having them . . . when all at once the brother of the children knocked one of the Williamses down with his gun, and raised his gun to strike the other, but before he could do so . . . [the other Williams] stooped down and raised a trap-door. . . . The father . . . went down and found his children lying on a little bed with their mouths tied up with rags. He tore the rags away and brought them up. When my people saw their condition, they at once killed both brothers and set fire to the house.

Three days after the news was spread as usual. "The blood-thirsty savages had murdered two innocent, hardworking, industrious, kind-hearted settlers"; and word was sent to California for some army soldiers. . . . Major Ormsbey collected one hundred and sixty volunteers, and came up, and without asking or listening to any explanation demanded the [aggrieved] men. But my people would not give them up, and when the volunteers fired on my people, they flew to arms to defend the father and brother, as any human beings would do in such a case, and ought to do. And so the war began.

—Sarah Winnemucca, *Paiute*

After the soldiers had killed all but some little children and babies still tied up in their baskets, the soldiers took them also, and set the camp on fire and threw them into the flames to see them burn alive. I had one baby brother killed there. . . .

They went after my people all over Nevada. Reports were made everywhere throughout the whole country by the white settlers, that the red devils were killing their cattle, and by this lying of the white settlers the trail began which is marked by the blood of my people. . . .

—Sarah Winnemucca, *Paiute*

The only way the cattle-men and farmers get to make money is to start an Indian war, so that the troops may come and buy their beef, cattle, horses, and grain. The settlers get fat by it.

—Sarah Winnemucca, *Paiute*

Did the government tell you to come here and drive us off this reservation? Did the Big Father say, go and kill us all off, so you can have our land? . . . Is the government mightier than our Spirit-Father, or is he our Spirit Father? Oh, what have we done that he is to take all from us that he has given us? His white children have come and have taken all our mountains, and all our valleys, and all our rivers; and now, because he has given us this little place without our asking him for it, he sends you here to tell us to go away. Do you see that high mountain away off there? There is nothing but rocks

Romanticized by some, reviled as an educated savage by others,
Sarah Winnemucca captured the attention of the American
public with her 1883 autobiography, *Life Among the Paiutes*.

there. Is that where the Big Father wants me to go? If you scattered your seed and it should fall there, it will not grow for it is all rock there. Oh, what am I saying? I know you will come and say: Here, Indians, go away; I want these rocks to make me a beautiful home with!

—Egan, *Snake River Paiute*

We all like this land, and I want to send a letter to Washington not to sell the land. You must not think hard feelings against us. . . . I do not know the reason Washington wants my little land. . . . God gives us this land, and that is the reason I want my land yet, and it makes us feel bad when you ask us about it.

—Race Horse, *Bannock*

When God first put us on this land he gave us only one law to follow, and now you are going to change this law to-day and take a different course . . . it is hard for me to part with any of my land. How is it that you want me to do so?

—Gibson Jack, *Shoshone*

The white man, who possesses this whole vast country from sea to sea, who roams over it at pleasure and lives where he likes, cannot know the cramp we feel in this little spot, with the undying remembrance of the fact, which you know as well as we, that every foot of what you proudly call America, not very long ago belonged to the Red Man. . . . We . . . are cornered in little spots of the earth, all ours by right—cornered like guilty prisoners, and watched by men with guns who are more than anxious to kill us off.

—Washakie, *Shoshone*

The Plateau

*Do not become annoyed if the Frenchman and the Americans
laugh at us, the day will come when we will laugh at them.*
—*Skolaskin*, Sanpoil

In 1841 the first organized immigrant train trekked across the
Oregon Trail. From this tentative beginning, the little trickle
turned into a torrent. In 1845 three thousand travelers raced
across and in little more than three years, the influx of settlers
justified the creation of two new territories, Oregon and Washington. Preceding the newcomers were fur traders representing the
North West Company, John Jacob Astor's Pacific Fur Company,
and the Hudson Bay Company, along with Methodist and Pres-
byterian missionaries.

In 1836 the Reverend Marcus Whitman established a Presby-
terian mission in the country of the Cayuse and actively encouraged immigration and the settlement of Indian lands. In 1847
measles, transmitted by immigrants, swept through Oregon, deci-
mating the Cayuse and neighboring nations. Whitman was
blamed for its introduction. As a result, two Cayuse men by the
name of Tilokaikt and Tomahas sought redress and killed him,
triggering a war that ultimately involved the Cayuse, Nez Percé,
Spokane, Palouse, and Walla Walla nations. The situation was
escalated by an unprovoked attack upon the Palouse and Walla

Walla by Oregon volunteers led by notorious Indian-fighter Colonel Cornelius Gilliam. Preferring war and extermination to peace, Gilliam caused considerable bloodshed and anguish before the war finally was ended.

In 1855 Governor Isaac Stevens of Washington Territory held a peace council with the Cayuse, Umatilla, Walla Walla, Yakima, Nez Percé, and nations along the Columbia River. But peace with the United States always came with a price: reservations. In return for selling their countries, Indian nations were to receive a portion of them back again as reservations—along with agents, annuities, rations, teachers, and missionaries, all designed to replace traditional cultures with "American" ideals. Although this plan should have, and did, sound extremely unattractive to Indian leaders, in the end they were forced to sign after Stevens threatened to make them "walk in blood knee deep." Kamiakin, a Palouse leader who acted as head chief for the Yakima, was the last to sign. An interpreter later testified that Kamiakin's lips were covered with blood, having bitten them in suppressed rage.

If the nations suspected a raw deal before they signed the treaty, their suspicions were justified less than a year later when they were starving to death on the reservations. Food rations were nonexistent or grossly inadequate. Often the most they could hope for was a pound and a half of beef and a pound of flour per person, per week. Unable to live on such meager allowance, the nations were forced to hunt outside the reservations, where they were abused by ranchers who fanned rumors of an "Indian War." Promised farming tools were misappropriated by the same agents who pocketed annuity monies, and the nations were pauperized and robbed in the lands that once had been exclusively theirs.

War again broke out late in 1855. Disgusted by the Walla Walla councils and the grand promises that kept neither gold miners nor a railroad from stalking illegally across their lands, Yakima leader Kamiakin organized a confederacy to resist. His supporters included members of the Nez Percé, Palouse, Wenatchee, Umatilla, Yakima, Wanapam, Walla Walla, Chelan, Spokane, Colville, Coeur d'Alene, Sanpoil, Kalispel, Cayuse, and Flathead; and when the fighting ended in 1858, both the United States and the Indian nations had lost much. The nations lost the hope of recovering their lands, but the United States lost the approbation of history.

By 1861 ten thousand miners had invaded the Nez Percé country alone, and plans were begun to reduce the extent of existing reservations. White settlers purposely moved onto Indian lands, fully knowing that the action was illegal, but confident that the government would buy them out to preserve peace. This scam in the Wallowa Valley backfired when the government announced that it had no interest in annexing the region as part of Washington Territory. No settlers would be reimbursed for the trouble of settling illegally on Indian land. Tremendous pressure immediately was brought to bear upon Indian commissioners and military, and in 1877 the official position was reversed. The Wallowa Nez Percé, under the leadership of Chief Joseph, were ordered to remove. Although the desire to possess the Wallowa Valley was a crucial factor in the decision, the military had grown afraid of a religious movement within the Nez Percé nation whose practitioners were known to whites as "Dreamers."

Supported in their belief by the Wanapam prophet Smohalla, who argued that the settlers despoiled Creation by ravaging the land, the "Dreamers" adhered to a traditional philosophy directly at odds with the United States government plan for removal. The military blamed a growing resistance among the younger Nez Percé on the influence of this religion and—foreshadowing the massacre of practitioners of the Ghost Dance at Wounded Knee thirteen years later—determined to stamp out the "Dreamer" faith in the Wallowa Valley.

The relentless 1,800-mile pursuit of Joseph's band over the Rocky Mountains and across the Montana plains remains a great

blemish upon the honor of the United States in a history of U.S./
Indian relations riddled with dishonor. When Joseph eloquently
told his side of the story in Washington, D.C., after his surrender,
the entire nation was held up to shame.

[The] sky has wept tears of compassion on our fathers for centuries untold and [that] which to us looks eternal, may change. My words are like the stars that never set. What Seattle says the Great Chief [in] Washington can rely upon with as much certainty . . . as the return of the seasons. . . . The White Chief [in Washington] sends us greetings of friendship and good-will. This is kind, for we know he has little need of our friendship in return, because his people are many. They are like the grass that covers the vast prairies, while my people are few, and resemble the scattering trees of a storm-swept plain.

The great white chief sends us word that he wants to buy our lands. . . . There was a time when our people covered the whole land as the waves of a wind-ruffled sea cover its shell-paved floor. But that time has long since passed away with the greatness of tribes almost forgotten. I will not mourn over our untimely decay. . . . Our Great Father in Washington sends word . . . that if we do as he desires, he will protect us. . . . But can this ever be? Your god loves your people and hates mine; . . . he makes your people wax strong every day, and soon they will fill the land; while our people are ebbing away like a fast receding tide, that will never flow again. [We] seem to be orphans and can look nowhere for help. . . .

Your god seems to us to be partial . . . he had no word for his red children whose teeming millions filled this vast continent as the stars fill the firmament. No, we are distinct races and must ever remain so. There is little in common between us. The ashes of our ancestors are sacred and their final resting place is hallowed ground, while you wander away from the tombs of your fathers seemingly without regret. . . . Our religion is the traditions of our ancestors, the dreams of our old men, given them by [God] . . . and is written in the hearts of our people.

Your dead cease to love you and the homes of their nativity

as soon as they pass the portals of the tomb. . . . Our dead never forget the beautiful world that gave them being. They still love its winding rivers, its great mountains and its sequestered vales, and they ever yearn in tenderest affection over the lonely-hearted living and often return to visit and comfort them.

Day and night cannot dwell together. The red man has ever fled the approach of the white man, as the changing mists on the mountainside flee before the blazing morning sun. . . . It matters little where we pass the remainder of our days. They are not many. The Indians' night promises to be dark. No bright star hovers about the horizon. Sad-voiced winds moan in the distance. . . . A few more moons, a few more winters, and not one of all the mighty hosts that once filled this broad land, or that now roam in fragmentary bands through these vast solitudes, will remain to weep over the tombs of a people once as powerful and as hopeful as your own.

But why should we repine? Why should I murmur at the fate of my people? Tribes are made up of individuals and are no better than they. Men come and go like the waves of the sea. A tear . . . a dirge, and they are gone from our longing eyes forever. Even the white man . . . is not exempt from the common destiny. We may be brothers after all. We shall see.

Every part of this country is sacred to my people. Every hillside, every valley, every plain and grove has been hallowed by some fond memory or some sad experience of my tribe. Even the rocks that seem to lie dumb as they swelter in the sun along the silent seashore in solemn grandeur thrill with memories of past events connected with the fate of my people, and the very dust under your feet responds more lovingly to our footsteps than to yours, because it is the ashes of our ancestors, and our bare feet are conscious of the sympathetic touch, for the soil is rich with the life of our kindred. . . . And when the last red man shall have perished from the earth and his memory among white men shall have become a myth, these shores shall swarm with the invisible dead of my tribe, and when your children's children shall think themselves alone in the field, the store, the shop, upon the highway, or in the silence of the woods, they will not be alone. In all the earth there is no place dedicated to solitude. At night, when the streets of your cities and villages shall be silent and you think them deserted, they will throng with the returning hosts that once filled and still love this beautiful land. The white man will never be alone. Let him be just and deal kindly with my people, for the dead are not altogether powerless.

—Seealth (Seattle), *Duwamish*

Puget Sound—the Treaty of Point-No-Point (1855)

I wish to speak my mind as to selling the land—Great Chief! What shall we eat if we do so? Our only food is berries, deer, and salmon—where then shall we find these? I don't want to sign away all my land, take half of it, and let us keep the rest. I am afraid that I shall become destitute and perish for want of food. I don't like the place you have chosen for us to live on. I am not ready to sign the paper.

—Ohelantehtat, *Skokomish*

I do not want to leave the mouth of the River. I do not want to leave my old home, and my burying ground. I am afraid I shall die if I do. —Shairatsehauk, *Toanhooch*

... I hope the Governor will tell the whites not to abuse the Indians as many are in the habit of doing; or ordering them to go away and knocking them down. . . .

   —Chitsamahan (The Duke of York), *S'Klallam*

Desecration of the Coquille (1856)

In the summer of 1856 . . . the Coquille Indians on the Siletz and . . . Yaquina Bay, became, on account of hunger and prospective starvation, very much excited and exasperated, getting beyond the control of their agent, and even threatening his life, so a detachment of troops was sent out to set things to rights. . . .

Having brought with me over the mountains a few head of beef . . . the Indians soon formed a circle about the sentinels, and impelled by starvation, attempted to take the beef before it could be equally divided . . . the possibility that the starving Indians might break out [of the reservation] was ever present, so to anticipate any further revolt, I called for more troops . . . it was deemed advisable to build a block-house for the better protection of the agent, and I looked about for suitable ground on which to erect it . . . the only good site that could be found was some level ground used as the burial-place of the Yaquina Bay Indians. . . .

Their dead were buried in canoes, which rested in the crotches of forked sticks a few feet above-ground. . . . I made known to the Indians that we would have to take this piece of ground for the block-house. They demurred at first, for there is nothing more painful to an Indian than disturbing his dead . . . at last they gave in, consenting . . . as much because they could not help themselves, as for any other reason. . . .

[I decided] I should take my men and place the canoes in the bay, and let them float out on the tide across the ocean to the happy hunting-grounds. . . . We anticipated great fun watching the efforts of [the wood-rats] . . . when the canoes should be launched on the ocean. . . . When the work of taking down the canoes and carrying them to the water began . . . not a rat was to be seen. . . . The Indians said the rats understood Chinook. . . .

—General Philip H. Sheridan, *United States Army*

Puget Sound

These represent the number of my people killed by the whites during the past year, all Indian chiefs, fifteen of them, and yet nothing has been done by the Government to punish these wicked white men who killed my people. . . . The whites now scare all the Indians, and we look now wondering when all the Indians will be killed. . . . We never saw any man as agent on the reservation who had pity on the Indians; they all frighten them. . . . The whites say, "You will all be killed soon," and the Indians don't care to work the land.

—Napoleon, *Tulalip*

You commissioners from Washington, look at that blanket. . . . I got it from the Government. Is that what bought our land? Is that money?   —Clum Shelton, *Tulalip*

One of our employers treats us like dogs; he uses us like slaves . . . he struck an Indian on the face, and the blood gushed out. . . . The whites cheat us, and some of our agents cheat us. . . . I have no land now. I am a poor old man. God made me; the whites took our land. Here is my country below this reservation; near it is Tulalip. I want a paper to keep any white

men away when they come. They scare the old men and want
to kill us.　　　　　　　　　　　　　　—William, *Tulalip*

My heart is sorry all the time; it cries every day. All the Indian
country feels sad.　　　　　　　　　—Big John, *Skokomish*

Governor Isaac Stevens　　(1855–1856)

Governor Isaac Stevens, superintendent of Indian affairs in Washington Territory, and General Joel Palmer, holder of the same office in Oregon, chair the Walla Walla councils. Settlers in the newly created Washington and Oregon territories want land, and the Nez Percé, Cayuse, Walla Walla, Yakima, Colville, Palouse, Spokane, Pisquose, Methow, Okanagan, Dalles, and nations on the Columbia River will have to provide it.

The Nez Perses . . . fed my men driven out of the mountains by snow: the Cayuses and Walla Wallas received my men kindly; Pee-o-pee-mox-a-mox saw us in his country and gave us guides: the Young Chief and his people had nothing but smiles and kindness for us . . . there sits a Flat Head and there a Coeur D-Alene on the route across the Bitter Root; there are Poulouses and Colvilles and Spokanes away to the North . . . all were kind . . . The Great Father has learned much of you. He first learned of you from Lewis & Clarke; Pee-o-pee-mox-a-mox remembers Lewis & Clarke, the Lawyer does: they came through your country finding friends and meeting no enemies.
　　. . . The Great Father has been for many years caring for his red children across the mountains . . . many treaties have been made. . . . Andrew Jackson . . . said I will take the red man across a great river into a fine country where I can take

330

care of them; they have been there twenty years; they have their government, they have their schools . . . the Great Father and his chiefs; they did much for John Ross and his [Cherokee] people twenty years ago.

. . . This brings us now to the question. What shall we do at this council? We want you . . . to agree upon tracts of land where you will live. . . . On each tract we wish to have one or more schools . . . blacksmiths . . . carpenters . . . we want you and your children to learn to make plows, to learn to make wagons. . . .

—Isaac Stevens, *Washington Territory governor*

Do you speak true that you call me brother? We have but one Father in Heaven; it is He who has made all the earth; He made us of earth on this earth: He made our Fathers; when he gave us this earth. He gave no garden . . . we were divided into different countries; It was He, the Almighty that passed the law. . . . —Five Crows, *Cayuse*

I know the value of your speech from having experienced the same in California, having seen treaties there. We have not seen in a true light the object of your speeches; as if there was a post set between us, as if my heart cried from what you have said; as if the Almighty came down upon us here this day; as if He would say, What are you saying? . . .

You see this earth that we are sitting on; this country is small in all directions. . . . Should I speak to you of things that have been long ago as you have done? . . . From what you have said I think you intend to win our country, or how is it to be? In one day the Americans become as numerous as the grass; this I learned in California; I know that is not right. You have spoken in a round about way; speak straight. I have ears to hear you and here is my heart. Suppose you show me goods, shall I run up and take them? That is the way we are, we Indians, as you know us. Goods and the Earth are not equal; goods are for using on the Earth. I do not know where they have given lands for goods. We require time to think, quietly, slowly. . . . You have spoken in a manner partly tending to Evil. Speak plain to us.   —Peopeomoxmox, *Walla Walla*

Besides all these things, these shops, these mills and these schools which I have mentioned; we must pay you for the land which you give to the Great Father; these schools and mills and shops, are only a portion of payment . . . we also want to provide you with tools for your farms, with ploughs and hoes and shovels . . . we want in your houses plates and cups and brass and tin kettles; frying pans to cook your meat and bake ovens to bake your bread, like white people.

—Isaac Stevens, *Washington Territory governor*

It is but fifty years since the first white man came among you, those were Lewis and Clark who came down the Big River— the Columbia. . . . then came the Hudson Bay Co. who were traders. Next came missionaries; those were followed by emigrants with wagons across the plains; and now we have a good many settlers in the country below you.

If there were no other whites coming into the country we might get along in peace: You may ask, why do they come? Can you stop the waters of the Columbia River from flowing on its course? Can you prevent the wind from blowing? Can you prevent the rain from falling? Can you prevent the whites from coming? You are answered No!

—General Joel Palmer, *United States*
superintendent of Indian Affairs

How long will these people remain blind? We came to try to open their eyes [and] they refuse the light.

—General Joel Palmer, *United States superintendent of Indian Affairs*

I wonder if this ground has anything to say: I wonder if the ground is listening to what is said . . . the earth says, God has placed me here. The Earth says, that God tells me to take care of the Indians on this earth: the Earth says to the Indians that stop on the Earth feed them right. God named the roots that he should feed the Indians on: the water speaks the same way. . . . the grass says the same thing. . . . The Earth and water and grass say God has given our names and we are told those names: neither the Indians [n]or the Whites have a right to change those names: the Earth says, God has placed me here to produce all that grows upon me, the trees, fruit, etc. The same way the Earth says, it was from her man was made. God, on placing them on the Earth, desired them to take good care of the earth and do each other no harm. God said. —Weatenatenamy (Young Chief), *Cayuse*

God named this land to us, that is the reason I am afraid to say anything about this land. . . . Shall I steal this land and sell it? or what shall I do? this is the reason that my heart is sad. My friends, God made our bodies from the earth, as if they were different from the whites. What shall I do? Shall I give the lands that are a part of my body and leave myself poor and destitute? Shall I say I will give you my lands? I cannot say. —Owhi, *Yakima*

How is it I have been troubled in mind? If your mothers were here in this country who gave you birth and suckled you and, while you were sucking, some person came and took away your mother and left you alone and sold your mother, how would you feel then? This is our mother, this country, as if we drew our living from her. My friends, all of this you have taken.

—Stachas, *Cayuse*

What would I be glad about if I were to take a thing and throw it away? . . . How do you show your pity by sending me and my children to a land where there is nothing to eat but wood? That is the kind of land up there, that is the reason I cry. . . . The laws of God are not alone for you, they are for me as well.

—Camaspello, *Cayuse*

At last, we are faced with those awful people, the coming of whom was foretold by the old medicine man, Wa-tum-nah, long ago. Pe-peu-mox-mox, who has been in California, says that the Indians are dying off. . . . So it will be with us, if we allow the whites to settle in our country. . . . Now, when that pale-faced stranger, Gov. Stevens, from a distant land, sends to us such words as you have brought me, I am for war. If they take our lands, their trails will be marked with blood.

—Kamiakin, *Yakima*

We wish to be left alone in the lands of our forefathers, whose bones lie in the sand hills and along the trails, but a pale-face stranger has come from a distant land and sends words to us that we must give up our country, as he wants it for the white man. Where can we go? There is no place left. Only a single mountain now separates us from the big salt water of the setting sun. Our fathers, from the hunting grounds of the other world, are looking down on us today. Let us not make them ashamed! My people, the Great Spirit has his eyes upon us. He will be angry if, like cowardly dogs, we give our lands to the whites. Better to die like brave warriors on the battlefield, than live among our vanquishers, despised. —Kamiakin, *Yakima*

Why should we want a few goods in exchange for our lands? . . . We love our country—it is composed of the bones of our people, and we will not part with it.

—Cayuse delegation

. . . you selected this country for us to live in without our having any voice in the matter. We will think slowly over the different streams that run through the country. . . . I cannot take the whole country and throw it to you. . . . You embraced all my country, where was I to go, was I to be a wanderer like a wolf? Without a home, without a house I would be compelled to steal, consequently I would die. I will show you lands that I will give you, we will then take good care of each other. —Weatenatenamy (Young Chief), *Cayuse*

. . . there have been tracks on my ground. . . . I am not going [to the president] to trample on his grounds, and I do not expect anyone to tramp on mine. . . . Why do you want to separate my children and scatter them all over the country? I do not go into your country and scatter your children in every direction. —Looking Glass, *Nez Percé*

The one-armed white chief [Oliver O. Howard] has a smooth tongue and speaks softly and nicely to the Indians, but his good words have no power to reach their hearts. The Indians laughed at the General and his fine speeches saying that they would never persuade them to give up the Wallowa Valley which they were resolved to keep at every hazard.

—Howlish Wampo, *Cayuse*

You alone arranged the Indians' land. The Indians did not speak. Then you struck the Indians to the heart. You thought they were only Indians. That is why you did it.

—Quinquinmoeso, *Spokane*

For a great many years [my people] have listened to your teachings. These people's fathers were not without instruction. The earth was their teacher. That is the true teacher. That is where the Indian first discovered that he was a human being. Our forefathers taught their successors that were left on the earth. In the same way, from the earth, your fathers spring, and the earth taught you in the same way . . . when they hunted for happiness, they searched the ground first.

—Homli, *Walla Walla*

I know we cannot stop the river from running, nor the wind from blowing, and I have heard that you whites are the same. We could not stop you. I only speak to show my heart. I am done.

—Peter John, *Colville*

I have no faith in anything the governor has said, for I have been told that . . . the Americans are not our friends.

—Tleyuk, *Chehalis*

I am alone; all my people have left me; my friends are dead. They tried to do as the whites.　　　—Holoquila, *Tenino*

My young men shall never work. Men who work cannot dream, and wisdom comes to us in dreams. You ask me to plow the ground. Shall I take a knife and tear my mother's bosom? You ask me to dig for stone. Shall I dig under her skin for her bones? You ask me to cut grass and make hay and sell it and be rich like white men. But how dare I cut off my mother's hair?　　　—Smohalla, *Wanapam*

We are friends. We never spilt the blood of one of you. I never saw your blood. I want my country. I thought no one would ever want to talk about my country. Now you talk, you white men. . . . If I were to go to your country and say, "Give me a little piece," I wonder would you say, "Here, take it." I expect that is the same way you want me to do here. . . . You tell us, "Give us your land." . . . This is all the small piece I have got. I am not going to let it go.　　—Big Canoe, *Kalispel*

God created the Indian Country and it was like he spread out a big blanket. He put the Indians on it. They were created here in this Country . . . and that was the time this river started to run. Then God created fish in this river and put deer in the mountains and made laws through which has come the increase of fish and game. Then the Creator gave us Indians Life; we walked, and as soon as we saw the game and fish we knew they were made for us. For the women God made roots and berries to gather, and the Indians grew and multiplied as a people.

When we were created we were given our ground to live on, and from this time these were our rights. . . . We had the fish before the Missionaries came, before the white man came. We were put here by the Creator and these were our rights as far as my memory to my grandfather. . . . My strength is from the fish; my blood is from the fish, from the roots and berries. The fish and game are the essence of my life. I was not brought from a foreign country and did not come here. I was put here by the Creator.   —Meninick, *Yakima*

Since our forefathers first beheld him, more than seven times ten winters have snowed and melted. . . . We were happy when he first came. We first thought he came from the light; but he comes like the dusk of the evening now, not like the dawn of the morning. He comes like a day that has passed, and night enters our future with him. . . . To take and to lie should be burned on his forehead, as he burns the sides of my stolen horses with his own name. . . . He has filled graves with our bones . . . his course is destruction; he spoils what the spirit who gave us this country made beautiful and clean. . . .

His laws never gave us a blade, nor a tree, nor a duck, nor a grouse, nor a trout. . . . How often does he come? You know he comes as long as he lives, and takes more and more, and dirties what he leaves . . . this curse [is] on us and on the few that may see a few days more.   —Charlot, *Flathead*

Chief Joseph   (1877)

Uncommon times produce uncommon valor. Joseph, chief of the Wallowa Valley Nez Percé, is a man of both uncommon valor and extraordinary ability. In defense of his nation, he is driven from his homeland. He and his brother Ollokot, leaders White Bird, Toohoolhoolzote, Looking Glass, and their bands of Nez Percé

Chief Joseph and other Nez Percé militants were exiled by the U.S. government to an agency in Washington Territory away from the rest of their nation. His impassioned pleas for justice rank among the greatest oratory of his day.

will be pursued by a relentless cavalry eighteen hundred miles across the Bitterroot Mountains toward freedom in Canada. Across this distance, they fight more than twenty skirmishes against well-supplied soldiers armed with howitzers and cannon who are unencumbered by women, children, and old people. Yet Nez Percé military skill is so impressive, it is taught at West Point to the very soldiers who will fight Indian nations. In the Bear Paw Mountains of Montana, only thirty miles short of the Canadian line, the Nez Percé are forced to surrender; but only because Joseph has compassion for the elderly. They cannot run. The Nez Percé make a valiant stand and nearly win. Survivors are shipped to a malaria-infested reservation in Oklahoma. The government has taken away the Wallowa Valley forever. Eventually exiled to the rocky Colville Reservation in Washington, Joseph dies, reportedly of a broken heart.

My father was the first to see through the schemes of the white men. . . . [One day] my father sent for me. I saw he was dying. He said, . . . When I am gone, think of your country. You are the chief of these people. They look to you to guide them. Always remember that your father never sold his country. You must stop your ears whenever you are asked to sign a treaty selling your home. A few more years and the white men will be all around you. They have their eyes on this land. My son, never forget my dying words. This country holds your father's body. Never sell the bones of your father and your mother.   —Inmutooyahlatlat (Chief Joseph), *Nez Percé*

The Great Spirit Chief made the world as it is, and as he wanted it, and he made a part of it for us to live upon. I do not see where you get authority to say that we shall not live where he placed us.

—Inmutooyahlatlat (Chief Joseph), *Nez Percé*

The earth was created by the assistance of the sun, and it should be left as it was. . . . The country was made without lines of demarcation, and it is no man's business to divide it. . . . I see the whites all over the country gaining wealth, and see their desire to give us lands which are worthless. . . . Perhaps you think the Creator sent you here to dispose of us as you see fit. If I thought you were sent by the Creator I might be induced to think you had a right to dispose of me. Do not misunderstand me, but understand me fully with reference to my affection for the land. I never said the land was mine to do with it as I chose. The one who has the right to dispose of it is the one who has created it. I claim a right to live on my land, and accord you the privilege to live on yours.

—Inmutooyahlatlat (Chief Joseph), *Nez Percé*

It was lonesome, the leaving. Husband dead, friends buried or held prisoners. I felt that I was leaving all that I had, but I did not cry. You know how you feel when you lose kindred and friends through sickness—death. You do not care if you die. With us it was worse. Strong men, well women and little children, killed and buried. They had not done wrong to be so killed. We had only asked to be left in our own homes, the homes of our ancestors. Our going was with heavy hearts, broken spirits. But we would be free. . . . All lost, we walked silently on into the wintry night.   —Wetatonmi, *Nez Percé*

Let me be a free man—free to travel, free to stop, free to work, free to trade where I choose, free to choose my own teachers, free to follow the religion of my fathers, free to think and talk and act for myself. . . .

—Inmutooyahlatlat (Chief Joseph), *Nez Percé*

Treat all men alike. Give them all the same law. Give them all an even chance to live and grow. All men were made by the same Great Spirit Chief. They are all brothers. The earth is the mother of all people, and all people should have equal rights upon it. You might as well expect the rivers to run backward as that any man who was born a free man should be contented when penned up and denied liberty to go where he pleases. If you tie a horse to a stake, do you expect he will grow fat? If you pen an Indian up on a small spot of earth, and compel him to stay there, he will not be contented, nor will he grow and prosper. I have asked some of the great white chiefs where they get their authority to say to the Indian that he shall stay in one place, while he sees white men going where they please. They can not tell me.   —Inmutooyahlatlat (Chief Joseph), *Nez Percé*

Treat all men alike. Give them all the same law. Give them all an even chance to live and grow. All men were made by the same Great Spirit Chief. They are all brothers. The earth is the mother of all people, and all people should have equal rights upon it. You might as well expect the rivers to run backward as that any man who was born a free man should be contented when penned up and denied liberty to go where he pleases.

I do not understand why nothing is done for my people. I have heard talk and talk, and nothing is done. Good words do not last long unless they amount to something. Words do not pay for my dead people. They do not pay for my country, now overrun by white men. They do not protect my father's grave. They do not pay for all my horses and cattle. Good words will not give me back my children. Good words will not give my people good health and stop them from dying. Good words will not get my people a home where they can live in peace and take care of themselves. I am tired of talk that comes to nothing. It makes my heart sick when I remember all the good words and all the broken promises.

—Inmutooyahlatlat (Chief Joseph), *Nez Percé*

Epitaph

The following passages are not intended as an epilogue, but rather as an epitaph to the destructive foreign policies unleashed against Indian nations over the centuries, from the time Europeans first set foot upon the continent. What was begun by Cristóbal Colón received its finishing touches with forced deculturation, boarding schools, the allotment of Indian national lands, enrollment, and the vote. Today, Indian nations still await the time when the world recognizes their sovereign right to exist.

. . . the system of injustice, oppression, and robbery which the Government calls "its Indian Policy"; which has covered it with disgrace as incompetent, cruel, faithless, never keeping its treaties, and systematically and shamelessly violating its most solemn promises; has earned the contempt and detestation of all honest men and the distrust and hate of the Indian tribes. —Wendell Phillips, *United States*

The policy of the federal government has been, from the beginning, influenced by humane views towards the natives . . . it has made numerous treaties with them, with fair stipulations, which have been observed with good faith.
—William Tudor, *United States*

Epitaph

And suppose that, in some future day, our children should repay all these wrongs, would it not be doing as we, poor Indians, have been done to? But we sincerely hope there is more humanity in us, than that.   —William Apess, *Pequot*

If there was a crime . . . it was more your crime than ours. . . . You abolished our government, annihilated our laws, suppressed our authorities, took away our lands, turned us out of our houses, denied us the rights of men, made us outcasts and outlaws in our own land, plunging us at the same time into an abyss of moral degradation which was hurling our people to swift destruction.

—Stand Watie, *Cherokee*

I could not help thinking that there was a better way to deal with Indians than to begin with the conquering sword and follow it up with starvation, and justify every species of neglect and mismanagement in our dealing with them.

—General Oliver O. Howard, *United States Army*

The whole business is a monotonous piece of treachery and bloodstained villainy in which innocent persons suffer, while scoundrels who cheat and swindle the poor Indians keep out of danger and fill their pockets with money.

—Josephine Meeker, *United States*

There is no selfishness [among them], which is at the bottom of civilization.   —Henry Dawes, *United States*

Suppose the Federal Government should send a survey company into the midst of . . . Kansas or Colorado or Connecticut and run off the surface of the earth into sections and quarter sections and quarter quarter sections . . . rescinding and annulling all title to every inch of the earth's surface. . . . There is not an American citizen in any one of those States would submit to it, if it cost him every drop of his heart's blood. . . .   —Dewitt Duncan, *Cherokee*

No one certainly will rejoice more heartily than the . . . Commissioner when the Indians of this country cease to be in a position to dictate, in any form or degree, to the Government; when, in fact, the last hostile tribe becomes reduced to the condition of suppliants for charity. . . . If they stand up against the progress of civilization and industry, they must be relentlessly crushed. The westward course of population is neither to be denied nor delayed for the sake of all the Indians that ever called this country their home. They must yield or perish . . . the time shall come that the roving tribes are reduced to complete dependence and submission. . . . This is the true permanent Indian policy of the Government.

          —United States Secretary of the Interior report

I never yet knew an Indian chief to break his word!
          —General William S. Harney, *United States Army*

Every year's advance of our frontier takes in a territory as large as some of the kingdoms of Europe. We are richer by hundreds of millions; the Indian is poorer by a large part of the little that he has. This growth is bringing imperial greatness to the nation; to the Indian it brings wretchedness, destitution, beggary.

> —United States Secretary of the Interior report

All roving bands of Indians . . . will be required to go at once upon their reservations, and not leave them again upon any pretext whatever. So long as they remain upon their reservations in due subordination to the Government, they will be fully protected and provided for. . . . All male Indians will be enrolled, and their names will be recorded in a book kept for that purpose, with a full and accurate descriptive list of each person. Each Indian will be furnished with a copy of his descriptive list, and will be required to carry it always with him. . . . The presence on the reservation of every male adult will be verified once a day. . . .

Care will be taken to inform the Indians . . . that it is to their interest to assist in the detection of guilty individuals, so that the whole tribe may not suffer for the crimes of a few . . . when any enrolled Indian is found absent from his reservation without permission, all his family will be arrested and kept in close custody until he has been captured and punished according to his deserts. . . .

The ration for issue to adult Indians will consist of one pound of meat and one pound of breadstuffs . . . once a week. . . . An officer will always be present to witness and direct the slaughtering of beef and the distribution of food among the separate bands and families . . . the department commander will, in his discretion, make use of the friendly Indians to hunt out and destroy those who remain obstinately hostile.

> —Major General John M. Schofield, *United States Army*

All history admonishes us of the difficulty of civilizing a wandering race who live mainly upon game. To tame a savage you must tie him down to the soil. You must make him understand the value of property, and the benefits of its separate ownership. You must appeal to those selfish principles implanted by Divine Providence in the nature of man . . . and they should be taught to look forward to the day when they may be elevated to the dignity of American citizenship.

—United States Secretary of the Interior report

In January the issue of soup to the Indians commenced. It was made in a large cotton-wood vat, being cooked by steam carried from the boiler of the saw-mill in a pipe to the vat. . . . This soup was issued every other day. . . . [It consisted of] beef, beef-heads, entrails of the beeves, some beans, flour, and pork. . . . This mass was then cooked by the steam from the boiler passing through the pipe into the vat. When that was done, all the Indians were ordered to come with their pails to get it. . . . I passed there frequently when it was cooking, and was often there when it was being issued. It had a very offensive odor. It had the odor of the contents of the entrails of the beeves. I have seen the settlings . . . when they were cleaning the vat, and the settlings smelled like carrion—like decomposed meat. Some of the Indians refused to eat it, saying they could not, it made them sick.

—Samuel C. Haynes, *assistant surgeon, Fort Randall*

The agent . . . has almost absolute authority. . . . His power has grown to the overthrow of all self-government, and he is often an irresponsible despot, with no laws to execute but rules and orders from the Department at Washington.

The agent is rarely selected on account of his fitness for the place he is given. . . . The exigencies of politics, not the needs of the Indians, dictate the appointment of agents. . . . The Reservation line is a wall which fences out law, civil institutions, social order, and trade and commerce except through the Indian trader, and fences in savagery, despotism, greed, and lawlessness. The Indian under the Reservation system is a helpless and pauperized dependent, over whom the agent has even the power of life and death, with no restraints upon him except such as fear may exert. He has immense opportunities to demoralize those under his power and to enrich himself at their expense, and doing so is often largely his business. He knows that if his wards outgrow the necessity of a guardian, his occupation is gone. . . .

For a certain class of whites, an Indian Reservation is a veritable house of refuge. Here are no laws, no writs, no sheriffs, no jails. Here is the secure home of the forger, the horse-thief, and the murderer. . . .   —Editorial, *The Outlook*

I noticed . . . a small group of Indians who sat under a tree . . . all were dirty, ragged, and lean. . . . Soon an Indian woman and a young girl . . . hurried into the group, laid down . . . packs and opened them. . . . I could see spread out there some dingy meat, evidently waste from a butcher's shop, some discarded scraps of stale bread, and other stray odds and ends of food. . . . I felt a wave of fury toward our government's whole Indian policy. . . .

—Thomas Tibbles, *United States*

I know the Indian Ring. Your hair will be gray before the first law is passed that does away with the present system. Men of national reputation will attack you. You will have to endure and suffer and drink the cup of bitterness.

—Wendell Phillips, *United States*

It is an injustice to the character of the government and a wrong to the Indians that they should be compelled to remain on their reservations and there slowly starve, and it is a most painful and unhappy duty for the troops that they should be kept in large numbers in their presence with no power or authority except to force them to starve tranquilly.
—Brigadier General John Pope, *United States Army*

The rations we get are not nearly enough. We have one swallow, and then it is all gone. —Assadawa, *Wichita*

The call to labor must come to him, not through memorials or treaties, councils or presents, but through his necessities. He must be driven to toil by cold and the pangs of hunger. . . . Naturally, when a man begins to toil for that which he receives, he begins to learn the value of personal-property rights, and thus takes the first step in separating from his tribe, and toward individual manhood.
—United States commissioner of Indian Affairs

The only chance of saving any of this race, will be, by taking their children, at a very early age, and educating them in our habits, in a situation removed from the contagion of Indian pursuits. —William Tudor, *United States*

This [English] language which is good enough for a white man or a black man ought to be good enough for the red man. It is also believed that teaching an Indian youth in his own barbarous dialect is a positive detriment to him. The impracticability, if not impossibility, of civilizing the Indians of this country in any other tongue than our own would seem obvious.　　—United States commissioner of Indian Affairs

From all over the country thousands of little Indian boys and girls were rounded up and shipped hundreds of miles away to government boarding schools, to be recreated and humanized. They were forbidden to speak their native language. They were punished if they did. Parents were subjected to corporal punishment if they objected. The young ones were made to understand that all that "was before" was wrong. . . . How daring is stupidity!!

　　　　　—Metha Bercier, *Turtle Mountain Chippewa*

They told us that Indian ways were bad. They said we must get civilized. I remember that word too. It means "be like the white man." . . . And the books told how bad the Indians had been to the white men—burning their towns and killing their women and children. . . . We all wore white man's clothes and ate white man's food and went to white man's churches and spoke white man's talk. And so after a while we also began to say Indians were bad. We laughed at our own people and their blankets and cooking pots and sacred societies and dances. . . .　　　　　—Sun Elk, *Taos*

Who determines what civilization is the right one, I ask? Don't even the animals, the birds and all living creatures upon this earth have their own civilization? . . . And yet, they condemned us. . . .

　　　　　—Metha Bercier, *Turtle Mountain Chippewa*

The soldiers came and rounded up as many of the Blackfeet children as they could. The government had decided we were to get White Man's education by force. . . . Nobody waved as the wagons, escorted by the soldiers, took us toward the school at Ft. Shaw.   —Lone Wolf, *Blackfeet*

. . . you are taking my land from me; you are killing off our game, so it is hard for us to live. Now you tell us to work for a living. . . . We do not interfere with you, and again you say, why do you not become civilized? We do not want your civilization! We would live as our fathers did, and their fathers before them.   —Crazy Horse, *Oglala*

If we thought that the days were bad, the nights were much worse. This was the time when real loneliness set in. . . . Many boys ran away . . . but most of them were caught and brought back by the police. We were told never to talk Indian and if we were caught, we got a strapping with a leather belt. I remember one evening when we were all lined up in a room and one of the boys said something in Indian to another boy. The man in charge . . . caught him by the shirt, and threw him across the room. Later we found out that his collar-bone was broken. The boy's father, an old warrior, came to the school. He told the instructor that among his people, children were never punished by striking them. That was no way to teach children; kind words and good examples were much better.

                    —Lone Wolf, *Blackfeet*

And so the days passed by, and the changes slowly came to settle within me. . . . Gone were the vivid pictures of my parents, sisters and brothers. Only a blurred vision of what used to be. Desperately, I tried to cling to the faded past which was slowly being erased from my mind.

—Metha Bercier, *Turtle Mountain Chippewa*

You certainly must discover that the United States do not wish to injure you, but, on the contrary, that they wish to make you a people like themselves.

—United States commissioner of Indian Affairs

Read the books written during the past century and a quarter from the white man's standpoint, reviewing America's dealings with the Indian, and there is but one conclusion at which you can arrive, viz., that the North American Indian, in the main, is dull, stupid, unimpressionable, rude, dirty, brutal, treacherous, vindictive, murderous, and monstrously cruel; that he has no finer feelings to which one may appeal; that he has no religion, poetry, imagination, mythology, or legend. . . . Indeed, the very name, Indian, was synonymous, in the minds of the millions, with dirt, brutality, treachery, and murder. . . . In common parlance, "the only good Indian was the dead Indian," and many a man gained fame as an "Indian hunter" who should have been hung as a murderer.

. . . the Indian . . . has been maligned, misrepresented, and his real character denied, and there has been fastened upon him a fantastic, wickedly false, distorted mental and spiritual mask that cruelly belies his real self.

—George Wharton James, *United States*

"Every native Indian is now a citizen of the United States." . . . It has been a long road to legal absorption of the Red Man.   —Editorial

Epitaph

There may have been a reason in the weakness of the early colonies, and far superior numbers of their Indian foes, for recognizing this condition of Indian sovereignty. But that has long since passed away, and there is no longer any occasion for recognizing the tribes who remain with us as foreigners. Their own interests . . . require that they should be recognized and treated for what they are, an ignorant and helpless people.   —United States commissioner of Indian Affairs

I have lived on this frontier 50 years, and I have never yet known an instance in which war broke out between these tribes that the tribes were not in the right.
—General William S. Harney, *United States Army*

White   men—whiskey—tomahawks—scalping   knives—guns, powder and ball—small-pox—debauchery—extermination.   —George Catlin, *United States*

Does this generation love justice enough to ask that it be shown to the red men? Have we not as a people fixed the brutal maxim in our language, "the only good Indian is a dead Indian?" We laugh at the saying now as a good jest, but the cheeks of our descendants will redden with shame when they read the coarse brutality of our wit.
—Fletcher Johnson, *United States*

Notes

Introduction

xiii *Inmutooyahlatlat, "My Friends . . .":* "An Indian's View of Indian Affairs," *North American Review* (vol. 128, Apr. 1879), p. 415.

Epigraph

2 Phillips, "Why, fellow-citizens . . .": *Report of the Secretary of the Interior,* 42nd Congress, 2nd session, 1871, H. Exec. Doc. 1, vol. 3, serial set 1505, p. 455.

The Caribbean

5 Las Casas, "How much damage . . .": Lyman S. Tyler, *Two Worlds: The Indian Encounter with the European, 1492–1509* (Salt Lake City: University of Utah Press, 1988), p. 16.

6 Colón, "They are fit . . .": Marion Lansing, *Liberators and Heroes of the West Indian Islands* (Boston: L. C. Page & Co., 1953), p. 37.

7 Las Casas, "from 1494 . . .": Bartolomé de Las Casas, *History of the Indies,* Book Two, trans. Andrée Collard (New York: Harper & Row, Torchbook Library, 1971), p. 154.

8 Colón, ". . . neither better people . . .": Oliver Dunn and James E. Kelley, Jr., eds., *The Diario of Christopher Columbus's First Voyage to America 1492–1493* (Norman: University of Oklahoma Press, 1989), pp. 273, 275, 281.

   Colón, "Now I have ordered . . .": *Diario of Christopher Columbus's First Voyage,* p. 289.

   Las Casas, "And this may . . .": Bartolomé de Las Casas, *The Tears of the Indians; being an historical and true account of the cruel massacres and slaughters of above twenty millions of innocent people; committed by the Spaniards* (London: J. C. Printer, 1656).

9 Las Casas, "The worst and gravest . . .": *History of the Indies,* Book One, trans. Andrée Collard, pp. 52–53.

10 Las Casas, ". . . [The Taíno] began . . .": *Tears of the Indians.*

Notes

11 Las Casas, "Once the Indians . . .": *History of the Indies,* Book Two, trans. Andrée Collard, p. 94.

  Las Casas, "Thus [the Spaniards] . . .": *History of the Indies,* Book Two, trans. Andrée Collard, pp. 79–80.

12 Las Casas, "And who . . .": *History of the Indies,* Book Two, trans. Andrée Collard, p. 82.

13 Las Casas, "It is not possible . . .": *Liberators and Heroes of the West Indian Islands,* p. 38.

14 Hatuey, "You know that . . .": *Liberators and Heroes of the West Indian Islands,* p. 33.

  Las Casas, ". . . they were so relentlessly . . .": Samuel Wilson, *Hispaniola: Caribbean Chiefdoms in the Age of Columbus* (Tuscaloosa: University of Alabama Press, 1990), pp. 95–96.

  Benzoni, "Wherefore many went . . .": Girolamo Benzoni, *History of the New World* (London: Hakluyt Society, 1857), pp. 77–78.

15 Las Casas, ". . . [Ovando] decided . . .": *History of the Indies,* Book Two, trans. Andrée Collard, pp. 98–99.

16 Las Casas, ". . . they used to stuff . . .": *History of the Indies,* Book Two, trans. Andrée Collard, p. 158.

  Las Casas, "I stood there staring . . .": *History of the Indies,* Book Two, trans. Andrée Collard, pp. 160–61.

17 Las Casas, "In a more just world . . .": Bartolomé de Las Casas, *Historia de las Indias,* Book Three, ed. José M. Vigio (Mexico City: Imprenta y Litographia de Ireneo Paz, 1877). Translated from the original by Blair Sullivan.

  Las Casas, "The Spanish came . . .": *Historia de las Indias,* Book Three. Translated from the original by Blair Sullivan.

19 Las Casas, ". . . the Indian kings . . .": *History of the Indies,* Book Three, trans. Andrée Collard, p. 249.

  (Name not given), *Taíno,* "You have come . . .": *History of the Indies,* Book One, trans. Andrée Collard, p. 55.

  Mayobanex, "[The Spaniards] . . .": Peter Martyr D'Anghera, *De Orbe Novo: The Eight Decades of Peter Martyr D'Anghera,* vol. 1, book 7, trans. Francis Augustus MacNutt (New York: G. P. Putnam's Sons, 1912), p. 145.

  Enrique, "I know the Spanish . . .": *Historia de las Indias,* Book Three. Translated from the original by Blair Sullivan.

Mexico

21 *Nezahualcoyotl, "I am intoxicated . . .":* Miguel León-Portilla, *Fifteen Poets of the Aztec World* (Norman: University of Oklahoma Press, 1992), p. 81.

Notes

23 Aztec poem, *"Extended lies the city . . .":* John Bierhorst, *In the Trail of the Wind: American Indian Poems and Ritual Orations* (New York: Farrar, Straus, & Giroux, 1971), p. 44.

25 Aztec chronicler, "They gave the Spaniards . . .": F. Bernardino de Sahagun, *The Florentine Codex,* trans. Dr. Catherine Good, manuscript, Biblioteca Medicea Laurenziana, Florence, Italy.

Aztec chronicler, "Then there arose . . .": F. Bernardino de Sahagun, *The War of Conquest: How It Was Waged Here in Mexico,* trans. Arthur J. O. Anderson and Charles E. Dibble (Salt Lake City: University of Utah Press, 1978), p. 23.

26 Aztec chronicler, "[The city] rose . . .": *War of Conquest,* p. 23.

Aztec chronicler, "Shocked, terrified . . .": *War of Conquest,* p. 20.

Aztec chronicler, "The iron of their lances . . .": *War of Conquest,* p. 23.

27 Díaz, "We were astounded . . .": Kate Stephens, *The Mastering of Mexico* (New York: Macmillan, 1916), p. 145.

Cortés, "[Your Highness,] . . .": Hernán Cortés, *Letters from Mexico,* trans. Anthony Pagden (New Haven, Conn.: Yale University Press, 1986), pp. 107–8.

Moctezuma, "What now . . .": *War of Conquest,* p. 26.

Moctezuma, "Do the former rulers . . .": *War of Conquest,* p. 33.

29 Aztec chronicler, "Moctezuma's own property . . .": *War of Conquest,* p. 36.

Aztec chronicler, ". . . they charged the crowd . . .": *War of Conquest,* pp. 43–44.

30 Aztec chronicler, "That night, at midnight . . .": *War of Conquest,* p. 53.

31 Aztec chronicler, "The canal was filled . . .": *War of Conquest,* pp. 54–56.

Aztec chronicler, ". . . at about the time . . .": *War of Conquest,* p. 64.

32 Cuauhtémoc, "Ah, captain . . .": *In the Trail of the Wind,* p. 152.

Aztec chronicler, "Fighting continued . . .": *War of Conquest,* pp. 79, 86.

Aztec chronicler, "Great was the stench . . .": Adrian Recinos and Delia Goetz, *The Annals of the Cakchiquels: Title of the Lords of Totonicapan* (Norman: University of Oklahoma Press, 1953), p. 116.

33 Aztec chronicler, "Finally the battle . . .": *War of Conquest,* pp. 87, 89.

Aztec poem, *"Proudly stands . . .":* Ronald Wright, *Stolen Continents* (Boston: Houghton Mifflin Co., Penguin Books; Canada: John Murray, Ltd., 1992), p. 15.

The North Atlantic

34 (*Name not given*), Micmac, *"Learn now, my brother . . .":* Chrestien Le Clercq, *New Relations of Gaspesia, with the Customs and Religion of the Gaspesian Indians,* ed. and trans. William Ganong (Toronto: Champlain Society, 1910), p. 106.

34 Cartier, "sawe two companies . . .": Richard Hakluyt, ed., *The Principal Navigations, Voyages, Traffiques, and Discoveries . . .*, vol. 8 (New York: Macmillan, 1904), p. 197.

38 Capitanal, "I am only . . .": Reuben Gold Thwaites, ed., *Jesuit Relations and Allied Documents: Travels and Explorations of the Jesuit Missionaries in New France, 1610–1791*, vol. 5 (Cleveland: Burrow's Brothers Co., 1896–1901), pp. 205–11. Translated from the original by Lee Miller.

Nicolar, "[The] . . . event created . . .": Joseph Nicolar, *The Life and Traditions of the Red Man* (Bangor, Maine: C. H. Glass & Co., 1893), pp. 106–7, 128–29.

40 Cartier, ". . . then did their legges . . .": *Principal Navigations, Voyages, Traffiques, and Discoveries*, pp. 247–48.

41 Cartier, "After this medicine . . .": *Principal Navigations, Voyages, Traffiques, and Discoveries*, pp. 250–51.

Bedagi, "The earth is . . .": Natalie Curtis, *The Indians' Book* (New York: Harper & Brothers, 1907), p. 11.

42 (Name not given), *Micmac*, "I am greatly astonished . . .": *New Relations of Gaspesia*, p. 103.

Cartier, "About two of the clocke . . .": *Principal Navigations, Voyages, Traffiques, and Discoveries*, p. 255.

43 Cartier, ". . . the people of [Stadacona] . . .": *Principal Navigations, Voyages, Traffiques, and Discoveries*, p. 265.

(Name not given), *Micmac*, "Thou reproachest us . . .": *New Relations of Gaspesia*, pp. 104–6.

45 (Name not given), *Montagnais*, "The beaver does everything . . .": *Jesuit Relations and Allied Documents*, vol. 6, pp. 297–99.

47 Pigarouich, "Who do you think . . .": *Jesuit Relations and Allied Documents*, vol. 16, p. 158. Translated from the original by Lee Miller.

Agouachimagan, ". . . I understand that your town . . .": *Jesuit Relations and Allied Documents*, vol. 26, p. 302. Translated from the original by Lee Miller.

48 Bomazeen, "Although several missionaries . . .": Samuel Drake, *Biography and History of the Indians of North America, from its first discovery* (Boston: B. B. Mussey & Co., 1848), p. 309.

Micmac delegation, "The place where . . .": *Collection de Documents Inédits sur le Canada et l'Amérique, publiés par le Canada-Français*, vol. 1 (Quebec: L. J. Demers & Brothers, 1888), pp. 17–18. Translated from the original by Lee Miller.

49 Madokawando, "We were driven . . .": *Biography and History of the Indians of North America*, p. 288.

Neptune, "You know your people . . .": *Biography and History of the Indians of North America*, p. 321.

50 Wentworth, "[The raid was] . . .": James Phinney Baxter, ed., *Documentary History of the State of Maine*, Collections of the Maine Historical Society, 2nd series, vol. 10 (Portland: Maine Historical Society, 1869–1916), p. 222.

Penhallow, "The *Indians* . . .": Samuel Penhallow, *The History of the Wars of New England with the Eastern Indians* (Boston: T. Fleet, 1726), pp. 105–6.

51 Atiwaneto, "We hear . . .": E. B. O'Callaghan, ed., *Documents Relative to the Colonial History of the State of New York*, vol. 10 (Albany: Weed, Parsons, & Co., 1858), pp. 252–54.

52 Panaouamskeyen, "I Panaouamskeyen . . .": *Documents Relative to the Colonial History of the State of New York*, vol. 9, pp. 966–67.

53 Nonosbawsut's murderer, "It is only an Indian . . .": James P. Howley, *The Beothuks or Red Indians: The Aboriginal Inhabitants of Newfoundland* (Cambridge, England: Cambridge University Press, 1915), p. 100. Changed from third person to first person.

Harvey, "The rude fishermen . . .": Rev. Moses Harvey, "Memoirs of an Extinct Race," *Maritime Monthly Magazine* (June 1875).

New England

55 *(Name not given)*, Mohegan, *"The times are Exceedingly . . .":* "Harry Quaduaquid and Robert Ashpo to the Most Honourable Assembly of the State of Connecticut" (May 14, 1789).

Morton, "the hand of God . . .": Thomas Morton, *New English Canaan; Or, New Canaan, containing an abstract of New England*, book 1 (n.p.: Charles Green, 1632), pp. 18–19; reprinted in Peter Force, *Tracts and Other Papers, relating principally to the origin, settlement, and progress of the colonies in North America, from the discovery of the country to the year 1776* (Washington, D.C.: Peter Force, 1838).

56 Bradford, "there is neither man . . .": Alexander Young, *Chronicles of the Pilgrim Fathers of the Colony of Plymouth, from 1602–1625* (Boston: Little, Brown, 1894), pp. 182–83.

60 Tappan delegation, "We wonder how . . .": John Brodhead, *History of the State of New York*, vol. 1 (New York: Harper & Brothers, 1853), p. 310. Changed from third person to first person.

Montauk delegation, "Are you our friends? . . .": *History of the State of New York*, vol. 1, p. 355.

Hackensack delegation, "Why do you sell . . .": *History of the State of New York*, vol. 1, p. 348.

61 DeVries, "When it was day . . .": David Peterszoon DeVries, *Voyages from Hol-*

land to America, A.D. 1632 to 1644, Collections of the New-York Historical Society, 2nd Series, vol. 3 (New York: D. Appleton & Co., 1857), pp. 115–16.

62   Montauk delegation, "Our chief has . . .": *History of the State of New York,* vol. 1, p. 358.

(Name not given), *Montauk,* "When you first came . . .": *History of the State of New York,* vol. 1, p. 358.

(Name not given), *Lenape,* "When the [English] arrived . . .": John Hecke-welder, *The History, Manners, and Customs of the Indian Nations Who Once Inhabited Pennsylvania and the Neighbouring States,* Memoirs of the Historical Society of Pennsylvania, vol. 12 (Philadelphia: Historical Society of Pennsylvania, 1876), pp. 77–78.

63   New Netherland, "clouded brains . . .": E. B. O'Callaghan and Berthold Fernow, eds., *Documents Relative to the Colonial History of the State of New York,* vol. 13 (Albany: Weed, Parsons, & Co., 1881), p. 70.

Tschoop, "Once a preacher came . . .": George H. Loskiel, *History of the Mission Among the United Brethren Among Indians in North America,* vol. 2 (London: Brethren's Society for the Gospel, 1794), p. 14.

64   "Mourt's Relation," "We brought sundry . . .": *Biography and History of the Indians of North America,* p. 107.

Chickataubut, ". . . much troubled . . .": *Biography and History of the Indians of North America,* p. 107.

66   Apess, "These Indians had not . . .": William Apes, *Eulogy on King Philip* (Boston: the author, 1836), pp. 18–19.

67   King Philip, "[My] brother . . .": Charles Lincoln, *Narratives of the Indian Wars, 1675–1699* (New York: Charles Scribner's Sons, 1913), pp. 10–11. Changed from third person to first person; changed to modern English spelling.

68   Apess, ". . . the pilgrims landed . . .": *Eulogy on King Philip,* pp. 10–11.

Apess, ". . . the people were . . .": *Eulogy on King Philip,* p. 25.

King Philip, "We have been the first . . .": *Narratives of the Indian Wars, 1675–1699,* p. 10. Changed from third person to first person; changed to modern English spelling.

69   English eyewitness, "like the lightning . . .": Samuel Goodrich, *Lives of Celebrated American Indians* (Boston: George C. Rand, 1852), p. 200.

71   English soldier, "if young Indians . . .": *Biography and History of the Indians of North America,* p. 286.

King Philip, "Brothers,—You see . . .": *Eulogy on King Philip,* pp. 35–36.

Peksuot, "I understand the captain . . .": *Biography and History of the Indians of North America,* p. 100. First sentence changed from third person to first person. Second sentence already rendered first person.

Notes

72 James the Printer, "Know by this paper . . .": *Biography and History of the Indians of North America*, p. 221.

Miantunnomoh, "Brothers, we must . . .": *Biography and History of the Indians of North America*, p. 127.

73 Caunbitant, "If your love . . .": *Biography and History of the Indians of North America*, p. 95.

74 Canonchet, "I like it well . . .": *Biography and History of the Indians of North America*, p. 234.

75 King Philip, "My heart breaks . . .": Samuel Goodrich, *Lives of Celebrated American Indians* (Boston: Bradbury, Soden & Co., 1843), p. 205.

76 Apess, ". . . they took a part . . .": *Eulogy on King Philip*, pp. 45–46.

Apess, "How they could go . . .": *Eulogy on King Philip*, p. 9.

77 Apess, "It is said . . .": *Eulogy on King Philip*, p. 57.

Apess, ". . . during the bloody . . .": *Eulogy on King Philip*, pp. 48–49.

The Northeast

78 Long, "The Iroquois laugh . . .": John Long, *Voyages and Travels of an Indian Interpreter and Trader* (London: n.p., 1791), p. 30.

82 Penn, "I will justifie . . .": "Report of a Conference between Col. Talbot and William Penn," *Maryland Historical Magazine* (vol. 3, 1908), p. 25.

(Name not given), *Susquehannock*, "My brother . . .": *Biography and History of the Indians of North America*, p. 42.

(Name not given), *Susquehannock*, "Our forefathers . . .": Helen Hunt Jackson, *A Century of Dishonor* (New York: Harper & Brothers, 1881), pp. 300–1.

83 Garangula, "You must have believed . . .": Benjamin B. Thatcher, *Indian Biography*, vol. 2 (New York: Harper & Brothers, 1848), pp. 42–44.

85 Furniss, "And indeed . . .": Chester Sipe, *Indian Chiefs of Pennsylvania* (Butler, Pa.: Ziegler Printing Co., 1927), p. 169.

Teedyuscung, ". . . this very ground . . .": *Indian Chiefs of Pennsylvania*, p. 336.

86 Maryland Assembly, "Our kindness to you . . .": William Hand Browne, ed., *Archives of Maryland. Proceedings of the Council of Maryland 1732–1753*, vol. 28 (Baltimore: Maryland Historical Society, 1908), p. 270.

Heckewelder, ". . . they were known . . .": *History, Manners, and Customs of the Indian Nations*, vol. 12, p. 92.

Canassatego, "We now speak . . .": Samuel Hazard, ed., *Minutes of the Provincial Council of Pennsylvania (Pa. Colonial Records)*, vol. 5 (Harrisburg, Pa.: T. Fenn & Co., 1851–53), pp. 401–2.

87 Tokahaio, "About seven Years ago . . .": *Minutes of the Provincial Council of Pennsylvania*, vol. 8, p. 651.

88 Thoyanoguen, "If they are to . . .": *Biography and History of the Indians of North America*, p. 536.

Tanacharison, "The Colonel . . .": *Indian Chiefs of Pennsylvania*, pp. 209–10.

89 Canassatego, ". . . we told them . . .": *Minutes of the Provincial Council of Pennsylvania*, vol. 5, p. 23.

Tanacharison, ". . . it is you . . .": *Biography and History of the Indians of North America*, p. 531.

Ogaushtosh, ". . . [The Grand Council] . . .": *Minutes of the Provincial Council of Pennsylvania*, vol. 5, p. 389.

Tokahaio, "[The English] have called . . .": *Minutes of the Provincial Council of Pennsylvania*, vol. 8, p. 212.

90 Canassatego, "When you mentioned . . .": *Minutes of the Provincial Council of Pennsylvania*, vol. 4, pp. 706–7.

Thoyanoguen, "We thought the Boundaries . . .": *Minutes of the Provincial Council of Pennsylvania*, vol. 8, p. 115.

93 Pontiac, "I stand . . .": *Lives of Celebrated American Indians*, 1843, p. 211.

Pontiac, "It is important . . .": "The Pontiac Manuscript," *Michigan Pioneer Society*, Lansing, Mich. (vol. 8, 1885), pp. 273–74.

Ecuyer, "I have warriors . . .": Francis Parkman, *The Conspiracy of Pontiac and the Indian War after the Conquest of Canada*, vol. 2 (Boston: Little, Brown, & Co., 1913), p. 24.

94 Bouquet, "I wish . . .": *Conspiracy of Pontiac and the Indian War*, vol. 2, p. 39, footnote 1.

Shingas and Turtle's Heart, "Why do you complain . . .": *Conspiracy of Pontiac and the Indian War*, vol. 2, p. 23.

Mihnehwehna, "Englishman! . . .": Alexander Henry, *Travels and Adventures in Canada and the Indian Territories Between the Years 1760 and 1776* (New York: I. Riley, 1809), p. 44.

Kahkewaquonaby, "I do not see . . .": Peter Jones, *History of the Ojibway Indians, with especial reference to their Conversion to Christianity* (London: A. W. Bennett, 1861), p. 230.

95 Amherst, "Could it not . . .": *Conspiracy of Pontiac and the Indian War*, vol. 2, p. 39.

Bouquet, "I will try . . .": *Conspiracy of Pontiac and the Indian War*, vol. 2, p. 40.

Notes

Amherst, "You will do well . . .": *Conspiracy of Pontiac and the Indian War*, vol. 2, p. 40.

96 Mashipinashiwish, "When I view . . .": *American State Papers: Indian Affairs*, vol. 7, Office of Indian Affairs, p. 572.

Blackbird, "The Ottawas . . .": Andrew Blackbird, *History of the Ottawa and Chippewa Indians of Michigan* (Ypsilanti, Mich.: Ypsilanti Job Printing House, 1887), pp. 9–10.

97 Penn, "Those cruel men . . .": Leonard Labaree, ed., *The Papers of Benjamin Franklin*, vol. 11 (New Haven, Conn.: Yale University Press, 1967), pp. 47, 52–53.

98 Henry, "Near the back door . . .": *Century of Dishonor*, p. 306.

Franklin, "These poor people . . .": *Papers of Benjamin Franklin*, vol. 11, p. 65.

Cataradirha, "Many of our old . . .": *Minutes of the Provincial Council of Pennsylvania*, vol. 5, p. 432.

99 Thatcher, "In the spring . . .": *Indian Biography*, vol. 2, p. 167.

Tahgahjute, "I appeal to any . . .": *Indian Biography*, vol. 2, p. 171.

100 Canassatego, "We heartily recommend . . .": National Archives, Papers of the Continental Congress, "Proceedings of the Commissioners Appointed by the Continental Congress to Negotiate a Treaty with the Six Nations, 1775" (Aug. 25, 1775), RG 360, M-247, roll 144.

101 Pachgantschihilas, "At first I looked . . .": John Heckewelder, *A Narrative of the Mission of the United Brethren Among the Delaware and Mohegan Indians; from its commencement, in the year 1740, to the close of the year 1808* (Philadelphia: M'Carty & Davis, 1820), pp. 216–17.

Sagoyewatha, "You have told us . . .": *Indian Biography*, vol. 2, p. 286.

102 Little Abraham, "The resolutions . . .": *Documents Relative to the Colonial History of the State of New York*, vol. 8, pp. 621–22.

Guyashuta, "I am appointed . . .": *Indian Chiefs of Pennsylvania*, p. 403.

Hopocan, "Some time ago . . .": *Indian Biography*, vol. 2, pp. 146–48.

105 Washington, "The expedition . . .": Jared Sparks, *The Writings of George Washington; being his correspondence, addresses, messages & other papers, official & private*, vol. 6 (New York: Harper & Brothers, 1847), pp. 264–66.

Dickewamis, "A part of our . . .": James E. Seaver, *A Narrative of the Life of Mrs. Mary Jemison* (New York: J. D. Bemis & Co., 1824), pp. 73–74.

Cornplanter, "Father: The voice . . .": *American State Papers: Indian Affairs*, vol. 7, pp. 206–7.

106 Sagoyewatha, "They must have . . .": *Indian Biography*, vol. 2, p. 284.

Skenando, "The news that came . . .": Draper Manuscript, 2D139–41, chapter

13, Draper Manuscript Collection, State Historical Society of Wisconsin, Madison.

107 Ohnawiio et al., "Formerly we enjoyed . . .": *American State Papers: Indian Affairs*, vol. 7, p. 618.

Ohnawiio et al., "At our meeting . . .": *American State Papers: Indian Affairs*, vol. 7, p. 617.

108 Waowowanoonk, "That land of Ganono-o . . .": Waowowanoonk, address to the New-York Historical Society (May 1847).

110 Sagoyewatha, "With sweet voices . . .": *Indian Biography*, vol. 2, pp. 280–81.

Sagoyewatha, "Brother, listen . . .": *Indian Biography*, vol. 2, pp. 291–94.

The South

112 *Cornell, "It was a strange . . .": American State Papers: Indian Affairs*, vol. 7, p. 607.

113 Hariot, "within a few days . . .": Thomas Hariot, *A Briefe and True Report of the Newfound Land of Virginia* (Frankfurt am Main, Germany: Theodore DeBry, 1590), pp. 28–29.

117 Smith, "Powhatan, you must knowe . . .": Captain John Smith, *Travels and Works of Captain John Smith*, ed. Edward Arber (Edinburgh: John Grant, 1910), p. 137.

Smith, ". . . but a foul trouble . . .": Captain John Smith, "The General History of Virginia, New England, and the Summer Isles," in John Pinkerton, *A General Collection of the Best and Most Interesting Voyages and Travels in All Parts of the World*, vol. 13 (London: n.p., 1812), p. 75.

Wahunsonacock, "Yet, Captain *Smith* . . .": *Travels and Works of Captain John Smith*, p. 134.

118 Wahunsonacock, "Captaine *Smith*, I never . . .": *Travels and Works of Captain John Smith*, pp. 136–37.

Tomocomo, "Count the stars . . .": *Biography and History of the Indians of North America*, p. 355.

Brooke, "[The Powhatan are] . . .": J. Frederick Fausz, "The Powhatan Uprising of 1622: An Historical Study of Ethnocentrism and Cultural Conflict," vol. 2 (Ph.D. diss., Dept. of History, College of William and Mary, 1977), p. 434.

Wahunsonacock, "I have seen . . .": *Lives of Celebrated American Indians*, 1843, pp. 179–80.

120 Wannis, "I will not bid . . .": *Biography and History of the Indians of North America*, p. 41.

Mattagund, "Let us have . . .": William Hand Browne, ed., *Archives of Maryland. Proceedings and Acts of the General Assembly April 1666–June 1676*, vol. 2 (Baltimore: Maryland Historical Society, 1884), p. 15.

Notes

121 White, "It is much more . . .": [Father White?], *A Relation of Maryland*, ed. Francis L. Hawks (New York: Joseph Sabin, 1865), p. 44.

(Name not given), *Patuxent*, "I am a Native . . .": *Relation of Maryland*, pp. 41–43.

Andrew, ". . . [The Creator] was sorry . . .": "Description of Cypress Swamps in Delaware and Maryland States," *Delaware History* (vol. 3, Mar. 1949), pp. 136–37.

122 Choctaw/Chickasaw delegation, "If your countrymen . . .": H. B. Cushman, *History of the Choctaw, Chickasaw, and Natchez Indians* (Greenville, Tex.: Headlight Printing House, 1899), p. 75.

Bienville, "The Choctaws, whom I . . .": *History of the Choctaw, Chickasaw, and Natchez Indians*, p. 454.

123 Choctaw delegation, "We neither respect . . .": *History of the Choctaw, Chickasaw, and Natchez Indians*, p. 455.

Bienville, "Do you not remember . . .": Charles Gayarre, *History of Louisiana: the French domination* (New Orleans: Armand Hawkins, 1885), pp. 144–45.

124 Long Panther, "Thou knowest . . .": Jean-Bernard Bossu, *Travels through that part of North America formerly called Louisianna*, vol. 1 (London: T. Davies Printers, 1771), pp. 29–30.

125 Old Hair, "Brother, such language . . .": *History of the Choctaw, Chickasaw, and Natchez Indians*, p. 541.

Chopart, "Insolent barbarian! . . .": *History of the Choctaw, Chickasaw, and Natchez Indians*, p. 541.

Old Hair, "My white brother . . .": *History of the Choctaw, Chickasaw, and Natchez Indians*, p. 541.

Périer, ". . . the [Chawasha] . . .": *History of the Choctaw, Chickasaw, and Natchez Indians*, p. 545.

126 Guardian of the temple, ". . . in order to live . . .": Le Page DuPratz, *The History of Louisiana, or of the Western Parts of Virginia and Carolina* (London: T. Becket, 1774), p. 331.

Natchez Council, "We have noticed . . .": Seymour Feiler, ed., *Jean-Bernard Bossu's Travels in the Interior of North America, 1751–1762* (Norman: University of Oklahoma Press, 1962), pp. 39–40.

127 Moncachtape, "The cold was . . .": *Biography and History of the Indians of North America*, p. 382.

128 Arataswa, "As to our Liveing . . .": William Saunders, ed., *Colonial Records of North Carolina*, vol. 5, 1752–1759 (Raleigh: Josephus Daniels, Minister to the State, 1887), p. 144a.

Arataswa, ". . . many times . . .": *Colonial Records of North Carolina*, vol. 5, 1752–1759, pp. 142–43.

130 Marion, "We proceeded . . .": John Brown, *Old Frontiers* (Kingsport, Tenn.: Southern Publishers, 1938), p. 111.

Jefferson, "I tremble . . .": *Stolen Continents*, p. 212.

Dunmore, "[The settlers] do not . . .": *Documentary History of Dunmore's War, 1774*, eds. Reuben Gold Thwaites and Louise Phelps Kellogg (Madison: Wisconsin Historical Society, 1905), p. 371.

Onitositah, "It is a little surprising . . .": Samuel C. Williams, ed., "Tatham's Characters Among the North American Indians," *Tennessee Historical Magazine* (vol. 7, no. 3, [Oct.] 1921), pp. 176–78.

132 Shawnee et al., "When we passed . . .": *Old Frontiers*, p. 142.

133 Cornstalk, "In a few years . . .": *Old Frontiers*, p. 144.

Attakullakulla, "I pity the white people . . .": *Old Frontiers*, pp. 130–31.

Little Turkey, "We must inform you . . .": *American State Papers: Indian Affairs*, vol. 7, p. 46.

Cherokee Council, ". . . but what is the reason . . .": *American State Papers: Indian Affairs*, vol. 7, p. 47.

134 Blount, ". . . I am surprised . . .": *American State Papers: Indian Affairs*, vol. 7, p. 281.

Martin, "I have certain accounts . . .": *American State Papers: Indian Affairs*, vol. 7, p. 48.

135 Tsiyu Gansini, "Our Nation was alone . . .": *Old Frontiers*, p. 176.

Tickagiska King, "We are neither birds . . .": *American State Papers: Indian Affairs*, vol. 7, p. 57.

Tsiyu Gansini, "We had hoped . . .": *Old Frontiers*, p. 10.

136 Unsuckanail, "The encroachments . . .": *American State Papers: Indian Affairs*, vol. 7, p. 41.

Chescoenwhee, "Formerly, when I . . .": *American State Papers: Indian Affairs*, vol. 7, p. 42.

Doublehead, "I am still . . .": *American State Papers: Indian Affairs*, vol. 7, p. 460.

Ballew, ". . . [I am] encouraged . . .": *American State Papers: Indian Affairs*, vol. 7, p. 56.

138 McGillivray, ". . . a general convention . . .": *American State Papers: Indian Affairs*, vol. 7, p. 18.

Instructions to commissioners, "If the Creeks . . .": *American State Papers: Indian Affairs*, vol. 7, p. 65.

Creek delegation, "We are told . . .": *American State Papers: Indian Affairs*, vol. 7, p. 604.

139 McGillivray, ". . . we were invited . . .": *American State Papers: Indian Affairs*, vol. 7, p. 18.

Cornell, "As for talking . . .": *American State Papers: Indian Affairs*, vol. 7, p. 604.

United States commissioners, ". . . we recommended to you . . .": *American State Papers: Indian Affairs*, vol. 7, p. 674.

140 Georgia commissioners, ". . . I must inform you . . .": *American State Papers: Indian Affairs*, vol. 7, p. 22.

Seagrove, "[The hostages] are . . .": *American State Papers: Indian Affairs*, vol. 7, p. 398.

Hallowing King, ". . . these last strides . . .": *American State Papers: Indian Affairs*, vol. 7, p. 23.

Efau Harjo, "The thing that was . . .": *American State Papers: Indian Affairs*, vol. 7, p. 674.

141 McGillivray, ". . . and, if, after every . . .": *American State Papers: Indian Affairs*, vol. 7, p. 18.

Creek Council, "You well know . . .": *American State Papers: Indian Affairs*, vol. 7, p. 371.

142 Georgia Commission, "[You] yourselves must . . .": *American State Papers: Indian Affairs*, vol. 7, pp. 32–33.

143 Georgia State Assembly, "On what principle . . .": *American State Papers: Indian Affairs*, vol. 7, p. 33.

Hallowing King and The Fat King, "We minded nothing . . .": *American State Papers: Indian Affairs*, vol. 7, p. 32.

The Fat King, ". . . in the late affairs . . .": *American State Papers: Indian Affairs*, vol. 7, p. 33.

144 Hawkins, "I hear you are . . .": *American State Papers: Indian Affairs*, vol. 7, p. 848.

145 Jackson, "Our enemies are not . . .": John Eaton, *The Life of Andrew Jackson* (Philadelphia: Samuel F. Bradford, 1824), p. 168.

Tsali, "[The Creator] says . . .": Thomas McKenney and James Hall, *Biographical Sketches and Anecdotes of Ninety-five of 120 Principal Chiefs from the Indian Tribes of North America* (Washington, D.C.: U.S. Department of the Interior, 1967), pp. 191–92. Changed from third person to second person.

Red Eagle, "I am in . . .": *Life of Andrew Jackson*, pp. 177–78.

146 Blount, "You have been told . . .": *American State Papers: Indian Affairs*, vol. 7, p. 285.

Piamingo, "Could I once see . . .": *American State Papers: Indian Affairs*, vol. 7, p. 287.

146 Wolf's Friend, "I must explain . . .": *American State Papers: Indian Affairs*, vol. 7, p. 285.

Wolf's Friend, "The Americans . . .": *American State Papers: Indian Affairs*, vol. 7, p. 285. Changed from third person to first person.

147 Tunnahthoomah, "The whites . . .": *American State Papers: Indian Affairs*, vol. 7, p. 285.

Webb, "Brother, when you were . . .": "Speech of Colonel Webb," *The Friend, a religious and literary journal* (Philadelphia, vol. 17, no. 8, Nov. 18, 1843), p. 59.

148 Harkins, "We were hedged . . .": "A chieftain's 'Farewell Letter' to the American people," *The American Indian* (Tulsa, vol. 1, no. 3, Dec. 1926), pp. 7, 12.

149 Wall, "Though you have . . .": Letter from William Wall to Robert Anderson, Tuskegee, Ala., Aug. 19, 1836, Papers of Robert Anderson, vol. 2, Ms. Division, Library of Congress.

Chinnebey, ". . . our . . . reason . . .": Letter from Chinnebey, Creek chief, to General L. Lanney, June 21, 1838, Papers of Robert Anderson, vol. 2.

150 Jones, "We have gloomy tidings . . .": Gary Moulton, ed., *The Papers of Chief John Ross*, vol. 1, *1807–1839* (Norman: University of Oklahoma Press, 1985), p. 600.

Menewa, "Last evening . . .": Thomas L. McKenney and James Hall, *History of the Indian Tribes of North America, with biographical sketches and anecdotes of the principal chiefs*, vol. 2 (Philadelphia: Daniel Rice & James G. Clark, 1842), p. 105.

Speckled Snake, "When he first came . . .": *Niles Weekly Register* (Baltimore, vol. 36, no. 36, June 20, 1829), p. 274.

152 Creek delegation, ". . . in the spirit . . .": National Archives, Office of Indian Affairs, "Opothleyoholo and others, Creek Delegation to the Secretary of War 16th December 1825, relative to the Treaty of Indian Springs" (Dec. 16, 1825), RG 75, T-494, roll 1, pp. 798–99.

Burnett, "Murder is murder . . .": "Original Birthday Story of Private John G. Burnett," mss. 87–83, Museum of the Cherokee Indian Archives, Eastern Band of the Cherokee Nation, Cherokee, N.C.

153 Burnett, "I fought through . . .": James Mooney, *Myths of the Cherokee*, 19th BAE (Washington, D.C.: Government Printing Office, 1897–98), p. 130.

Jackson, "They have neither . . .": *Message from the President of the United States to the Two Houses of Congress*, 23rd Congress, 1st session, 1833, H. Doc. 1, vol. 1, serial set 254, pp. 14–15.

Van Buren, "No State can achieve . . .": *Stolen Continents*, p. 218.

(Name not given), *Cherokee*, ". . . news come . . .": "The Trail of Tears," *Oklahoman*, Apr. 7, 1929, p. 6F.

154 Ross, "But I am still . . .": *Papers of Chief John Ross*, vol. 1, p. 636.

Ross, ". . . We have been made . . .": *Papers of Chief John Ross*, vol. 1, p. 285.

Cherokee Council, "We are deprived . . .": *Report from the Secretary of War*, 25th Congress, 2nd session, 1837–38, S. Doc. 120, vol. 2, serial set 315, pp. 799–802.

Ridge, ". . . notwithstanding the cries . . .": National Archives, Office of Indian Affairs (June 30, 1836), RG 75, M-234, roll 80, pp. 488–89.

155 Cherokee Council, "Of late years . . .": *Niles Weekly Register* (Baltimore, 4th series, vol. 2, no. 26, Aug. 21, 1830) (vol. 38, whole no. 988), p. 455.

Florida

156 Hirrihigua, *"I will willingly receive . . ."*: Garcilaso de la Vega, el Inca, *The Florida of the Inca*, eds. and trans. John Grier Varner and Jeannette Johnson Varner (Austin: University of Texas Press, 1951), p. 61. Changed from third person to first person.

160 Acuera, "I have long since . . .": *Florida of the Inca*, pp. 118–19.

Vitachuco, "The bondage in which . . .": *Florida of the Inca*, pp. 134–35.

162 Juanillo, "The friar is dead. . . .": Andrés Gonzales de Carballido y Zuñiga Barcia, *Barcia's Chronological History of the Continent of Florida* (Gainesville: University of Florida Press, 1951), pp. 181–82.

163 The young chief, "If you are not . . .": John Hann, *Missions to the Calusa* (Gainesville: University of Florida Press, 1991), p. 43. Changed from third person to first person.

The young chief, ". . . just as the Christians . . .": *Missions to the Calusa*, p. 44. Changed from third person to first person.

López, ". . . when I told them . . .": *Missions to the Calusa*, p. 43.

164 Estéva, ". . . the young [chief] . . .": *Missions to the Calusa*, pp. 197–98.

165 Osceola, "I have done nothing . . .": Charles Coe, *Red Patriots: the story of the Seminoles* (Cincinnati: Editor Publishing Co., 1898), p. 91.

Arpeika, "I have never made . . .": *Red Patriots*, p. 120. Changed from third person to first person.

Micanopee, "I have no intention . . .": *Biography and History of the Indians of North America*, p. 412.

Osceola, "You have guns . . .": *Red Patriots*, pp. 65–66.

Editorial, "We learn . . .": *History of the Ojibway*, appendix A, pp. 247–48.

167 Editorial, "We have been unable . . .": *History of the Ojibway*, appendix A, p. 248.

168 Masters, "I shall never forget . . .": *Red Patriots*, p. 84.

169 Coe, ". . . he sometimes talked . . .": *Red Patriots*, p. 103.

169 Welch, "Never was a more . . .": *Red Patriots*, p. 89.

Coacoochee, "When I was taken . . .": John Sprague, *The Origin, Progress, and Conclusion of the Florida War* (New York: D. Appleton & Co., 1848), p. 327.

Coacoochee, "I was once . . .": *Origin, Progress, and Conclusion of the Florida War*, pp. 288–89.

170 Coacoochee, "If Coacooche is . . .": *Origin, Progress, and Conclusion of the Florida War*, p. 290.

Seminole Council, "We have listened . . .": Minnie Moore Willson, *The Seminoles of Florida* (Philadelphia: American Printing House, 1896), p. 45.

The Ohio Valley

171 *Red Pole*, "[The Creator] . . .": *American State Papers: Indian Affairs*, vol. 7, p. 581.

174 Kenton, "I have killed . . .": Draper Manuscript, 21S109, Draper Manuscript Collection, State Historical Society of Wisconsin, Madison.

Scott, "To the various . . .": *American State Papers: Indian Affairs*, vol. 7, pp. 132–33.

Peau de Chat, "Father, do you ask . . .": *Advocate* (Green Bay, Wisc.), Nov. 30, 1848.

175 Main Poc, ". . . you have caught me . . .": Clarence Carter, ed., *Territorial Papers of the United States*, vol. 7, *The Territory of Indiana, 1800–1810* (Washington, D.C.: Government Printing Office, 1939), p. 556.

176 Heckewelder, "[There is] a class . . .": *Narrative of the Mission of the United Brethren*, 1820, p. x.

Wingenund, "Colonel Crawford! . . .": John Heckewelder, *A Narrative of the Mission of the United Brethren Among the Delaware and Mohegan Indians; From Its Commencement, in the Year 1740, to the Close of the Year 1808.* (New York: Arno Press and The New York Times, 1971), pp. 286–88.

177 Leaders of the Hodenosaunee et al., "In the course . . .": *American State Papers: Indian Affairs*, vol. 7, pp. 8–9.

178 Harmar, ". . . I was induced . . .": *American State Papers: Indian Affairs*, vol. 7, p. 91.

179 Washington, "The President . . .": *American State Papers: Indian Affairs*, vol. 7, p. 230.

Wyandot et al., ". . . we are sensible . . .": *American State Papers: Indian Affairs*, vol. 7, p. 575.

Pachgantschihilas, "I admit . . .": *History, Manners, and Customs of the Indian Nations*, p. 81.

180 Lenape delegation, "We desire . . .": *Century of Dishonor*, pp. 42–43.

Council between Hodenosaunee et al., "Brothers: now . . .": *American State Papers: Indian Affairs*, vol. 7, pp. 323–24.

Sawaghdawunk, "You mentioned the treaties . . .": *American State Papers: Indian Affairs*, vol. 7, p. 354.

181 Mishikinakwa, "We have beaten . . .": *Biography and History of the Indians of North America*, p. 572.

182 Captain Charley, "You were the first . . .": *American State Papers: Indian Affairs*, vol. 7, p. 832.

Wabash Council, "Money to us . . .": *American State Papers: Indian Affairs*, vol. 7, p. 356.

183 Treaty of Greenville, "A treaty of peace . . .": *American State Papers: Indian Affairs*, vol. 7, p. 562.

Wayne, "what yesterday might . . .": *American State Papers: Indian Affairs*, vol. 7, p. 565.

Wayne, ". . . all the people . . .": *American State Papers: Indian Affairs*, vol. 7, p. 566.

184 New Corn, ". . . our hearts are sorry . . .": *American State Papers: Indian Affairs*, vol. 7, p. 565.

Wayne, "The New Corn . . .": *American State Papers: Indian Affairs*, vol. 7, p. 565.

Masass, "When you yesterday . . .": *American State Papers: Indian Affairs*, vol. 7, p. 570.

Mishikinakwa, "I now take . . .": *American State Papers: Indian Affairs*, vol. 7, p. 570.

Mishikinakwa, "You have pointed . . .": *American State Papers: Indian Affairs*, vol. 7, pp. 570–71.

185 Little Beaver, "Here are papers . . .": *American State Papers: Indian Affairs*, vol. 7, p. 577.

Ausimethe, "You know we have . . .": *American State Papers: Indian Affairs*, vol. 7, p. 576.

186 New Corn, "The heavens and earth . . .": *American State Papers: Indian Affairs*, vol. 7, pp. 580–81.

187 Tecumseh, "These lands are ours. . . .": E. O. Randall, "Tecumseh, the Shawnee Chief," *Ohio Anthropological and Historical Quarterly* (vol. 15, no. 4, Oct. 1906), p. 464.

Le Maiquois, "I created . . .": *American State Papers: Indian Affairs*, vol. 7, p. 798.

187 Letter, "The prophet has selected . . .": *American State Papers: Indian Affairs*, vol. 7, p. 798.

188 Tecumseh, ". . . unless we support . . .": *History of the Choctaw, Chickasaw, and Natchez Indians*, p. 311.

Wyandot delegation, "We thought the land . . .": *American State Papers: Indian Affairs*, vol. 7, p. 796.

Tecumseh, "Once there were no . . .": "Tecumseh, the Shawnee Chief," p. 470.

189 Tecumseh, "I have made myself . . .": "Tecumseh, the Shawnee Chief," p. 470.

190 Harrison, "The implicit obedience . . .": "Tecumseh, the Shawnee Chief," p. 472.

Tecumseh, "Where to-day . . .": *History of the Choctaw, Chickasaw, and Natchez Indians*, pp. 311–13.

192 Letter, "I have received . . .": *American State Papers: Indian Affairs*, vol. 7, p. 799.

Jefferson, ". . . as we have learnt . . .": *American State Papers: Indian Affairs*, vol. 7, p. 745.

Letter, "There appears to be . . .": *American State Papers: Indian Affairs*, vol. 7, p. 798.

193 Letter, "From the Ioways . . .": *American State Papers: Indian Affairs*, vol. 7, p. 799.

Letter, "Winemac assured me that . . .": *American State Papers: Indian Affairs*, vol. 7, p. 799.

Letter, "From the hostile appearance . . .": *American State Papers: Indian Affairs*, vol. 7, p. 800.

Letter, ". . . [At the Prophet's town] . . .": *American State Papers: Indian Affairs*, vol. 7, p. 800.

Letter, "All the information . . .": *American State Papers: Indian Affairs*, vol. 7, p. 800.

194 Letter, "The Shawanee chief . . .": *American State Papers: Indian Affairs*, vol. 7, p. 800.

Letter, ". . . the [Great Lakes] Sioux . . .": *American State Papers: Indian Affairs*, vol. 7, p. 808.

Letter, ". . . the major part . . .": *American State Papers: Indian Affairs*, vol. 7, p. 808.

Tecumseh, "*Brothers*—We are friends . . .": John D. Hunter, *Memoirs of a Captivity Among the Indians of North America, from childhood to the age of 19* (London: Longmans, Hurst, Rees, Orme, & Brown, 1823), pp. 45–46.

196 Elliott, ". . . in consequence . . .": Rev. Charles Elliott, *Indian Missionary Reminiscences: principally of the Wyandot Nation, in which is exhibited the efficacy of the gospel in elevating ignorant and savage men* (New York: Lane & Scott, 1850), pp. 212–13.

Wyandot delegation, "Several black robes . . .": *American State Papers: Indian Affairs*, vol. 7, p. 795.

Wyandot delegation, "We know that some . . .": *American State Papers: Indian Affairs*, vol. 7, p. 796.

197 Hicks, "I feel myself . . .": *Indian Missionary Reminiscences*, pp. 28–29.

198 Mononcue, "I doubt not . . .": *Indian Missionary Reminiscences*, pp. 29–30.

Warpole, "Why does your religion . . .": *Indian Missionary Reminiscences*, p. 65.

199 Tecumseh, "If there be one . . .": *History of the Choctaw, Chickasaw, and Natchez Indians*, p. 313.

Tecumseh, "My cause will not . . .": "Tecumseh, the Shawnee Chief," p. 472.

Tenskwatawa, "Have [you] not heard . . .": John Frost, *Thrilling Adventures Among the Indians* (Philadelphia: John C. Porter & Co., 1850), pp. 181–82. Italics removed.

200 Keshena, "But a few years . . .": *Oshkosh (Wisc.) Weekly Times*, Feb. 23, 1870.

Oshkosh, "The only time . . .": Patricia K. Ourada, *The Menominee Indians: A History* (Norman: University of Oklahoma Press, 1979), p. 71.

Grizzly Bear, "We see your Council House . . .": Samuel Hazard, ed., "Indian Visit," *The Register of Pennsylvania, devoted to the preservation of facts and documents, and every other kind of useful information respecting the State of Pennsylvania* (Philadelphia, vol. 7, no. 15, Apr. 9, 1831), p. 230.

Hole-in-the-Day, ". . . It takes time . . .": National Archives, ratified treaty no. 287, documents relative to the negotiation of the treaty of February 22, 1855 with the Mississippi Pillager Lake, Winibigoshish bands of Chippewa Indians, RG 75, T-494, roll 5, p. 314.

201 Hole-in-the-Day, "The [Creator] . . .": National Archives, ratified treaty no. 287, RG 75, T-494, roll 5, p. 319.

Hole-in-the-Day, "Our people must . . .": National Archives, ratified treaty no. 287, RG 75, T-494, roll 5, p. 321.

Buffalo, ". . . You must remember . . .": National Archives, ratified treaty no. 287, RG 75, T-494, roll 5, p. 362.

Hole-in-the-Day, ". . . I know what . . .": National Archives, ratified treaty no. 287, RG 75, T-494, roll 5, p. 375.

202 Mackkatananamakee, "My father, restrain . . .": *Biography and History of the Indians of North America*, p. 632.

Notes

202 Makataimeshekiakiak, "How smooth must be . . .": Black Hawk, *Life of Black Hawk, or Ma-ka-tai-me-she-kia-kiak*, ed. J. B. Patterson (Boston: Russell, Odiorne & Metcalf, 1834), pp. 90, 96.

Makataimeshekiakiak, "You know the cause . . .": *Lives of Celebrated American Indians*, 1843, p. 311.

203 Decorah, "Our people once owned . . .": *Wisconsin Historical Society Collections* (vol. 13, 1895), pp. 458–59.

The Grasslands

204 *Moanahonga*, ". . . a brave man . . .": *History of the Indian Tribes of North America*, vol. 1 (Philadelphia: Frederick W. Greenough, 1838), p. 159.

205 Taylor, ". . . thousands of mounted warriors . . .": Alfred A. Taylor, "The Medicine Lodge Peace Council," *The Chronicles of Oklahoma* (Oklahoma City, vol. 2, no. 2, June 1924), p. 103.

208 Duncan, "It had, he said . . .": National Archives, Office of Indian Affairs, St. Louis Superintendency, "Council with the Kickapoos" (June 13, 1836), RG 75, LR, M-234, roll 751.

Patsachi, "Since we made . . .": National Archives, "Council with the Kickapoos," RG 75, LR, M-234, roll 751.

209 Catlin, "In a former Letter . . .": George Catlin, *Letters and Notes on the Manners, Customs, and Conditions of the North American Indians*, vol. 1 (New York: Putnam and Riley, 1844), letter no. 21.

Mahto Topah, "My friends . . .": Chardon's journal, entry of July 30, 1837, Collection of Joseph Nicollet, Ms. Division, Library of Congress.

210 Maximilian, ". . . we have . . . the most frightful . . .": Maximilian, Philip Prince Von Wied-Neuwied, "Travels in the Interior of North America, 1832–1834," part 1, in Reuben Gold Thwaites, *Early Western Travels 1748–1846*, vol. 22 (Cleveland: Arthur H. Clark Co., 1906), pp. 33–35.

211 Crow Belly, "When the great . . .": Philippe Regis de Trobriand, *Army Life in Dakota*, ed. Milo Milton Quaife (Chicago: R. R. Donnelley & Sons Co., 1941), pp. 241–42.

Waheenee, "Our camp . . .": Gilbert L. Wilson, *Waheenee: An Indian Girl's Story* (Lincoln: University of Nebraska Press, 1981), pp. 13–14, 16–17.

212 Waheenee, "I am an old . . .": *Waheenee*, pp. 175–76.

213 Reverend, "Did it ever . . .": George Catlin, *Notes of Eight Years' Travel and Residence in Europe*, vol. 2 (New York: Burgess, Stringer & Co., 1848), p. 41.

Neumonya, ". . . If the [Creator] . . .": *Notes of Eight Years' Travel*, vol. 2, p. 41.

Neumonya, "As to the white . . .": *Notes of Eight Years' Travel*, vol. 2, pp. 40–42.

214 Neumonya, "I am willing . . .": *Notes of Eight Years' Travel*, vol. 2, p. 176.

215 Catlin, "The ostrich . . .": *Notes of Eight Years' Travel*, vol. 2, p. 88.

Catlin, "[The Indian delegation] reflect[ed] . . .": *Notes of Eight Years' Travel*, vol. 2, p. 91.

216 Washkamonya, "What have all . . .": *Notes of Eight Years' Travel*, vol. 2, p. 91.

Curtis, "I want no peace . . .": *Sand Creek Massacre*, 39th Congress, 2nd session, 1867, S. Exec. Doc. 26, vol. 2, serial set 1277, p. 173.

218 Bent, "I heard shouts . . .": George E. Hyde, *Life of George Bent: Written from His Letters* (Norman: University of Oklahoma Press, 1968), pp. 151–58.

219 Chivington, "The Cheyennes . . .": Chivington dispatch to Major Wynkoop, May 31, 1864, U.S. War Dept., *The War of the Rebellion: a compilation of the official records of the Union and Confederate Armies*, series 1, vol. 34—"Correspondence" (Washington, D.C.: Government Printing Office, 1891), p. 151.

Motavato, "On sight . . .": *Sand Creek Massacre*, p. 213.

Buffalo Good, "I have heard . . .": *Report of the Secretary of the Interior*, 42nd Congress, 2nd session, 1871, H. Exec. Doc. 1, vol. 3, serial set 1505, p. 32.

220 Motavato, "I once thought . . .": *Report of the Secretary of the Interior*, 39th Congress, 1st session, 1865, H. Exec. Doc. 1, vol. 2, serial set 1248, p. 704.

Southern Cheyenne Council, "But what do we . . .": *Sand Creek Massacre*, p. 73.

Anthony, "There was one . . .": *Massacre of the Cheyenne Indians*, 38th Congress, 2nd session, 1865, S. Rep. 142, vol. 2, serial set 1214, p. 27.

221 Connor, ". . . I did not see . . .": *Sand Creek Massacre*, p. 129.

Richmond, "I never heard . . .": *Sand Creek Massacre*, p. 212.

Joint Special Committee, "It is difficult . . .": *Massacre of the Cheyenne Indians*, appendix 3.

223 Allegawahu, "Be-che-go, great father . . .": William Unrau, *The Kaw People* (Phoenix: Indian Tribal Series, 1975), p. 16.

Heckaton, "The land we now . . .": *Arkansas Gazette*, Nov. 11, 1824.

Powderface, "When I was . . .": U.S. Senate, *Testimony taken by a Select Committee of the Senate concerning the removal of the Northern Cheyenne Indians* (Washington, D.C.: Government Printing Office, 1879), p. 27.

224 Deroin, ". . . [the] chiefs . . .": National Archives, Office of Indian Affairs, Special Case 147 (Apr. 25, 1895), L 18666-1895.

White Eagle, "The soldiers came . . .": "Removal of the Ponca Indians," 46th Congress, 3rd session, 1880–81, S. Exec. Doc. 30, vol. 1, serial set 1941, p. 15.

Machunazha, "I thought God . . .": Thomas Tibbles, *Buckskin and Blanket Days: Memoir of a Friend of the Indians* (Garden City, N.Y.: Doubleday & Co., 1957), p. 198.

225 Machunazha, "[My] hand is not . . .": T. R. Porter, "How the Indian Finally Became a Man," 1909 newspaper clipping, Papers of William Ghent, container 37, Ms. Division, Library of Congress.

227 Satanta, "I have heard . . .": James Mooney, *Calendar History of the Kiowa Indians,* BAE annual report 17, 1895–96 (Washington, D.C.: Government Printing Office, 1898), p. 208.

Parrawasamen, "But there are things . . .": National Archives, Office of Indian Affairs, United States Peace Commission, recorded copy of the Proceedings of the Indian Peace Commission (Oct. 19–20, 1867), I, 104.

228 Sheridan, "[The buffalo hunters] . . .": Wayne Gard, *The Great Buffalo Hunt* (New York: Alfred A. Knopf, 1959), p. 215.

Dodge, "Kill every buffalo . . .": Mari Sandoz, *The Buffalo Hunters* (Lincoln: University of Nebraska Press, 1954), p. 88.

Satanta, "Has the white man . . .": *Calendar History of the Kiowa Indians,* p. 207.

229 Old Lady Horse, "Everything the Kiowas had . . .": Alice Marriott and Carol Rachlin, *American Indian Mythology* (New York: Thomas Y. Crowell Co., 1968), p. 139.

230 Satanta, "This is our country. . . .": *Calendar History of the Kiowa Indians,* p. 208.

Satanta, "Yes, I led . . .": Lawrie Tatum, *Our Red Brothers and the Peace Policy of President Ulysses S. Grant* (Philadelphia: John C. Winston & Co., 1899), pp. 116–17.

231 Satank, "I wish to send . . .": *Our Red Brothers,* p. 118.

Wood Fire, "I think all . . .": Francis Stanley, *Satanta and the Kiowas* (Borger, Tex.: Jim Hess Printers, 1968), p. 241.

Arapooish, "The Crow country . . .": Washington Irving, *The Adventures of Captain Bonneville* (New York: R. Worthington Co., 1884), pp. 135–36.

Aleekchea-ahoosh, "They spoke very loudly . . .": Frank Linderman, *Plentycoups of the Crows* (New York: John Day Co., 1930), pp. 227–28.

233 Curly, "The Great Father . . .": Joseph Dixon, *The Vanishing Race* (Garden City, N.Y.: Doubleday, Page & Co., 1913), p. 141.

Seen-From-Afar, ". . . what the Blackrobe . . .": Father Nicholas Point, *Wilderness Kingdom: Indian life in the Rocky Mountains: 1840–1847,* trans. Joseph P. Donnelly, 1867 (New York: Holt, Rinehart & Winston, 1967; copyright held by Loyola University Press, Chicago), p. 116.

234 One Spot, "We are going after . . .": *Benton Record* (Ft. Benton, Mont.), Aug. 25, 1881.

Crowfoot, "Our land is more . . .": *Benton Record* (Ft. Benton, Mont.), Aug. 24, 1877.

Notes

White Calf, "The Agency issued . . .": Richard Lancaster, *Piegan* (Garden City, N.Y.: Doubleday & Co., 1966), p. 93.

235 Report of the commissioners, ". . . three years . . .": *Report of the Commissioners of Indian Affairs*, 42nd Congress, 3rd session, 1872–73, H. Exec. Doc. 1, vol. 3, serial set 1560.

Man-Who-Walks-Under-The-Gound, "By these my people . . .": "The Indian Commission," *Cincinnati Commercial*, Sept. 19, 1867.

Editorial, "[Washington should] open . . .": *Battle River Pilot* (Hermosa, S.D.), Mar. 16, 1889.

237 Mahpiua Luta, "The white men . . .": Francis C. Carrington, *My Army Life and the Ft. Phil Kearney Massacre* (Philadelphia: J. B. Lippincott, 1910), p. 292. Changed from third person to first person.

Mahpiua Luta, "Whose voice was . . .": "The Indians. Great Council of Chiefs with Secretary Cox," New York *Herald*, June 8, 1870.

Pawnee Killer, "I am an Oglalla . . .": "The Indian Commission "

Sinte Gleshka, "There is no fun . . .": "The Indian Commission."

238 Little Chief, "The [Creator] brought . . .": *Record of a conference between the Honorable Senator Vest . . . and the chiefs and headmen of the Gros Ventres and Assinaboine Indian tribes, held at Ft. Assinaboine, Montana, September 19, 1883*, 48th Congress, 1st session, 1883, S. Rept. 283, vol. 2, serial set 2174, p. xxxiv.

239 Mahpiua Luta, "When I went . . .": *Condition of the Indian Tribes in Montana and Dakota*, 48th Congress, 1st session, 1883, S. Rept. 283, vol. 2, serial set 2174, p. 135.

240 Tatanka Yotanka, "What is it . . .": Stanley Vestal, *New Sources of Indian History, 1850–1891* (Norman: University of Oklahoma Press, 1934), pp. 303–4.

Bear Ribs, "Tell the Grandfather . . .": Stanley Vestal, "Sitting Bull's Maiden Speech," *The Frontier, Magazine of the Northwest* (vol. 12, no. 3, Mar. 1932), p. 271.

John Glass, "We talked with them . . .": *Condition of the Indian Tribes in Montana and Dakota*, p. 65.

242 Mahpiua Luta, "The Great Father . . .": Mahpiua Luta, speech at Cooper Institute, N.Y., New York *Tribune*, Jan. 16, 1870.

243 Tatanka Yotanka, "Tell them at Washington . . .": *Century of Dishonor*, p. 179.

White Thunder, "Now my friends . . .": *Condition of the Indian Tribes in Montana and Dakota*, p. 157.

Sinte Gleshka, "This war did not . . .": W. Fletcher Johnson, *The Red Record of the Sioux: Life of Sitting Bull and history of the Indian war of 1890–91* (Philadelphia: Edgewood Pub. Co., 1891), pp. 384–85.

Notes

244 Tashunka Witko, "One does not . . .": Mari Sandoz, *Crazy Horse: The Strange Man of the Oglalas* (Lincoln: University of Nebraska Press, 1942), p. 295.

Iron Teeth, "Our tribe were . . .": Iron Teeth, *Cheyenne and Sioux: The Reminiscences of Four Indians and a White Soldier*, ed. Thomas Marquis (Stockton, Calif.: Pacific Center for Western Historical Studies, 1973), p. 17.

Tatoke Inyanke, "The land known . . .": U.S. Commissioner, *Annual Report of the Commissioner of Indian Affairs, 1875* (Washington, D.C.: Government Printing Office, 1875), p. 190.

245 Wanigi Ska, "You have driven . . .": *Sioux Tribe of Indians vs. the United States: no. c-531-(7) Black Hills. Dakota Indians: Plaintiffs. U.S. Court of Claims*, vol. 1 (n.p.: Ralph Case, 1937), pp. 422–23.

Tatanka Yotanka, "Look at me . . .": "Sitting Bull's Maiden Speech," p. 270.

246 Murray, "I knew this man . . .": *Red Record of the Sioux*, p. 195.

Tatanka Yotanka, "Yet hear me . . .": Paul Jacobs and Saul Landau, *To Serve the Devil*, vol. 1 (New York: Random House, 1971), p. 4.

Two Moons, ". . . we all went . . .": Hamlin Garland, "General Custer's Last Fight As Seen by Two Moon," *McClure's Magazine* (vol. 11, no. 5, Sept. 1898), pp. 445–48.

247 Iron Teeth, "Our men did not . . .": *Cheyenne and Sioux*, pp. 18–19.

248 Wild Hog, "We were *always* hungry . . .": *U.S. Congress Senate Select Committee re: the removal of the Northern Cheyenne Indians*, pp. 6, 8.

249 Tahmelapashme, "All we ask . . .": Dee Brown, *Bury My Heart at Wounded Knee: An Indian History of the American West* (New York: Holt, Rinehart & Winston, 1970), p. 332.

250 Wild Hog, "From the motions . . .": *U.S. Congress Senate Select Committee re: the removal of the Northern Cheyenne Indians*, p. 12.

Iron Teeth, "The men decided . . .": *Cheyenne and Sioux*, p. 22.

Tangled Hair, "From the actions . . .": *U.S. Congress Senate Select Committee re: the removal of the Northern Cheyenne Indians*, p. 13.

251 Murray, "The land grabbers . . .": *Red Record of the Sioux*, p. 195.

Johnson, "I read that . . .": *Red Record of the Sioux*, pp. 202–3.

252 Tatanka Yotanka, "I wish all . . .": Stanley Vestal, *Sitting Bull, Champion of the Sioux* (Boston and New York: Houghton Mifflin, 1932), p. 97.

254 Tatanka Yotanka, "When I was . . .": *Red Record of the Sioux*, p. 201.

Standing Bear, "The white man . . .": Luther Standing Bear, *Land of the Spotted Eagle* (Lincoln: University of Nebraska Press, 1978), p. 248.

255 Standing Bear, "As yet I know . . .": *Land of the Spotted Eagle*, pp. 165–66.

256 Editorial, "The Indians must . . .": *Black Hills Daily Times* (Deadwood, S.D.), Nov. 26, 1890.

Masse Hadjo, "You say . . .": "An Indian on the Messiah Craze," Chicago *Tribune,* Dec. 5, 1890.

257 Mahpiua Luta, "There was no hope . . .": *Red Record of the Sioux*, p. 465.

Tatanga Mani, ". . . You whites assumed . . .": J. W. Grant MacEwan, *Tatanga Mani, Walking Buffalo of the Stonies* (Edmonton, Alberta: M. J. Hurtig, 1969), pp. 5, 181.

258 Tibbles, "Suddenly I heard . . .": *Buckskin and Blanket Days*, pp. 312–14.

American Horse, "The men were separated . . .": James Mooney, *The Ghost Dance Religion and the Sioux Outbreak of 1890*, BAE annual report 14 (Washington, D.C.: U.S. Government Press, 1892–93), pp. 885–86.

259 Black Elk, "It was a good . . .": John G. Neihardt, *Black Elk Speaks: Being the Life Story of a Holy Man of the Oglala Sioux* (Lincoln: University of Nebraska Press, 1989), p. 262.

Maskepetoon, "Talk not . . .": Egerton R. Young, *Indian Life in the Great North-West* (London: S. W. Partridge & Co., n.d.), p. 125.

The Southwest

260 Victorio, *"Every struggle . . .":* Cheewa James, *Catch the Whisper of the Wind* (Sacramento: Horizon 2000, 1992), quote 38.

264 Taos tradition, *"When Earth was still . . .":* Glenebah Martinez, Albuquerque, N.M.

265 Hopi elders of Shongopovi, "Always vital . . .": Hopi elders, National Archives, 1951 letter to commissioner of Indian Affairs, Hopi Nation.

267 Lucas, ". . . they say . . .": Charles Hackett, *Revolt of the Pueblo Indians of New Mexico and Otermin's Attempted Reconquest, 1680–1682* (Albuquerque: University of New Mexico Press, 1942), p. 244.

Estrada, "The destruction . . .": *Revolt of the Pueblo Indians*, p. 45.

268 Antonio, "On reaching [Santa Fé] . . .": *Revolt of the Pueblo Indians*, p. 20. Changed from third person to first person.

Nanboa, ". . . the Indians . . .": *Revolt of the Pueblo Indians*, p. 61.

Nanboa, ". . . the resentment . . .": *Revolt of the Pueblo Indians*, p. 61. Changed from third person to first person.

Juan, "Popé came . . .": *Revolt of the Pueblo Indians*, pp. 234–35.

269 Hopi delegation, "What we say . . .": National Archives, Box 99, 57A-185, file no. 8155 1949 260.

Hopi delegation, "Great Spirit made . . .": National Archives, Box 99, 57A-185, file no. 17053 1950 066.

Hopi elders of Hotevilla, ". . . we . . . will not . . .": National Archives, Box 99, 57A-185, file no. 17053 1950 066.

269 Hopi delegation, "Our tradition . . .": National Archives, Box 99, 57A-185, file no. 8155 1949 260.

Hopi elders of Shongopovi, "The Hopi people . . .": National Archives, Box 99, 57A-185, file no. 17053 1950 066.

270 Hopi delegation, "We, the traditional leaders . . .": National Archives, Box 99, 57A-185, file no. 8155 1949 260.

271 Barboncito, ". . . when we had . . .": "Proceedings of a Council between General W. T. Sherman and Samuel F. Tappan Commissioners on the part of the United States and the Chiefs and head men of the Navajo Tribe of Indians," U.S. Peace Commission, May 28, 1868.

Ganado Mucho, "We think we were . . .": Virginia Hoffman, *Navajo Biographies*, vol. 1 (Phoenix: Navajo Curriculum Center, 1974), p. 141.

Armijo, "Is it American . . .": Frank McNitt, *Navajo Wars: Military Campaigns, Slave Raids, and Reprisals* (Albuquerque: University of New Mexico Press, 1972), p. 209.

Barboncito, "I hope to God . . .": "Proceedings of a Council between General W. T. Sherman and Samuel F. Tappan Commissioners on the part of the United States and the Chiefs and head men of the Navajo Tribe of Indians."

Big Mouth, "After the Bosque Redondo . . .": Eve Ball, *Indeh: An Apache Odyssey* (Norman: University of Oklahoma Press, 1988), pp. 284–85.

272 Peso, "The surest way . . .": *Indeh*, p. 81.

Price, "In 1867 . . .": National Archives, Special Case 1, Supai (Havasupai) and Walapai (Hualapai), extract from a report of Lieutenant Colonel Price, Sixth Cavalry, Whipple Barracks, Prescott, Arizona Territory (July 1, 1881), envelope 14489 1882.

273 Sherum, "My people cannot . . .": National Archives, Special Case 1, "Annual Report of Colonel August V. Kautz (8th infantry) Brevet Major-General United States Army commanding the Department of Arizona, Prescott, Arizona, August 31, 1875," envelope 14489 1882, p. 8. Changed from third person to first person.

Sherum et al., ". . . in the country . . .": National Archives, Special Case 1, extract from a report of Lieutenant Colonel Price, envelope 14489 1882, p. 9.

274 (Name not given), *Cocomaricopa*, "Behold, to give . . .": Herbert Bolton, *Anza's California Expeditions: An Outpost of Empire*, vol. 1 (Berkeley: University of California Press, 1930), p. 268.

Chiparopai, "In the old times . . .": *Indians' Book*, p. 569.

Chiparopai, "Why not knock . . .": *Indians' Book*, p. 340.

275 Carleton, "There is to be . . .": Robert N. Scott, *The War of Rebellion: a compilation of the official records of the Union and Confederate Armies*, series 1, vol. 15 (Washington, D.C.: Government Printing Office, 1886), p. 580.

Notes

Goyathlay, "The Indians always . . .": S. M. Barrett, *Geronimo's Story of His Life* (New York: Duffield & Co., 1907), pp. 116–17.

Cochise, "The Americans . . .": *Arizona Miner*, Mar. 20, 1869.

Cochise, "I do not think . . .": David C. Cooke, *Fighting Indians of America* (New York: Dodd, Mead & Co., 1954), p. 40.

276 Cochise, "When I was young . . .": A. N. Ellis, "Recollections of an Interview with Cochise," *Kansas State Historical Society Collections* (vol. 13, 1913–14), p. 392.

Mangas Coloradas, "I come into . . .": *Fighting Indians of America*, p. 10.

277 Daklugie, "He went into . . .": *Indeh*, p. 20.

Tucson *Arizona Star*, "His head was severed . . .": *Geronimo's Story*, p. 125.

278 Eskiminzin, "If it had not . . .": *Report of the Secretary of the Interior*, 42nd Congress, 2nd session, 1871, H. Exec. Doc. 1, vol. 3, serial set 1505, p. 470. Changed from third person to first person.

(Name not given), *Aravaipa*, "I no longer . . .": *Report of the Commissioner of Indian Affairs 1870/71* (Washington, D.C.: Government Printing Office, 1872), p. 71.

Whitman, "That evening . . .": *Report of the Commissioner of Indian Affairs 1870/71*, p. 70.

279 Cochise, "We were once . . .": Oliver Howard, *My Life and Personal Experiences among Our Hostile Indians* (Hartford, Conn.: A. D. Worthington & Co., 1907), pp. 207–8.

Lyman, ". . . and the story . . .": *Report of the Secretary of the Interior*, 1871, p. 460.

United States commissioner, "The Arizona Citizen . . .": *Report of the Commissioner of Indian Affairs 1870/71*, p. 55.

280 Daklugie, "[Juh] told them . . .": *Indeh*, p. 34.

Kaywaykla, "The Creator did not . . .": Eve Ball, *In the Days of Victorio: Recollections of a Warm Springs Apache*, narr. James Kaywaykla (Tucson: University of Arizona Press, 1970), p. 50. Kaywaykla quoting Owen Wister.

281 Cochise, "Why shut me up . . .": *My Life and Personal Experiences among Our Hostile Indians*, p. 208.

Goyathlay, "During my [childhood] . . .": *Geronimo's Story*, p. 34.

Goyathlay, "They never explained . . .": *Geronimo's Story*, p. 116.

Goyathlay, "In the summer . . .": *Geronimo's Story*, pp. 43–46.

283 Goyathlay, "We were reckless . . .": *Geronimo's Story*, p. 141.

284 Delche, ". . . now the very rocks . . .": Martin Schmitt and Dee Brown, *The Fighting Indians of the West* (New York: Charles Scribner's & Sons, 1948), p. 94.

284 Goyathlay, "I give myself . . .": *Conference . . . Between General Crook and the Chiricahua Chiefs*, 51st Congress, 1st session, 1889–90, S. Exec. Doc. 88, vol. 9, serial set 2686, p. 16.

Kanseah, "At that time . . .": *Indeh*, p. 110.

285 Daklugie, ". . . above all living men . . .": *Indeh*, p. 134.

Goyathlay, "When I had given . . .": *Geronimo's Story*, pp. 177–78.

Goyathlay, "There is no climate . . .": *Geronimo's Story*, pp. 215–16.

Goyathlay, "What is the matter . . .": *Conference . . . Between General Crook and the Chiricahua Chiefs*, p. 12.

286 Goyathlay, "We are vanishing . . .": *Geronimo's Story*, pp. 15–16.

Nednhi song, *"Ussen gave us . . .": Indeh*, p. 62.

287 Havasupai, "Our case is clear . . .": *Statement of the Havasupai Tribe to the United States Senate Committee on Interior and Insular Affairs, Subcommittee on Parks and Recreation*, 93rd Congress, 1st session, 1973, serial set 1296, p. 75.

Hanna, "Not too many . . .": *Grand Canyon National Park Hearing before the Subcommittee on Parks and Recreation*, 93rd Congress, 1st session, 1973, serial set 1296, p. 72.

Ouray, "Agreements the Indian makes . . .": Charles Marsh, *People of the Shining Mountains* (Boulder, Colo.: Pruett Publishing Co., 1982), p. 64.

Ouray, "I realize . . .": P. David Smith, *Ouray, Chief of the Utes* (Ouray, Colo.: Wayfinder Press, 1986), p. 11.

288 Colorado *Banner*, "There is no . . .": Jan Petit, *Utes: The Mountain People* (Boulder, Colo.: Johnson Books, 1990), p. 120.

Ouray, "We do not . . .": *Utes*, p. 119.

The West

289 *Anonymous*, Yokuts, *"Do you see me! . . .":* Jules Billard, ed., *The World of the American Indian* (Washington, D.C.: National Geographic Society, 1974), p. 24.

293 Font, "In fine . . .": *Anza's California Expeditions*, p. 325.

294 Font, ". . . sometimes [the neophytes] . . .": *Anza's California Expeditions*, p. 340.

Towendolly, "God is called . . .": Helen Hogue, *Wintu Trails* (Redding, Calif.: Shasta Historical Society, 1977), p. 39.

Freeman, "My grandfather . . .": Walter Goldschmidt, *Nomlaki Ethnography*, University of California Publications in American Archaeology and Ethnology, vol. 42, no. 4 (Berkeley: University of California Press, 1951), p. 312.

Janitin, "I and two . . .": Jack Forbes, *The Indian in America's Past* (New York: Simon and Schuster, 1964), pp. 62–63.

295 (Name not given), *Luiseno*, "You see . . .": Marguerite Eyer Wilbur, ed., *Duflot De Mofras' Travels on the Pacific Coast*, vol. 1 (Santa Ana: Fine Arts Press, 1937), p. 179.

296 Kitsepawit, "Another person . . .": Fernando Librado, *Breath of the Sun: Life in Early California as Told by a Chumash Indian, Fernando Librado to John P. Harrington* (Morongo Indian Reservation: Malki Museum Press, 1979), p. 15.

Kitsepawit, "Donociana and Nolberto . . .": *Breath of the Sun*, p. 33.

(Name not given), *Miwok-Costanoan*, "I am very old . . .": J. P. Dunn, Jr., *Massacres of the Mountains: a history of the Indian wars of the far West* (New York: Harper & Brothers, 1886), p. 132.

297 Carleton, "The miners will go . . .": *Massacres of the Mountains*, p. 125.

Johnston, "The majority . . .": National Archives, Office of Indian Affairs, California Superintendency (1849–52), LR, M-234, roll 32.

Lucas, "Before the Spanish . . .": Lora Cline, *The Kwaymi: A Reflection on a Lost Culture* (El Centro, Calif.: IVC Museum Society, 1979), p. 111.

298 Luckie, "The white people . . .": Cora DuBois, *Wintu Ethnography*, University of California Publications in American Archaeology and Ethnology, vol. 36, no. 1 (Berkeley: University of California Press, 1935), pp. 75–76.

Thompson, "When the present . . .": Lucy Thompson, *To the American Indian: Reminiscences of a Yurok Woman* (Berkeley, Calif.: Heyday Books, 1916), p. 84.

299 Rey, "My people are now . . .": LaFayette Houghton Bunnell, *Discovery of Yosemite and the Indian War of 1851 Which Led To That Event* (New York: Fleming H. Revell Co., 1897), p. 5.

Tomkit and Frederico, "The white soldiers . . .": *Discovery of Yosemite and the Indian War*, p. 135. Changed from third person to first person.

300 (Name not given), *Miwok*, "Where can we . . .": *Discovery of Yosemite and the Indian War*, p. 231.

Tenieya, "My people do not . . .": *Discovery of Yosemite and the Indian War*, pp. 45–46.

Tenieya, "Kill me, sir Captain! . . .": *Discovery of Yosemite and the Indian War*, pp. 172–73.

301 Dunn, "The largest . . .": *Massacres of the Mountains*, pp. 136–37.

303 Antonio, "The Americans . . .": *Indian Affairs on the Pacific*, 34th Congress, 3rd session, 1856, H. Exec. Doc. 76, vol. 9, serial set 906, p. 126. Captain H. S. Burton to Captain D. R. Jones, June 15, 1856.

Blacktooth, "We thank you . . .": Zephyrin Engelhardt, *San Luis Rey Mission* (San Francisco: James H. Barry, 1921), p. 192.

303 Beckwith, ". . . a promise was made . . .": *Western Watchman* (Eureka, Calif.), Feb. 21, 1891.

304 Editorial, ". . . the only correct . . .": *Humboldt Register* (Winnemucca, Nev.), Aug. 5, 1865.

Editorial, "I promised . . .": "Indian Hunting in Washington Territory," *Porter's Prairie* (Washington Territory), May 28, 1856, newspaper clipping, Papers of August V. Kautz, container 5, Ms. Division, Library of Congress.

306 Editorials, "Good Haul of Diggers . . .": *Humboldt Times* (Eureka, Calif.), Apr. 11 and Jan. 17, 1863.

Bell, "My grandfather . . .": Gladys Nomland, *Sinkyone Notes*, University of California Publications in American Archaeology and Ethnology, vol. 36, no. 2 (Berkeley: University of California Press, 1935), p. 166.

307 Adams, "Well, soldier come . . .": Edward Curtis, *The Hupa, Yurok, Karuk, Wiyot, Tolowa and Tututni, Shasta, Klamath; The North American Indian: Being a Series of Volumes Picturing and Describing the Indians of the United States and Alaska*, ed. Frank Webb Hodge, vol. 13 (Cambridge, England: Cambridge University Press, 1924), p. 95.

Beeson, "When those claiming . . .": John Beeson, "Are we not men and Brethren? An Address to the People of the United States" (Boston, 1859), Beinecke Library, Yale University.

308 Benham, ". . . that we, yes . . .": *Modoc War*, 43rd Congress, 1st session, 1873–74, H. Exec. Doc. 122, vol. 9, serial set 1607, p. 271.

Captain Jack's father, "My people, we [were] . . .": Frank Riddle, *The Indian History of the Modoc War, and the Causes That Led to It* (San Francisco: Marnell & Co. Printers, 1914), p. 19.

309 Legugyakes, "I am a Combutwaush. . . .": *Indian History of the Modoc War*, p. 19.

Riddle, "Ben Wright . . . told them . . .": *Indian History of the Modoc War*, pp. 27, 29–30.

311 Luttrell, ". . . the Indians were compelled . . .": *Modoc War*, p. 297.

Captain Jack, "I cannot talk . . .": *Indian History of the Modoc War*, p. 187.

313 Captain Jack, "Life is mine only . . .": *Indian History of the Modoc War*, pp. 187–89.

315 Winnemucca, "Two of them . . .": Sarah Winnemucca Hopkins, *Life Among the Paiutes: their wrongs and claims* (New York: G. P. Putnam's Sons, 1883), pp. 59–61.

316 Winnemucca, "Oh, such a scene . . .": *Life Among the Paiutes*, pp. 62–64.

317 Winnemucca, "Two little girls . . .": *Life Among the Paiutes*, pp. 70–72.

318 Winnemucca, "After the soldiers . . .": *Life Among the Paiutes*, p. 78.

Winnemucca, "The only way . . .": *Life Among the Paiutes*, p. 78.

Egan, "Did the government . . .": *Life Among the Paiutes*, pp. 133–34.

320 Race Horse, "We all like . . .": *Presidential Message on Agreement with Shoshone and Bannock Indians*, 50th Congress, 1st session, 1888, H. Exec. Doc. 140, vol. 26, serial set 2558, pp. 19–20.

Gibson Jack, "When God first . . .": *Presidential Message on Agreement with Shoshone and Bannock Indians*, p. 20.

Washakie, "The white man . . .": Clark Wissler, *Indians of the United States: Four Centuries of Their History and Culture* (New York: Doubleday, Doran & Co., 1940), p. 227.

The Plateau

321 *Skolaskin, "Do not become annoyed . . .":* Robert H. Ruby and John A. Brown, *Dreamer-Prophets of the Columbia Plateau: Smohalla and Skolaskin* (Norman: University of Oklahoma Press, 1989), p. 199.

325 Seealth, "[The] sky has wept . . .": H. A. Smith, "Scraps From a Diary—Chief Seattle," Seattle *Sunday Star*, Oct. 29, 1887.

327 Ohelantehtat, "I wish to speak . . .": National Archives, ratified treaty no. 284, "Treaty of Hahd-skus, or Point no Point," documents relative to the negotiation of the treaty of January 26, 1855, with the S'Klallam, Skokomish, Toanhooch, and Chimakum Indians, RG 75, T-494, roll 5, p. 291.

Shairatsehauk, "I do not want . . .": National Archives, ratified treaty no. 284, "Treaty of Hahd-skus, or Point no Point," RG 75, T-494, roll 5, p. 291.

328 Chitsamahan, ". . . I hope the Governor . . .": National Archives, ratified treaty no. 284, "Treaty of Hahd-skus, or Point no Point," RG 75, T-494, roll 5, pp. 292–93.

Sheridan, "In the summer . . .": Philip H. Sheridan, *Personal Memoirs of P. H. Sheridan*, vol. 1 (New York: Charles L. Webster & Co., 1888), pp. 97–103.

329 Napoleon, "These represent . . .": *Report of the Commissioner of Indian Affairs 1870/71*, p. 137.

Shelton, "You commissioners from Washington . . .": *Report of the Commissioner of Indian Affairs 1870/71*, p. 138.

William, "One of our employers . . .": *Report of the Commissioner of Indian Affairs 1870/71*, p. 138.

330 Big John, "My heart is sorry . . .": *Report of the Commissioner of Indian Affairs 1870/71*, p. 146.

Stevens, "The Nez Perses . . .": "Record of the Official Proceedings at the Council in the Walla Walla Valley, June 9 and 11, 1855," Umatilla Indian Nation Archives, Pendleton, Ore.

331 Five Crows, "Do you speak true . . .": "Record of the Official Proceedings at the Council in the Walla Walla Valley."

Peopeomoxmox, "I know the value . . .": "Record of the Official Proceedings at the Council in the Walla Walla Valley."

332 Stevens, "Besides all these things . . .": "Record of the Official Proceedings at the Council in the Walla Walla Valley."

Palmer, "It is but fifty . . .": "Record of the Official Proceedings at the Council in the Walla Walla Valley."

333 Palmer, "How long . . .": "Record of the Official Proceedings at the Council in the Walla Walla Valley."

Weatenatenamy, "I wonder if . . .": "Record of the Official Proceedings at the Council in the Walla Walla Valley."

Owhi, "God named . . .": "Record of the Official Proceedings at the Council in the Walla Walla Valley."

334 Stachas, "How is it . . .": "Record of the Official Proceedings at the Council in the Walla Walla Valley."

Camaspello, "What would I . . .": "Record of the Official Proceedings at the Council in the Walla Walla Valley."

Kamiakin, "At last, we . . .": Andrew Splawn, *Ka-mi-akin: The Last Hero of the Yakimas* (Portland, Ore.: Kilham Stationery & Printing Co., 1917), p. 20.

Kamiakin, "We wish to be . . .": *Ka-mi-akin*, p. 24.

335 Cayuse delegation, "Why should we want . . .": National Archives, Office of Indian Affairs, Oregon Superintendency, "Record of the Council in the Walla Walla Valley with Isaac Stevens, Governor and Supt., Washington Territory, and Joel Palmer, Supt. Indian Affairs, Oregon Territory, June 9 and 11, 1855" (1848–73), LR, M-2, roll 5.

Weatenatenamy, ". . . you selected this country . . .": "Record of the Official Proceedings at the Council in the Walla Walla Valley."

Looking Glass, ". . . there have been tracks . . .": "Record of the Official Proceedings at the Council in the Walla Walla Valley."

336 Howlish Wampo, "The one-armed white chief . . .": *East Oregonian* (Pendleton, Ore.), July 7, 1877, p. 2.

Quinquinmoeso, "You alone arranged . . .": National Archives, Office of Indian Affairs, Oregon Superintendency, LR, RG 75, T-494, roll 5.

Homli, "For a great many . . .": *Report of the Commissioner of Indian Affairs 1870/71*, p. 109.

John, "I know we cannot . . .": Hazard Stevens, *The Life of Isaac Ingalls Stevens*, vol. 2 (Boston: Houghton Mifflin & Co., 1900), p. 138.

Tleyuk, "I have no faith . . .": *Life of Isaac Ingalls Stevens*, vol. 2, p. 7.

Notes

337   Holoquila, "I am alone . . .": *Report of the Commissioner of Indian Affairs 1870/71*, p. 129.

Smohalla, "My young men . . .": *Ghost Dance Religion and the Sioux Outbreak*, p. 716.

Big Canoe, "We are friends. . . .": *Life of Isaac Ingalls Stevens*, vol. 2, p. 83.

Meninick, "God created the Indian . . .": Francis Garrecht, "An Indian Chief," *Washington State Historical Quarterly* (Tacoma, vol. 19, 1928), p. 170.

338   Charlot, "Since our forefathers . . .": *Missoula Missoulian*, Apr. 26, 1876.

340   Inmutooyahlatlat, "My father was . . .": "An Indian's View of Indian Affairs," *North American Review* (vol. 128, Apr. 1879), pp. 416, 419.

Inmutooyahlatlat quoting Toohoolhoolzote, "The Great Spirit Chief . . .": "Indian's View of Indian Affairs," p. 421.

341   Inmutooyahlatlat, "The earth was created . . .": "Indian's View of Indian Affairs," pp. 428–29.

Wetatonmi, "It was lonesome . . .": Lucullus V. McWhorter, *Hear Me, My Chiefs!* (Caldwell, Idaho: Caxton Printers, 1952), pp. 510–11.

Inmutooyahlatlat, "Let me be . . .": "Indian's View of Indian Affairs," p. 433.

342   Inmutooyahlatlat, "Treat all men alike. . . .": "Indian's View of Indian Affairs," p. 432.

Inmutooyahlatlat, "I do not understand . . .": "Indian's View of Indian Affairs," p. 432.

Epitaph

343   Phillips, ". . . the system of injustice . . .": Thomas Tibbles, *The Ponca Chiefs* (Boston: Lockwood, Brooks & Co., 1880), dedication page.

Tudor, "The policy . . .": William Tudor, *Letters on the Eastern States* (Boston: Wells & Lilly, 1821), p. 295.

344   Apess, "And suppose that . . .": *Eulogy on King Philip*, pp. 16–17.

Watie, "If there was . . .": *Cherokee, Disturbances, with Map*, 29th Congress, 1st session, 1845–46, H. Doc. 185, vol. 6, serial set 485, p. 104.

Howard, "I could not help . . .": *My Life and Personal Experiences among Our Hostile Indians*, p. 130.

Meeker, "The whole business . . .": *Utes*, p. 120.

Dawes, "There is no selfishness . . .": *Board of Indian Commissioners Annual Report, 1885* (Washington, D.C.: Government Printing Office, 1885), p. 91.

345   Duncan, "Suppose the Federal Government . . .": *Report on Affairs in Indian Territory, with Hearings*, 59th Congress, 2nd session, 1906–7, S. Rept. 5013, part 1, vol. 3, serial set 5062, p. 186.

345 U.S. Secretary of the Interior, "No one certainly . . .": *Report of the Commissioner of Indian Affairs,* 42nd Congress, 3rd session, 1872, H. Exec. Doc. 1, vol. 3, serial set 1560, p. 397.

Harney, "I never yet knew . . .": *Report of the Commissioner of Indian Affairs 1870/71,* p. 40.

U.S. Secretary of the Interior, "Every year's advance . . .": *Report of the Commissioner of Indian Affairs,* 42nd Congress, 3rd session, 1872, H. Exec. Doc. 1, vol. 3, serial set 1560, p. 398.

346 Schofield, "All roving bands . . .": *Report of the Commissioner of Indian Affairs 1870/71,* pp. 94–95.

347 U.S. Secretary of the Interior, "All history admonishes us . . .": *Century of Dishonor,* p. 74.

Haynes, "In January the issue . . .": *Century of Dishonor,* pp. 394–95.

Editorial, "The agent . . . has almost . . .": *The Outlook,* Sept. 19, 1903, Papers of William Ghent.

348 Tibbles, "I noticed . . .": *Buckskin and Blanket Days,* pp. 154–55.

Phillips, "I know the Indian . . .": *Buckskin and Blanket Days,* pp. 209–10.

349 Pope, "It is an injustice . . .": *Report of the Secretary of War,* 45th Congress, 2nd session, 1877–78, H. Exec. Doc. 1, vol. 2, serial set 1794, p. 60.

Assadawa, "The rations we get . . .": *Our Red Brothers,* pp. 112–13.

U.S. commissioner, "The call to labor . . .": U.S. Commissioner, *Annual Report of the Commissioner of Indian Affairs, 1875,* p. 24.

Tudor, "The only chance . . .": *Letters on the Eastern States,* p. 293.

U.S. commissioner, "This [English] language . . .": U.S. Commissioner, *Annual Report of the Commissioner of Indian Affairs, 1887* (Washington, D.C.: Government Printing Office, 1887), p. xxiii.

350 Bercier, "From all over . . .": Metha Parisien Bercier, "Tomorrow, My Sister Said, But Tomorrow Never Came," 1993 (unpublished ms., Belcourt, N.D.). In memory of her daughter—Monica Bercier.

Sun Elk, "They told us . . .": Edwin R. Embree, *Indians of the Americas* (Boston: Houghton Mifflin, 1939), pp. 227–28.

Bercier, "Who determines what civilization . . .": "Tomorrow, My Sister Said."

351 Lone Wolf, "The soldiers came . . .": "Lone Wolf Returns . . . To That Long Ago Time" as related to Paul Dyck by Lone Wolf, *Montana, The Magazine of Western History* (Helena: Montana Historical Society, vol. 22, no. 1, Jan. 1972).

Crazy Horse, ". . . you are taking . . .": Stephen Ambrose, *Crazy Horse and Custer: The Parallel Lives of Two American Warriors* (Garden City, N.Y.: Doubleday, 1975), pp. 465–66.

Lone Wolf, "If we thought . . .": "Lone Wolf Returns."

Bercier, "And so the days . . .": "Tomorrow, My Sister Said."

352 U.S. commissioner, "You certainly must discover . . .": *American State Papers: Indian Affairs*, vol. 7, p. 445.

James, "Read the books written . . .": George Wharton James, "The American Indian Question," June 21, 1923, undisclosed clipping, Papers of William Ghent.

Editorial, " 'Every native Indian . . .' ": "Absorbing the Indian," Mar. 7, 1926, undisclosed clipping, Papers of William Ghent.

353 U.S. commissioner, "There may have been . . .": *Report of the Commissioner of Indian Affairs, 1875*, pp. 23–24.

Harney, "I have lived . . .": *Report of the Commissioner of Indian Affairs 1870/71*, p. 40.

Catlin, "White men—whiskey . . .": *Letters and Notes on the Manners, Customs, and Conditions of the North American Indians*, vol. 1, letter no. 13.

Johnson, "Does this generation . . .": *Red Record of the Sioux*, p. 202.

Index

Index

Index

Index

Grateful acknowledgment is made to the following for permission to reprint previously published and unpublished material:

Ayer Company Publishers Inc.: Excerpts from *Old Frontiers* by John Brown (Southern Publishers, 1938); excerpts from "Wingenund Speech" from *A Narrative of the Mission of the United Brethren Among the Delaware and Mohegan Indians; From Its Commencement, in the Year 1740, to the Close of the Year 1808* by John Heckewelder (Arno Press and The New York Times, 1971). Reprinted by permission of Ayer Company Publishers Inc., P.O. Box 958, Salem, New Hampshire 03079.

Metha Bercier: Excerpts from unpublished manuscript "Tomorrow, My Sister Said, But Tomorrow Never Came" by Metha Bercier. Reprinted in memory of her daughter Monica Bercier by Metha Parisien Bercier, Belcourt, North Dakota.

Cambridge University Press: Excerpt from *The Hupa, Yurok, Karuk, Wiyot, Tolowa and Tututni, Shasta, Klamath* (The North American Indian Series, Vol. 13) by Edward Curtis (1924). Reprinted by permission of Cambridge University Press.

The Caxton Printers, Ltd.: Excerpt from *Hear Me, My Chiefs!* by L. V. McWhorter (1952). Reprinted by permission of The Caxton Printers, Ltd., Caldwell, Idaho.

David C. Cooke: Excerpts from *Fighting Indians of America* by David C. Cooke (Dodd, Mead & Co.), copyright © 1954, 1957, 1959, 1966, 1992 by David C. Cooke. Reprinted by permission of the author.

Dr. J. Frederick Fausz: Excerpts from dissertation "The Powhatan Uprising of 1622: An Historical Study of Ethnocentrism and Cultural Conflict" by Dr. J. Frederick Fausz. Reprinted by permission of Dr. J. Frederick Fausz, University of Missouri, St. Louis, Missouri.

Sallie Foster: Excerpt from *The Fighting Indians of the West* by Martin Schmitt and Dee Brown (Charles Scribner's & Sons, 1948). Reprinted by permission of Sallie Foster.

Blanche C. Gregory, Inc.: Excerpt from *Piegan* by Richard Lancaster (Doubleday & Co., 1966). Reprinted by permission of Blanche C. Gregory, Inc., for the author, Richard Lancaster.

Textual Acknowledgments

HarperCollins Publishers, Inc.: Excerpts from History of the Indies by Bartolomé de Las Casas, translated by Andrée Collard (Torchbook Library, 1971). Reprinted by permission of Harper-Collins Publishers, Inc.

Anna Rose Octavia Heil: Excerpts from Cheyenne and Sioux: The Reminiscences of Four Indians and a White Soldier, edited by Thomas Marquis (Pacific Center for Western Historical Studies, 1973). Reprinted by permission of Anna Rose Heil for Dr. Marquis Custer Publications.

Henry Holt and Company, Inc., and Sterling Lord Literistic, Inc.: Excerpt by Tahmelapashme (Dull Knife) from Bury My Heart at Wounded Knee by Dee Brown, copyright © 1970 by Dee Brown. Reprinted by permission of Henry Holt and Company, Inc., and Sterling Lord Literistic, Inc.

Houghton Mifflin Company: Excerpt by Sun Elk from Indians of the Americas by Edwin Embree, copyright © 1939 by Edwin Embree, copyright renewed 1967 by Kate C. Embree. Reprinted by permission of Houghton Mifflin Company. All rights reserved.

Imperial Valley College Desert Museum Society: Excerpt from quote by Tom Lucas, Kumeyaay, from The Kwaymi: A Reflection on a Lost Culture by Lora Cline (IVC Museum Society, 1979). Reprinted by permission of Imperial Valley College Desert Museum Society.

Johnson Books: Excerpts from Utes: The Mountain People by Jan Petit (1990). Reprinted by permission of Johnson Books, Boulder, Colorado.

Malki Museum Press: Excerpts from Breath of the Sun: Life in Early California as Told by a Chumash Indian, Fernando Librado to John P. Harrington by Fernando Librado (1979). Reprinted by permission of Malki Museum Press, Malki Museum, Inc.

McIntosh and Otis, Inc.: Excerpts from The Buffalo Hunters by Mari Sandoz (University of Nebraska Press), copyright © 1954 by Mari Sandoz. Reprinted by permission of McIntosh and Otis, Inc.

Montana, The Magazine of Western History: Excerpts from "Lone Wolf Returns . . . To That Long Ago Time" as related to Paul Dyck by Lone Wolf (Montana, The Magazine of Western History, Vol. 22, January 1972), pp. 18–41. Reprinted by permission.

Oklahoma Historical Society: Excerpt from "The Medicine Lodge Peace Council" by A. A. Taylor (The Chronicles of Oklahoma, 2, June 1924). Reprinted by permission of Oklahoma Historical Society.

The Oklahoma Publishing Company: Excerpt from April 7, 1929, issue of The Oklahoman, copyright © 1929 by The Oklahoma Publishing Company. Reprinted by permission of The Oklahoma Publishing Company.

Pruett Publishing Company: Excerpt from People of the Shining Mountains by Charles Marsh. Reprinted by permission of Pruett Publishing Company, Boulder, Colorado.

Carol K. Rachlin: Excerpts from American Indian Mythology by Alice Marriott and Carol Rachlin (Thomas Y. Crowell Company, 1968). Reprinted by permission of Carol K. Rachlin, co-author and heir to Alice Marriott.

Textual Acknowledgments

Rough Rock School Board, Inc.: Excerpt by Ganado Mucho from *Navajo Biographies*, Vol. 1, by Virginia Hoffman (Phoenix: Navajo Curriculum Center, 1974). Reprinted by permission of Rough Rock School Board, Inc., Rough Rock, Arizona.

Shasta Historical Society: Excerpt from *Wintu Trails* by Helen Hogue (1977). Reprinted by permission of Shasta Historical Society, Redding, California.

Simon & Schuster, Inc.: Excerpt from *The Indian in America's Past* by Jack Forbes, copyright © 1964 by Jack Forbes, copyright renewed 1992 by Jack Forbes. Reprinted by permission of Simon & Schuster, Inc.

P. David Smith: Excerpt from *Ouray, Chief of the Utes* by P. David Smith (Wayfinder Press, 1986). Reprinted by permission of P. David Smith.

Blair Sullivan: English translations of excerpts from *Historia de las Indias* by Bartolomé de Las Casas. Reprinted by permission of Blair Sullivan.

The Tennessee Historical Society: Excerpt from "Tatham's Characters Among the North American Indians" by Samuel C. Williams (*Tennessee Historical Magazine*, Vol. 7, No. 3, October 1921). Reprinted by permission of The Tennessee Historical Society, Nashville, Tennessee.

The University of Alabama Press: Excerpt from *Hispaniola: Caribbean Chiefdoms in the Age of Columbus* by Samuel Wilson (1990). Reprinted by permission of The University of Alabama Press.

The University of Arizona Press: Excerpt from *In the Days of Victorio: Recollec-tions of a Warm Springs Apache* by Eve Ball, narrated by James Kaywaykla, copyright © 1970 by The University of Arizona Press. Reprinted by permission of The University of Arizona Press.

University of California Press: Excerpts from *Anza's California Expeditions: An Outpost of Empire*, Vol. 1, by Herbert Bolton, copyright © 1930 by The Regents of the University of California. Reprinted by permission of the University of California Press.

University of Nebraska Press: Excerpt from *Land of the Spotted Eagle* by Luther Standing Bear (1978); excerpt from *Black Elk Speaks* by John G. Neihardt (1989, originally published 1932). Reprinted by permission of the University of Nebraska Press.

University of Oklahoma Press: Excerpt from *New Sources of Indian History* by Stanley Vestal, copyright © 1934 by the University of Oklahoma Press; excerpt from *The Annals of the Cakchiquels: Title of the Lords of Totonicapan* by Adrian Recinos and Delia Goetz, copyright © 1953 by the University of Oklahoma Press; excerpt from *Jean-Bernard Bossu's Travels in the Interior of North America, 1751–1762*, edited by Seymour Feiler, copyright © 1962 by the University of Oklahoma Press; excerpt from *Life of George Bent: Written from His Letters* by George E. Hyde, copyright © 1968 by the University of Oklahoma Press; excerpt from *The Menominee Indians: A History* by Patricia K. Ourada, copyright © 1979 by the University of Oklahoma Press; excerpt from *The Papers of Chief John Ross: Volume I, 1807–1839* by John Ross, copyright © 1985 by the University of Oklahoma Press; excerpts from *Indeh: An Apache Odyssey* by Eve Ball, copyright © 1988 by the

Textual Acknowledgments

University of Oklahoma Press; excerpts from *The Diario of Christopher Columbus's First Voyage to America 1492–1493* by Oliver Dunn and James E. Kelley, Jr., copyright © 1989 by Oliver Dunn and James E. Kelley, Jr.; excerpt from *Dreamer-Prophets of the Columbia Plateau: Smohalla and Skolaskin* by Robert H. Ruby and John A. Brown, copyright © 1989 by the University of Oklahoma Press; excerpts from *Fifteen Poets of the Aztec World* by Miguel León-Portilla, copyright © 1992 by the University of Oklahoma Press. Reprinted by permission of the University of Oklahoma Press.

University of Texas Press: Excerpts from *The Florida of the Inca* by Garcilaso de la Vega, translated and edited by John Grier Varner and Jeannette Johnson Varner, copyright © 1951 by the University of Texas Press. Reprinted by permission of the University of Texas Press, Austin, Texas.

University of Utah Press: Excerpts from *The War of Conquest: How It Was Waged Here in Mexico* by F. Bernardino de Sahagun, translated by Arthur J. O. Anderson and Charles E. Dibble (1978). Reprinted by permission of the University of Utah Press.

Washington State Historical Society: Excerpt by Meninick from "An Indian Chief" by Francis Garrecht (*Washington State Historical Quarterly*, Vol. 19, 1928). Reprinted by permission of the Washington State Historical Society, Tacoma, Washington.

Yale University Press: Excerpt from *Letters from Mexico* by Hernán Cortés (1986); excerpts from *The Papers of Benjamin Franklin*, Vol. 11 (1967). Reprinted by permission of Yale University Press.

ILLUSTRATION ACKNOWLEDGMENTS

Denver Museum of Natural History: page 28

Library of Congress, Prints and Photographs Division: page 232

Library of Congress, Rare Book and Special Collections Division: pages 18, 70, 151, 161

Smithsonian Institution, National Anthropological Archives: pages 104, 217, 226, 236, 305, 312, 339

Smithsonian Institution/Art Resource, N.Y., National Portrait Gallery: page 319

National Archives: pages 166, 253

North Wind Picture Archives: page 92

University of Cincinnati, Archives and Rare Books Department: page 302

University of Oklahoma Library, Western History Collections: page 282